THE STATE
OF THE STATES

THE STATE
OF THE STATES

Third Edition

Edited by
Carl E. Van Horn
Rutgers University

CQ
PRESS

A Division of Congressional Quarterly Inc.
Washington, D.C.

Printed in the United States of America

Library of Congress Cataloging-in-Publication Data

The state of the states/edited by Carl E. Van Horn. — 3rd. ed
   p. cm.
  Includes bibliographical references and index.
  ISBN 1-56802-158-5
  1. State governments—United States. I. Van Horn, Carl E.
  JK2408.S825 1996   96-12559
  353.9—dc20   CIP

To my wife, Christy Van Horn, who shares my enthusiasm for the art and science of politics and government

Contents

Tables and Figures

Tables

Figures

Preface

State governments are more important now than ever before. They were propelled into a central role in American government and politics by the election in 1994 of the first Republican-controlled Congress in forty years. Driven by a desire to balance the budget and an ideological preference for state government control, the new Republican Congress embraced a set of radical reforms that put more responsibility and pressure for performance on the shoulders of state governments. Even though many of these proposals were vetoed by President Clinton, the states have embarked on a new era that will enlarge their responsibilities and challenge their institutions.

The State of the States, third edition, with contributions by eleven leading observers of state government and politics, provides comprehensive coverage of politics, political institutions, and public policy in the states. Rather than attempting exhaustive summaries of the literature or the history and function of the institution or process, the authors have described and analyzed important trends, covering the period of state government resurgence that began in the 1960s but emphasizing more recent developments.

The authors consider the new challenges facing state governments in the second half of the 1990s. Prior to the major shift in responsibility delivered to the states by Congress and the president in 1995, state political institutions were already feeling the strains of a heightened role in the federal system. The shock of a national recession in the early 1990s exposed states' vulnerability to economic downturns as the golden era of state government expansion abruptly ended. Now, state policy makers are in the limelight in a way that few could have expected even a few years ago. The "Devolution Revolution" of 1995 will touch every state political institution and political actor. The stakes will be higher than ever before. Competition for the exercise of power—a permanent feature of politics—will grow more intense.

The chapters in *The State of the States* will help readers understand how well state political leaders have dealt with these difficult challenges and how they might handle their expanded responsibilities in the years ahead. Chapters on federalism, governors, legislatures, courts, bureaucracies, fiscal policy, and campaigns and elections highlight the profound changes that state governments are undergoing. The book includes new chapters on education and welfare policies. Education has been for many years an important state government responsibility, consuming a large share of state spending each year. Welfare programs are now squarely in the hands of the states and generating more controversy than ever.

I wish to express my appreciation to several individuals who helped me prepare the third edition. Margaret Koller and Cynthia Smith, my former research assistants, and Joanne Pfeiffer, my secretary at the Eagleton Institute, handled their duties with dispatch and good cheer. Working again with CQ Press also was a pleasure. Brenda Carter helped me through the revision and made many valuable suggestions, Tracy Villano provided excellent editorial guidance, and Talia Greenberg kept the production process running smoothly.

Contributors

Lawrence Baum is professor of political science at Ohio State University. He is author of *The Supreme Court* and *American Courts*. Subjects of his research include judicial elections and change in Supreme Court policy.

Thad L. Beyle is Thomas Pearsall Professor of Political Science at the University of North Carolina at Chapel Hill. He has worked in the North Carolina governor's office and for the National Governors' Association.

Margaret E. Goertz is professor in the Graduate School of Education and senior research fellow at the Consortium for Policy Research in Education at the University of Pennsylvania. Her research specializations include state and federal education policy and school finance.

William T. Gormley, Jr., is professor of government and public policy at Georgetown University. He is author of several books, including *Taming the Bureaucracy: Muscles, Prayers, and Other Strategies*.

Irene Lurie is associate professor of public administration and policy in the Rockefeller College at the State University of New York at Albany. She has analyzed welfare policy for many years and recently codirected a ten-state study of the implementation of the JOBS program for welfare recipients.

Richard P. Nathan is provost of the Rockefeller College of Public Affairs at the State University of New York at Albany. His most recent book is *Turning Promises into Performance: The Management Challenge of Implementing Workfare*.

Henry J. Raimondo is professor of public policy at the Eagleton Institute of Politics at Rutgers University. He is currently on leave serving as the chief economist of the Port Authority of New York and New Jersey.

Alan Rosenthal is professor of public policy and political science at the Eagleton Institute of Politics at Rutgers University. He has worked with legislatures throughout the nation. His latest book is *Drawing the Line: Legislative Ethics in the States*.

Barbara G. Salmore is professor of political science at Drew University. She has been associate dean of the college since 1992. She has coauthored, with Stephen Salmore, *Candidates, Parties, and Campaigns* and *New Jersey Politics and Government.*

Stephen A. Salmore is professor of political science at the Eagleton Institute of Politics at Rutgers University. He also serves as a campaign consultant to candidates for governor, the state legislature, and Congress.

Carl E. Van Horn is professor of public policy and political science at the Eagleton Institute of Politics and chair of the Department of Public Policy at the Bloustein School of Planning and Public Policy at Rutgers University. From 1990 to 1992 he was the director of policy in the office of the governor of the state of New Jersey.

1

The Quiet Revolution

Carl E. Van Horn

For more than two generations, from the 1930s through the 1960s, state governments languished in relative obscurity—overshadowed by a burgeoning national government responding to the crises of depression, war, and internal strife and overseeing an unprecedented and extended period of economic prosperity. Americans turned to Washington, D.C., for leadership and for their share of a growing federal pie.

In the first two-thirds of the twentieth century, sweeping national and international events and a cadre of political leaders shifted governmental activism to the federal level. State governments were bypassed as the federal government expanded beyond the limited role envisioned by the framers of the Constitution. State governments were scorned by many as racist, incompetent, inflexible, and politically and economically anemic.[1]

State governments changed profoundly between 1960 and 1995, and they will face further dramatic changes in the years ahead. Responding to the pressing concerns of their residents, states pioneered solutions to some of the country's most difficult problems and demonstrated effective leadership.[2] States reformed and strengthened their political and economic houses and, as a result, came to occupy a more important role in American life.

In the 1980s and 1990s, states were capable and willing to tackle tough problems. Governors, legislators, judges, and bureaucrats were setting national agendas. Innovative economic development, education, and health care programs laid the foundations for federal statutes. States were handling a wide range of vexing problems, from homelessness and Acquired Immune Deficiency Syndrome (AIDS) to fostering competitive industries and reducing automobile pollution. Increasingly, federal government officials expected state governments to assume greater policy and administrative responsibilities. States increased their commitment to manage and pay for such traditional local government services as law enforcement and education.

States became more politically significant, too. Several strong and effective governors rose to prominence. Lamar Alexander, former governor of Tennessee and secretary of education under President George Bush, helped galvanize a nationwide education reform movement. Two former governors—Jimmy Carter of Georgia and Ronald Reagan of California—occupied the White House from 1977 to 1989. And in 1992 former Arkansas governor Bill Clinton was elected president.

The rise of state governments came via a quiet revolution in American politics. The transformation was not always smooth, and it took several decades to reach full maturity. In the 1990s, state governments struggle to meet their new responsibilities. The boom years of increasing state revenues were replaced by the gloomy years of budget deficits, tax increases, and program reductions. Federal officeholders passed the buck, but not the bucks, to handle a broad array of public problems—cleaning the air, providing health care for the poor, and delivering services for the disabled.

The pace of change increased rapidly for state governments when, in 1994, the nation elected its first Republican-controlled Congress in forty years. Driven by a desire to balance the budget and by an ideological preference for state government control, the new Republican Congress embraced a set of radical reforms designed to put more responsibility and pressure for performance on the shoulders of state governments. President Clinton refused to approve many of these proposals so they did not become law.

However, sharp reductions in federal aid, which were endorsed by both the president and Congress, will have profound implications for state governments in the coming years. In the mid-1980s, when federal aid was cut deeply, states responded with huge tax increases that made up some of the shortfall. This time it will be different. In the mid-1990s, state governments are dominated by Republicans—thirty-one of the fifty governors and more than 50 percent of the legislative chambers. More often than not, these elected officials are cutting taxes and spending, not looking to enhance the government's role.

The Tidal Wave of Reform

Powerful and effective state governments did not emerge overnight. A series of reforms in the structure and process of state government—some carefully planned, others accidental—has come about since the 1960s. Cumulatively, these reforms enhanced the capacity of state governmental institutions and encouraged state government officials to broaden their responsibilities.

State government reform was not exclusively the accomplishment of enlightened state politicians. Two landmark federal policies—the reapportionment of state legislatures and the enactment of national civil rights laws—provoked much of the upheaval in state capitals. Initially, state officials regarded these policies as slaps in the face. Ultimately, they helped transform state politics and propelled state governments into a new era of growth.

In a sweeping 1962 decision, the U.S. Supreme Court mandated in *Baker v. Carr* that state legislatures be reapportioned so that political representation would be based on the principle of "one person, one vote."[3] Until that time, many state legislatures were dominated by rural and suburban lawmakers, intent on preserving the status quo of local government control, low taxes, and limited government. Over time, legislatures evolved into modern, representative institutions that more accurately reflected the broad range of interests and needs in their states.[4] Reformed legislatures then expanded the reach of government in accordance with the wishes of newly represented voters.

The enactment and implementation of landmark civil rights legislation—including the Civil Rights Act of 1964 and the Voting Rights Act of 1965—extended the influence of federal law throughout the federal system. Legally sanctioned discrimination in education, employment, business, and government was sharply reduced.[5] Gradually, the composition of the electorate, the membership of legislatures, and the direction of public policy more accurately reflected the citizenry of each state.

Prior to the civil rights statutes, federal lawmakers argued that state governments could not be trusted with the stewardship of the disadvantaged and minorities.[6] Less than a decade after their enactment the critical argument against giving state governments more power, and in favor of greater federal control, essentially evaporated from political discourse. In the early 1970s, southern governors such as Lester G. Maddox of Georgia and George C. Wallace of Alabama were symbols of state government intransigence when they refused black students admission to state universities. In the 1980s, Bill Clinton of Arkansas, with a coalition of support that included prominent blacks and members of other minorities, came to represent the new breed of progressive southern governors.

Pressure for modern and effective political and governmental institutions also came from state officials. Since the 1960s, nearly forty states have ratified new constitutions or significantly amended existing ones.[7] The office of governor has been enhanced by allowing for longer terms and increasing opportunities for succession, which have brought in better qualified individuals.[8] Statewide elections for many governmental positions, such as secretary of state, attorney general, and chief state school officer, have been eliminated. As a result, the governor's visibility and power has increased. Appointment and removal of important policy makers became the governor's responsibility. Chief executives took a greater role in the budget process, expanded planning and personal staffs, and turned the National Governors' Association into an advocate for stronger state governments.

Legislatures also became better prepared for governing. For decades, state legislatures were ridiculed as "inefficient and corrupt."[9] During the 1960s and 1970s, "legislatures undertook to rebuild themselves practically from scratch."[10] They devoted more time to lawmaking, streamlined rules and procedures, and tightened rules governing campaign financing and conflicts of interest. Turnover declined as legislators became careerists. Professional staff were hired to prepare legislation, review state budgets, and oversee program administration. By the mid-1990s, more than fifteen thousand people worked for legislatures on a full-time basis—an increase of more than 200 percent since the mid-1960s.[11]

State courts and state bureaucracies have also increased their ability to carry out the public's business. State courts have been strengthened through reforms that unified the judicial system and enhanced their administrative resources.[12] State bureaucracies have grown in size. During the 1980s, the U.S. population grew by 9 percent, while state government employment increased by 19 percent. Some states doubled their work forces in the 1980s, largely because of the need to monitor rapidly growing social service programs, such as Medicaid, and to guard convicts in state prisons. State government workers now are much more likely to be recruited on a merit system, and state employees are better trained and educated than ever before. The structure of state government has also changed in nearly all the states.[13] Almost two dozen states have experienced comprehensive reorganizations since 1965, and the rest have been partially reorganized.[14]

Fiscal Squeeze Play

State governments were the fiscal stepchildren of the federal system in the 1950s and 1960s. They depended heavily on the sales tax and user fees, and most were required to balance their budgets—a constitutional restriction then regarded as a liability. In contrast, the federal government enjoyed the powerful and progressive income tax, which tapped the rapid income growth of the post–World War II era. When revenues slumped during downturns in the business cycle, the federal government could pull itself out by borrowing money.

State government spending for public purposes have changed dramatically. In 1964, for example, state governments spent $24 billion; by 1990, more than $350 billion. During this same period, state spending increased at a slightly faster rate than federal government spending, somewhat faster than the rate of inflation, and considerably faster than local government spending.[15]

Federal aid to the states jumped sharply during the 1970s, then declined as a percentage of total state spending for more than a decade. Although often attributed to President Ronald Reagan, this trend actually started during Jimmy Carter's presidency and accelerated during the 1980s. In 1975, four out of every ten dollars spent by the states were passed down from the federal Treasury; by 1983, three out of every ten dollars.[16] Recently, federal aid has inched up again, but it has not reached the mid-1970s levels.[17] More important, federal aid has not kept pace with federal mandates to provide health care to the poor or to help deliver services for the disabled.

When federal officials halted the rapid increase in federal aid for states and localities, state governments picked up some of the slack. According to the Reagan philosophy, "federalism means that the central government speaks to the states and lets the states speak to the cities," said John Shannon, former executive director of the Advisory Commission on Intergovernmental Relations.[18] From 1980 to 1986, for example, total state spending for local government grew by 57 percent, from $83 billion to $130 billion. (Inflation over the same period was 32 percent.) Most state aid went to public elementary and secondary schools—five of every eight dollars. The balance was allocated for health and welfare, highways, public transit, housing, corrections, and general government support.[19]

The revenue raising power of states has been enhanced. Individual and corporate income taxes are now far more important than sales taxes and other fees. In 1967, only 22 percent of state government revenue derived from the income tax; by the 1980s, it was nearly 40 percent.[20] States also have found significant new sources of revenue in state lotteries, which have been created in twenty-two states. Setting up lotteries to raise funds thus far has not been considered a serious option by the federal government.[21]

State fiscal policy has followed six distinct paths.[22] From 1960 to 1977, state governments added new taxes and increased existing taxes to underwrite expenditure growth and to satisfy constituent demands for new and expanded services in health, education, environmental protection, and transportation.

During the late 1970s, many states experienced a tax revolt. Spurred by California's Proposition 13, which reduced property tax revenues by 57 percent and limited future increases to no more than 2 percent annually, citizens and legislators clamped down on the rapid growth in state spending. Between 1978 and 1984, only three of the nine states that voted on Proposition 13–type initiatives approved them. But voters in eleven states accepted moderate tax and spending limitation measures.[23] Legislatures in dozens of other states responded to the California message. No new taxes were added from 1978 to 1980, and taxes declined in dozens of states.[24]

Between 1981 and 1983, states imposed substantial tax increases to cope with an economic recession and deep reductions in federal aid. Unlike the federal government, each year the states must raise sufficient revenues to cover the costs of operating state programs. States responded by jacking up the sales tax, increasing income tax rates, adding a penny or two to the gasoline tax, extending the concept of user fees for services, and creating state-sponsored lotteries.

When the economy rebounded in the mid-1980s, many states reaped a fiscal bonanza.[25] The income and sales tax increases levied earlier to stave off financial disaster became the driving force behind expansionary government spending programs. Not much of the unanticipated "windfall government profit" was returned to taxpayers. A few states in the energy-producing regions of the country, such as Texas and Louisiana, and states heavily dependent on single revenue sources or weak industries, such as Oregon, did not experience a surge in financial horsepower, but many others did and they spent like mad.

In the early 1990s, state governments were plagued with soaring deficits brought on by the spending of the 1980s and by sharp reductions in revenues resulting from a deep national recession that lasted for nearly three years. In 1991, thirty-four states raised more than $16 billion in income, sales, and corporate taxes and cut more than $10 billion in programs just to try to keep their budgets in balance. California raised $7 billion in new revenues and cut $7 billion in programs, but still faced a $6 billion deficit the following year.[26]

The federal government's huge deficits and continuing appetite for mandating increases in state spending compounded the problem for state officials. Between 1981 and 1992, the total national debt quadrupled to more than $4 trillion.[27] Annual budget deficits rose from $25 billion in the $178 billion budget of 1968 to $200 billion in the $800 billion budget of 1983. By fiscal year 1991, the deficit had grown to $318 billion of the $1.4 trillion federal budget.[28]

The fallout from bloated federal deficits is still sending shock waves through state capitals. To pay for substantial increases in defense and entitlement programs, federal law makers have sharply cut aid to state and local governments. Consequently, states are receiving less money from the national government and more pleas for help from local governments.[29]

Federal officials are now reluctant or unable to mount new domestic program initiatives and pay for them with federal resources. Interest groups have turned up the heat on states to satisfy their demands. Unfortunately, state governments cannot "count on the federal cavalry to come charging over the hill with aid from Washington." The states are operating in "an atmosphere of fend-for-yourself federalism."[30]

During the 1960s, new domestic policies were created through federally funded categorical aid programs. The assistance often bypassed state governments and went directly to local governments or community organizations. Federal officials specified the what, when, and how of program administration and tried to monitor closely program compliance, which was consistent with the underlying distrust of state government capacity and intentions.[31]

Although devolution of responsibility to state governments in the 1980s was supposed to be accompanied by deregulation of federal control, the federal government continued to impose strict regulations. Federal mandates relating to health care for the poor, environmental protection, services for the disabled and senior citizens cost state governments billions of dollars annually. Congress and the president continued to satisfy constituent requests for assistance by imposing new demands on state capitals.[32]

The Devolution Revolution

The latest phase in the evolution of American federalism has been called the "Devolution Revolution" by Richard Nathan (see Chapter 2). The idea behind this revolution is simple: to reduce the size and influence of government by cutting taxes and spending and by sending federal responsibilities to the states. In 1995, the Republican-controlled Congress adopted a budget designed to reduce the federal operating deficit to zero in seven years, which included sharp reductions in aid to the states.

Just as Republicans were taking over Congress, they were sweeping into control in state capitols. In the mid-1990s, Republican governors headed all of the states with the largest populations, except Florida. In addition, Republicans controlled more than 50 percent of the legislative chambers for the first time since 1968. These officials were also committed to reducing government taxes and spending. In 1995, for the first time in ten years, state tax cuts exceeded state tax increases. As a result, states are now much less able or willing to replace lost federal revenues.[33]

The net effect of the Devolution Revolution remains unknown. What is certain is that these changes will influence state governmental institutions and public policy for years to come. States are being asked to assume important new responsibilities, generally with fewer resources than were previously available to remedy problems. State policy makers have been given much greater latitude to define policies and programs to fulfill broad federal objectives. The combination of constrained resources and expanded opportunities represents the upside and downside of the new reforms.

Struggle and Innovation

For more than fifty years—from Franklin Roosevelt's New Deal to Jimmy Carter's Urban Policy—the national government created progressive public policies. With large federal budget deficits and conservative Republican presidents in the White House during the 1980s and 1990s, however, the federal government often took a back seat to state governments in devising domestic policy innovations. States offered new policy initiatives in a broad range of areas—natural resources and energy policy, human services and health care, economic development, education, business, and insurance regulation. State governments became deeply engaged in issues that affected state residents on a daily basis—the quality of schools, the supply of water, and the condition of roads and waterways. States also tackled some of the nation's most difficult problems—surrogate motherhood, the care and treatment of the medically indigent, drug abuse in the public schools, teenage pregnancy, pay equity, the liability insurance crisis, and the right to die.

The importance of state policy leadership has recently been demonstrated in economic development, education, welfare, and environmental protection policies. The states initiated successful policy experiments that were copied or endorsed by the national government. State governments provided the lion's share of the funds needed to carry out new public strategies, although progress was slowed substantially by the national recession of the early 1990s.

Economic development has always been an important responsibility of state governments. States fund bridge and highway construction; maintain ports, rivers, airline terminals, and mass transit systems; support the education and training of the work force; and regulate basic financial institutions and utilities. During the 1980s and early 1990s, the states reconceived and expanded their economic development strategies. Facing double-digit unemployment and massive disruptions in communities, states initiated programs and policies to make their states economically competitive. States invested heavily in the development of new technologies, the retraining of workers, the development of small business opportunities, and the expansion of export markets. As journalist David Osborne noted: "While the national government debated whether it should develop a new industrial policy, the states were already implementing one."[34]

Clearly, however, state governments are limited in what they can accomplish when the national economy is not growing. For example, former New Jersey governor Jim Florio launched a major public works investment strategy to create 150,000 jobs over five years on projects designed to improve the state's roads, transit systems, airports, and ports. Despite this impressive commitment to capital spending, the state still lost more than 250,000 private sector jobs during the recession. Without the governor's program, the economy would have been in much worse shape, but state government policy alone cannot keep a state from sinking into a national recession.

Landmark environmental statutes mandating cleanup of the air, water, and land were enacted by the federal government in the 1960s and 1970s. The states were primarily responsible for the implementation of basic environmental statutes. Recent federal laws put the states in charge of some very tough problems, including dealing with the effects of automobile pollution. Decisions about where to dispose of toxic and low-level radioactive waste and how much Americans will be able to use their cars will be made by the states.[35]

Environmental policy innovations came from traditional sources—legislatures and governors—and from the voters, too. For example, former Arizona governor Bruce Babbitt was able to break a forty-year deadlock over water conservation policy in his state with effective public and private leadership. The New Jersey legislature passed sweeping legislation that required industries to inform employees about the potential health effects of chemicals in the workplace. And California voters supported an initiative that required the state government and industries to identify and stop the release of toxic chemicals into the groundwater.

More Power, More Conflict

As state governments grew in significance, conflict and competition within and across institutions also increased. This was followed by greater public skepticism of state officials and political institutions. The movement to limit the term of legislators has been an obvious outgrowth of this skepticism. In 1990, California voters imposed limitations on the number of terms state legislators may serve. By 1995, twenty other states followed their lead. The roller coaster of federal government expansion and contraction also increased pressure on state political institutions and processes.

The chapters that follow describe and assess how states cope with their new power and authority and the implications of the Devolution Revolution spawned by the 104th Congress. Some of the nation's leading students of state government and politics trained their skillful eyes on important trends in state political institutions and political processes. They provide perspectives on the impact of major changes that have taken place since the early 1960s, characterize the status of state politics and government today, and identify the challenges facing state political leaders in the late 1990s.

In Chapter 2, "The Role of the States in American Federalism," Richard P. Nathan describes the fall out from 1995's Republican-directed congressional shake-up of American federalism. Devolving responsibility and cutting federal spending on government entitlement programs for the poor represent a huge step into the unknown. Nathan predicts that the domestic policies initiated by Republicans in the 104th Congress will be a "bigger deal" for U. S. domestic policy than Lyndon Johnson's Great Society, Richard Nixon's New Federalism, and Ronald Reagan's 1981 budget cuts and block grants.

In Chapter 3, "State Budgeting: Problems, Choices, and Money," Henry J. Raimondo traces in detail the conflict-ridden landscape of state fiscal policy in the 1990s. The sustained period of economic growth in the 1980s enabled states to avoid the trap of budget deficits. When the recession arrived in the 1990s, states were caught in a vice of shrinking revenues and increasing demands for services. States responded by raising taxes, cutting services, and passing costs on to local governments, college students, and school districts. The "go-it-alone federalism" of the 1990s turned the United States into fifty small countries.

In Chapter 4, "The Transformation of State Electoral Politics," Stephen A. Salmore and Barbara G. Salmore describe the rise of candidate-centered campaigns, in which personal qualities and issues communicated directly to voters compete with party labels and organizations as the principal voting cues in state elections. As state governments become more important policy makers, state elections take on greater significance and attract more money with which to wage campaigns. Candidate-centered campaigns are most pronounced in gubernatorial elections because of the rise in split-ticket and cross-party voting, the use of direct primaries, the effective use of incumbency, the decoupling of federal and state elections, and the increases in spending on elections.

In Chapter 5, "Being Governor," Thad L. Beyle traces the strengthened role of governors, examines their growing significance on the national policy scene, and describes the difficulties of being a governor in the 1990s. As governors exercised more power in their respective states, they came into conflict with courts, legislatures, and other members of the executive branch. The mounting deficits that bring on program cuts and tax increases made life in the governor's office harder. Governors usually got their way on major policy initiatives, but they paid a high price in public opinion surveys. Beyle also chronicles the early impacts of the 1994 elections and the sharp increase in the number of Republican governors.

Chapter 6, "The Legislature: Unraveling of Institutional Fabric," by Alan Rosenthal, documents the "rise of the legislative institution" from the rural-dominated political backwaters of the 1950s to the modern, more representative institutions of today. New-generation legislators are unwilling to take a back seat to governors, judges, and bureaucrats. Instead, they are exercising greater influence on the allocation of money and the direction of state policy. Despite these positive developments, Rosenthal argues that careerism among state legislators, increased politicization of legislatures, greater fragmentation of decision making, term limits for incumbents, and an unfriendly political environment have put America's legislatures under siege.

Chapter 7, "Supreme Courts in the Policy Process," by Lawrence Baum, examines the institutions that often are called upon to referee conflicts between governors and legislatures or between governors and other executive branch agencies—the courts. State courts, however, also make policy and thus generate conflict with other governmental actors. A long-standing liberal trend in state supreme courts on such matters as civil rights and the rights of criminal defendants has faded, and the center of ideological gravity in state supreme courts has shifted to the right. When public opinion has disagreed with court decisions, initiatives and referendums have been used to overturn them, especially those that expanded the rights of criminal defendants. Voters have removed liberal justices from office in several states. Incumbent judges are rarely defeated, but they have become more vulnerable and more accountable for their actions.

In Chapter 8, "Accountability Battles in State Administration," William T. Gormley, Jr., summarizes the proliferation of controls intended to curb the power of state bureaucracies to make and carry out policy. As state governments, and hence state administrative agencies, took on greater responsibility for the implementation of public policy, other politicians, judges, and citizens began to demand more accountability from them. States have responded by increasing legislative oversight and executive management techniques and by involving citizens in a wider range of bureaucratic decisions. At the same time, federal agencies and federal and state judges have increased their control over the functions of state bureaucracies. As the competition for control has increased, accountability battles have emerged. These have pitted various state political institutions against one another in a bitter struggle over authority, with state bureaucracies as the ultimate prize.

The third edition of *The State of the States* adds two new chapters on education and welfare reform policy. In Chapter 9, "State Education Policy in the 1990s," Margaret E. Goertz explains the major expansion in state responsibilities for financing and regulation of public elementary and secondary education. Goertz argues that the intense politics of resource allocation and conflicts over the content of educational programs dominate the state policy agenda. Unfortunately, the by-product of these debates is often a confusing and fragmented educational system. Goertz traces the last fifteen years of state education reform and discusses the major issues that will characterize education policy making in the latter 1990s.

In Chapter 10, "State Welfare Policy," Irene Lurie explains why the shape of welfare for the poor has commanded so much attention from state policy makers. Beginning in the mid-1980s, state governments have attempted to reform welfare programs, successfully convincing the federal government that states should have more flexibility to experiment with strategies for moving welfare recipients into jobs. After candidate Bill Clinton promised to "end welfare as we know it," radical proposals from the White House, the Congress, and state capitols proliferated. Lurie describes the swift-changing domain of welfare policy and considers the implications for low-income people and state political institutions.

In Chapter 11, "Power to the States," I summarize the preceding chapters and consider the new challenges facing state governments in the 1990s. Even prior to the major shift in responsibility to the states delivered by Congress and the president in 1995, states' political institutions were feeling the strains of their new roles as central players in the federal system. The shock of a national recession in the early 1990s exposed how vulnerable states are to economic downturns as the golden era of state government expansion abruptly ended. Now, state policy makers are going to be on the spot in a way that few could have expected even just a few years ago.

The drive to balance the federal budget by cutting back on state aid will touch every state political institution and political actor. The stakes will be higher than ever before. Competition for the exercise of power—a permanent feature of politics—will grow more intense. How well state political leaders handle these difficult challenges will determine how the nation is to be governed and how its citizens are to be served in the coming decades.

Notes

1. Terry Sanford, *Storm over the States* (New York: McGraw-Hill, 1967).
2. Ann O'M. Bowman and Richard C. Kearney, *The Resurgence of the States* (Englewood Cliffs, N.J.: Prentice-Hall, 1986).
3. Timothy O'Rourke, *The Impact of Reapportionment* (New Brunswick, N.J.: Transaction Books, 1980).
4. Alan Rosenthal, *Legislative Life* (New York: Harper and Row, 1981).
5. Charles S. Bullock III and Charles M. Lamb, eds., *Implementation of Civil Rights Policy* (Monterey, Calif.: Brooks-Cole, 1984).
6. Carl E. Van Horn, *Policy Implementation in the Federal System* (Lexington, Mass.: D.C. Heath, 1979), 155–161.
7. Albert L. Sturm and Janice C. May, "State Constitutions and Constitutional Revisions: 1980–1981 and the Past Fifty Years," in Council of State Governments, *The Book of the States, 1982–1983* (Lexington, Ky.: Council of State Governments, 1982), 115–133.
8. Larry J. Sabato, *Goodbye to Good-time Charlie: The American Governor Transformed* (Washington, D.C.: CQ Press, 1983).
9. Sanford, *Storm over the States*, 39.
10. Rosenthal, *Legislative Life*, 3.
11. National Conference of State Legislatures, *Legislative Staff in the Fifty States* (Denver, Colo.: National Conference of State Legislatures, 1986).
12. Robert A. Kagan, Bloos Cartwright, Lawrence M. Friedman, and Stanton Wheeled, "The Evolution of State Supreme Courts," *Michigan Law Review* 76 (1978): 961–1005.
13. Deil S. Wright, *Understanding Intergovernmental Relations*, 2d ed. (Monterey, Calif.: Brooks-Cole, 1982).
14. Council of State Governments, *The Book of the States, 1982–1983*, 145–147; *The Book of the States, 1984–1985* (1984), 44–45; *The Book of the States, 1986–1987* (1986), 45–47; and *The Book of the States, 1988–1989* (1988), 47–48.

15. Advisory Commission on Intergovernmental Relations, *Significant Features of Fiscal Federalism, 1984* (Washington, D.C.: Advisory Commission on Intergovernmental Relations, 1984), 10.
16. Ibid., 62.
17. "Measuring Federal Aid: Whose Straw Is Shortest?" *Governing* (prototype 1987): 48.
18. Ibid., 49.
19. "More State Dollars for the Localities," *Governing* (May 1988): 60–61.
20. Advisory Commission on Intergovernmental Relations, *Significant Features of Fiscal Federalism,* 51.
21. Steven D. Gold, Brenda Erikson, and Michelle Kissell, *Earmarking State Taxes* (Denver, Colo.: National Conference of States Legislatures, 1987), 6.
22. Advisory Commission on Intergovernmental Relations, *Significant Features of Fiscal Federalism,* 71.
23. Patrick B. McGuigan, *The Politics of Direct Democracy in the 1980s* (Washington, D.C.: Free Congress Research and Education Foundation, 1985), 52, 54, 55.
24. Advisory Commission on Intergovernmental Relations, *Significant Features of Fiscal Federalism,* 71.
25. Steve D. Gold, ed., *Reforming State Tax Systems* (Denver, Colo.: National Conference of State Legislatures, 1986).
26. Earl C. Gottchalk, Jr., "Across the Country, Increased State Levies Hit Incomes Harder," *Wall Street Journal,* November 11, 1991, C1.
27. *Economic Report of the President* (Washington, D.C.: Government Printing Office, 1991), 375.
28. U.S. Congress, Joint Economic Committee, *The 1985 Joint Economic Report,* 99th Cong., 1st sess., 1985, 47; and Executive Office of the President, *Budget of the United States for Fiscal Year 1987* (Washington, D.C.: Government Printing Office, 1986). See also, *Budget of the United States, Fiscal Year 1992* (Washington, D.C.: Government Printing Office, 1991).
29. Richard P. Nathan and Fred C. Doolittle, *Reagan and the States* (Princeton, N.J.: Princeton University Press, 1987).
30. David Shribman, "Governors of Fiscally Strapped States, Seeing No Sign of Relief, Yearn for the Good Old Days," *Wall Street Journal,* August 19, 1991, 10.
31. James L. Sundquist, *Making Federalism Work* (Washington, D.C.: Brookings Institution, 1969).
32. Nathan and Doolittle, *Reagan and the States.*
33. Robert Rear, "Federal Impasse Saddling States With Indecision," *New York Times,* January 2, 1996, A1.
34. David Osborne, *Laboratories of Democracy* (Cambridge, Mass.: Harvard Business School Press, 1988).
35. National Conference of State Legislatures, *State Issues 1987* (Denver, Colo.: National Conference of State Legislatures, 1987), chapter 2.

2

The Role of the States in American Federalism
Richard P. Nathan

The question of the relation of the states to the federal government is the cardinal question of our constitutional system. It cannot be settled by one generation, because it is a question of growth, and every new successive stage of our political and economic development gives it a new aspect, makes it a new question.

—Woodrow Wilson (1908)

The 1994 election, which gave Republicans control of both bodies of the 104th Congress, is likely to represent a historic realigning moment for our governmental system comparable to realignments of the past. In 1800, the first Republicans (Jefferson and Madison) established a new party, which weakened the Hamiltonian system; 1828 saw the populist Jacksonian revolution capture the presidency; and 1860 saw the national emergence of Lincoln's new northern-based Republican party. The Bryan-McKinley election of 1896 and, in 1912, Wilson's election to the presidency and the maturation of the Progressive Movement, could be included on this list of realigning moments, as could Franklin Roosevelt's first election to the presidency, the emergence of his New Deal program in 1932, and the advent of Lyndon Johnson's Great Society in 1965. In each instance, historic shifts occurred that had strong manifestations in governmental structures not unlike what is happening right now as a result of actions by the 104th Congress to change the basic character of American federalism.

This chapter is divided into five parts: the first defines federalism as a governmental form and assesses the current condition of American federalism; the second discusses the "Devolution Revolution" encompassed in the changes in domestic policy and intergovernmental relations pressed forward by the leaders of the 104th Congress; the third considers issues for state governments in their relationship with the national government; the fourth discusses the role of state governments; and the fifth offers concluding observations.

Defining Contemporary American Federalism

American federalism emerged out of frustration with the earlier arrangement under the Articles of Confederation, which none other than the magisterial George Washington called "a shadow without substance."[1] Our brand of federalism was unique when it was created in precisely the sense that the word "unique" means—*one and only*. U.S. federalism, said the brilliant Madison (a proponent of centralization in 1787 at the Philadelphia Convention), was created as a "great composition"—partly federal and partly national *(Federalist No. 39)*. Unlike earlier confederal forms, which were essentially leagues of states, under the U.S. Constitution each citizen is a citizen of both the national government and the state. Over the two centuries of our history, the great battles of federalism have been fought over which citizenship—federal or state—should predominate. In this century, the clear victor has been the national government. There have been flurries of state activism—the Progressive Movement in the 1920s, under Richard Nixon's New Federalism, and during the Reagan years—but the great movement of government has been toward the center.

The "Devolution Revolution"—Why Now?

Now, however, we are in the midst of a dramatic shift toward what many political leaders believe is a correct, limited interpretation of the "enumerated powers" assigned to the national government in Article I of the U.S. Constitution and a correspondingly broad interpretation of the Tenth Amendment, which assigns residual (nonenumerated) powers to the states, or to the people. This shift is likely to involve basic changes at the core of the nation's governmental system.

Why is this happening now? Governors are demanding more responsibility and budget pressures are acute. Early in 1995, Republican leaders in Congress decided federal deficit-reduction targets could best be met by striking a deal whereby governors received more power in exchange for going along with cuts in spending. No matter what happens on headline-level policy disputes about block grants and budget cuts, a power shift is already under way that is not likely to be reversed soon. Congress passed and the president signed into law the Unfunded Mandates Reform Act of 1995 limiting the federal government's power to adopt future mandates for state, local, and tribal governments without paying them. This was promise "Number 8" in the House Republicans' "Contract with America." The law also requires a study of all existing mandates, and in other areas Congress is pulling back from regulatory regimes, notably for environmental programs.

The federal government is not simply loosening the regulatory apron strings, it is also tightening the purse strings. Cuts in discretionary spending for many domestic programs will be 15–20 percent or more for fiscal year 1996. Looking down the road to 2002, the reductions being discussed average 30 percent at the end of this seven-year period. Not only is federal spending being cut, it is no longer the *modus vivendi* of Washington to discover problems and provide money to solve them. The federal money machine is turned off. This is not just a fiscal event; it shifts the social policy agenda to others—mainly to the states.

The states are exhibiting a new readiness and capability for action. Republican governors (now 31 in number) are linked arm in arm with leaders of the Congress. Many governors are re-engineering state government, modernizing its administrative machinery, and taking steps to overhaul and integrate social programs. Many state governments are also hard at work on the "nuts and bolts" of good government, redesigning their civil service, procurement, training, and information systems and revising management procedures.

This devolutionary shift is rooted in frustration over stagnant wages. Voters, responding to their straitened circumstances, are supporting conservative economic policies aimed at reducing the size and cost of government. Part of the economic reason as to "Why now?" is international, tied to steps private corporations have taken in recent years to re-engineer and downsize their operations. The increasingly global economy puts pressure on not just private-sector costs, but on the cost of government as well. The Devolution Revolution can be seen as a way to push all of America's governments to cut costs and achieve efficiencies. A more political interpretation as to why the Devolution Revolution is under way relates to an idea emphasized in the political science writing of Robert D. Putnam.[2] Putnam believes that community identity matters. Neighborhoods, villages, cities, and states represent identities that give meaning to people's lives. Federalism as a device for reconciling unity and diversity is an instrument for enhancing this sense of belonging to a community.

American federalism, of course, is not just about the national government and the fifty states. There are 20,000 municipal governments, 17,000 towns and townships, and 3,000 county governments. In fact, a criticism of American federalism is that it is too diverse and fragmented and that this layering of multiple small governments frustrates the citizenry. But multiple governmental identities are intrinsic to who we are. The sense Americans have of living and self-governing with other people in communities is not a small item on the scale of values that citizens of the United States consider important.

In the literature on federalism, some scholars have taken the position that American federalism has three parts—national, state, and local. Roscoe Martin argued in the 1950s that U.S. federalism should be viewed as a three-cornered stool, unable to stand if there is not strength in all three legs.[3] However, while it is a mistake to ignore the role and importance of local units, federal systems of government should *not* be viewed this way.

Crucial Role of the Middle Level

What distinguishes federal systems of government from unitary systems is the existence of a middle level. It is the role and character of these governments (states in the United States, Australia, and India; Länder in Germany; provinces in Canada) that differentiate federalism from a unitary form of government. The relative strength of the role of these middle-level governments is what determines the overall strength of federal systems. A variety of aspects of the role of state governments should be the basis for assessing the strength of the federal form in different settings—for example, according to the relative strength of these governments in terms of their fiscal, legal, and programmatic role and powers; the strength of their political and cultural identity; the structure of the federal-state relationship; and the authority (both formal and informal) state governments exercise over local units.[4] In the United States, some states assign extensive home rule powers to local units. These are the powers local governments have to set their own tax rates, policies, and regulations. The critical point here is that this is basically (though not fully) each *state's* decision. It is to states that we must look to understand the balance of contemporary American federalism. The story line in recent years for the federalism changes now under way—and accelerating—has been the rising role of the states. At the outset of American history, states were the dominant governments in our political system. Today, they are coming into their own again.

Rising Role of the States

Five factors undergird this ascendance of the American states. One is the conservative and devolutionary policies adopted under the Reagan administration. A second, long-term factor underlying state activism is the modernization movement in state government, which first appeared in the mid-1960s. The phrase refers to reforms adopted by states to increase their managerial and technical capacity to take on new and expanded functions. In a 1985 report, the Advisory Commission on Intergovernmental Relations concluded that "state governments have been transformed in almost every facet of their structure and operations."[5] A third factor is the effect of the Supreme Court decision in *Baker v. Carr* (1962). This decision reduced the rural-urban political imbalance of state legislatures and increased public support for a stronger role for state governments. A fourth and related factor is "the end of southern exceptionalism." Martha Derthick believes that the civil rights revolution and integration in the South created a situation in which "the case for the states can at last begin to be discussed on its merits."[6] Finally, the strong recovery of the U.S. economy from the 1981–1982 recession contributed to the resurgence of the states in the 1980s. This factor interacted in an important way with Ronald Reagan's devolutionary policies to highlight the role of the state. Typically, state governments overreact to national recessions, battening down their fiscal hatches by cutting spending and raising taxes to balance their budgets. In late 1982 the strong recovery from recession meant that state coffers were filling up just as Reagan's federal aid retrenchment policies were being felt. This high volatility of state finances put state governments in a position to spend more and do more in those functional areas from which the federal government under Reagan was pulling back or signaling its intention to do so.

Taken together, these trends have produced a resurgence of the state role in American federalism. Evidence of this change appears in the states' response to Reagan's domestic budget cuts, his creation of new block grants, and related changes in federal grant-in-aid programs.[7] Data compiled by the U.S. Bureau of the Census show in the aggregate that state governments increased their role during the Reagan years. From 1983 to 1986, as the Reagan retrenchment and federalism policies took effect, state aid to localities increased by an average of 5.6 percent a year in real terms, that is, adjusted for inflation.[8] Total state spending rose by nearly the same percentage. Prior to that, from the mid-1970s to 1983, both state aid to localities and total state spending had been level in real terms. Considerable variation exists, however, in the character and mix of state expenditure increases, reflecting U.S. Supreme Court Justice Louis Brandeis's famous characterization of state governments as laboratories that can "try novel social and economic experiments without risk to the rest of the country."[9]

There are no ready calipers for measuring the activism and innovativeness of individual states. Studies by political scientists Jack L. Walker and Virginia Gray indicate that over time it has been the larger, older, and ideologically most liberal or pro-government states that have tended to be most innovative.[10] Other research suggests a broader distribution of state innovation in response to increasingly conservative national fiscal policies and devolutionary initiatives.[11] Southern and western states contributed to the rising role of state governments in the 1980s.

In the middle of the twentieth century, when state governments were in the doldrums, political scientist Morton Grodzins and other scholars downgraded their importance. In a famous essay, Grodzins said federalism is not a layer cake. Instead, he introduced the metaphor of a marble cake "characterized by an inseparable mingling of differently colored ingredients, the colors appearing in vertical and diagonal strands and unexpected swirls." Continuing, Grodzins said, "As colors are mixed in the marble cake, so functions are mixed in the American governmental system."[12] Even for its time, this theory downgrading the role of the states seemed a serious exaggeration. It is patently wrong today to ignore the distinctive and crucial role of states in American federalism. Events occurring now in national policy making in Washington are highly likely to enhance further the role of state governments in American federalism. State governments are challenged today to take on new roles and responsibilities as never before in the twentieth century.

Building Blocks of the "Devolution Revolution"

The best description of the domestic program of the Republican leadership of the 104th Congress is one of a "Devolution Revolution." A major aim of this revolution is the creation of block grants. Block grants are fixed amounts of money distributed to state (and sometimes local) governments on an automatic formula-allocation basis that can be spent flexibly within major functional areas of government. There are two ways to create block grants. One is the conventional way, by consolidating existing, narrower so-called "categorical" grants into lump-sum formula allocations to states and localities. The second way, new and more important, is to create block grants by closing the end on what had previously been open-ended grants-in-aid to the states, thereby placing a limit on federal aid payments. The two biggest block grants proposed in the 104th Congress are for Medicaid and the Aid to Families with Dependent Children (AFDC) program. Together Medicaid and AFDC account for half of total federal grant-in-aid spending. (The purpose of Medicaid is to provide health care services for the poor, including nursing home and other types of institutional care for the elderly and disabled. The AFDC program provides cash assistance to poor families with children. For more on AFDC, see Chapter 10.) Under both programs, the federal government pays the states a share of the benefits they provide to eligible families and individuals. Republican leaders in the Congress seek to convert these two programs into lump-sum payments to the states allocated on a formula basis with aggregate caps on their annual spending.

In addition to converting Medicaid and AFDC into block grants, leaders of the Congress have proposed measures to convert other entitlement-type grants (for example, for foster care, school nutrition, and welfare-related child care) into block grants; to convert food stamps (now federal vouchers) into a block grant; to create block grants in the conventional consolidation mode, as in the case of work force development, combining nearly ninety existing programs into a three-part block grant; and to reduce the size of other grants-in-aid, that is, grants that are not currently block grants or recommended to be converted into block grants.

The 104th Congress, as noted, has also cut back on the regulatory requirements of federal aid programs—that is, the conditions Congress places on the receipt of federal grant funds. These conditions, often referred to as mandates, can involve requirements tied to the use of federal aid funds. They can also involve requirements that are not intrinsic to the purpose of the funds provided. The mandates issue has created bad blood between national and state and local officials.

Taken together, this push to decentralize presents a challenge to the states. It rivals in historic importance the shifts made earlier in this century to centralize American governmental responsibilities during the New Deal era and the years of the Great Society. We don't know what the consequences will be. Predictions tend to be more influenced by ideology than by scholarship. Liberals predict a "race to the bottom," with states competing with each other to slash social benefits. Conservatives see a golden opportunity to integrate social programs, tone down social engineering, and generally enhance the efficiency of domestic government.

There is only one prediction that can be made with confidence, and that is that the response of state governments to the Devolution Revolution will be *varied*. Moreover, the effects of the changes in domestic policy now being contemplated in Washington are likely to shift over time.

Table 2-1 1995 Block Grants

Block Grant	Millions of Dollars (estimated)
Surface Transportation	18,773
Community Development Block Grant	3,186
Social Services Block Grant	2,800
Federal Transit Capital and Operating Assistance	2,284
CDBG States' Program	1,246
Low Income Home and Energy Assistance Program	1,319
Prevention and Treatment of Substance Abuse	1,234
Job Training Partnership Act, Title II-A	1,055
Child Care and Development Block Grant	935
Maternal and Child Health	684
Education (Federal-State-Local Partnerships)	370
Community Services	392
Community Mental Health Services	275
Preventative Health and Health Services	152
Assistance for Transition from Homelessness	29
Total	34,834

Source: Budget of the U.S. Government, Fiscal Year 1996, Budget Information for the States (Washington, D.C.: Government Printing Office, 1995).

History of Grants

One can go back to the pre-Constitutional period to find intergovernmental subventions to the states. During the period when the United States operated under the Articles of Confederation, the Continental Congress adopted the first grants-in-aid to the states, putting aside land for the support of public schools in territory west of the Ohio River. However, cash grants-in-aid were not significant until the twentieth century. The years of Woodrow Wilson's presidency started a slow and steady rise in cash grants to the states for major programmatic purposes. But even after Franklin Roosevelt's New Deal, federal aid accounted for only 10 percent of total state and local spending. It was under Lyndon Johnson that federal aid jumped to where it is now; from the mid-1960s to the present, federal grants-in-aid have represented about 30 percent of total state and local spending.

Federal grants-in-aid to states, localities, and nonprofit groups were estimated at $238.5 billion in the federal budget submitted for the fiscal year that began October 1, 1995. This included fifteen programs classified as block grants by the General Accounting Office and the Advisory Commission on Intergovernmental Relations (see Table 2-1). Over half of total outlays for current block grant programs is for surface transportation, provided as federal aid on a much more flexible and discretionary basis than in the past under the Intermodal Surface Transportation Efficiency Act of 1991.

Figure 2-1   1995 versus Proposed Block Grants

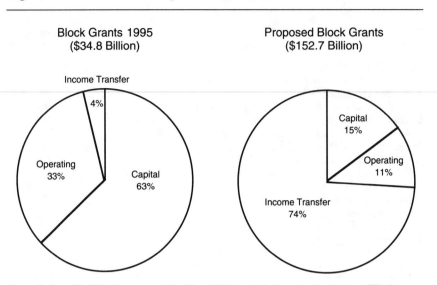

Block Grants 1995
($34.8 Billion)

Proposed Block Grants
($152.7 Billion)

Source: Budget of the U.S. Government, Fiscal Year 1996, Budget Information for the States (Washington, D.C., Government Printing Office, 1995).

The block grants now being debated in the 104th Congress represent a significant change in U.S. domestic policy because they mark a break with the past fifty years of steady accretion of entitlement-type federal grants-in-aid that operated on a fiscally open-ended basis. Under entitlement programs, states automatically receive payments equal to a fixed proportion of the income transfers (both cash and in-kind) they provide to poor families and individuals. These entitlement grants were actually entitlements to states. The states in turn determined the benefits eligible individuals and families received within the framework of federal laws and regulations.

Looked at on an across-the-board basis, there are three types of federal grants-in-aid: those for operational purposes (education, child care, etc.), those for capital purposes (surface transportation, wastewater treatment), and entitlement grants for income-transfer to families and individuals (Medicaid and AFDC). Figure 2-1 illustrates the dramatic shift that would occur with the blocking of entitlement (income transfer) grants.

Block Grants Emerge

It was during the Johnson administration that block grants first emerged in the modern era. Johnson saw the writing on the wall in the form of growing state and local government resentment towards narrow-gauged and particularistic federal grants. The idea of block grants began to take hold in answer to what chairman of Johnson's Council of Economic Advisors, Walter Heller, called "the hardening of the categories."

Responding to pressures from governors and mayors, President Johnson in 1966 proposed a block grant that would consolidate several public health grants into a single comprehensive grant for public health services. In 1967 Johnson took a bigger leap into grant blocking (although not enthusiastically) when his administration, with Republican urging, backed the creation of the law enforcement assistance grant. These funds were distributed on a formula basis to states with a requirement that 75 percent of the funds provided be passed on to localities.

Nixon's New Federalism

As already noted, contemporary block grants have generally been created through the consolidation of pre-existing categorical grants into broader grants with the combined stream of grant funds from the folded-in programs allocated to states and/or localities on an automatic formula basis. President Nixon's New Federalism successfully advocated the creation of several such block grants, notably for community development, employment and training, and social services. Nixon also won passage of a general revenue sharing program in 1972, which provided flexible aid on a formula basis to states and localities. But this was not called a block grant, because the use of this aid was not limited to a particular function of government (for example, law enforcement or community development).

Among the three basic types of federal grants mentioned earlier (entitlement grants, operating grants, and capital grants), Nixon's New Federalism called for blocking two types of grants—operating and capital grants—but not entitlement grants. Nixon was a spender when it came to grants and domestic policies in general. Besides his revenue sharing program (which involved distributing $5 billion per year in new funds to states and localities), Nixon's block grants included funds known as "sweeteners." The term referred to extra funds provided on top of the money contained in the categorical grants bundled together in a new block. Nixon added these sweeteners as an inducement to state and local officials to support his initiatives.

Again, Nixon did *not* recommend blocking entitlement grants. In advocating the sorting-out of functions in American federalism, Nixon argued that income transfers (cash, health care, foster care, school lunches, food stamps) should be made more—not less—national to assure equal treatment of the needy and to share this fiscal burden on a national basis. The consensus is that the community development block grant was the most successful of the block grants created under Nixon, moving away from huge renewal and slum clearance projects to more selective, targeted local development initiatives. Neither Nixon's Family Assistance Plan (FAP) for welfare reform nor his Family Health

Insurance Plan (FHIP, which was similar to Clinton's 1993 health-reform proposal) were enacted.

Reagan's New Federalism

President Reagan's brand of "new federalism" (he didn't use the term, but the press did) departed from Nixon's approach on the idea of blocking entitlements. Reagan was much less committed to the idea that what have come to be referred to as "safety net" functions should be exclusively or mainly carried out by the national government. In 1982 Reagan advanced a "swap and turnback" plan, which proposed that the national government take over Medicaid. In exchange, the states would pick up the responsibility for the AFDC program. In short, Reagan was on the fence on this federalism issue. He proposed centralizing one income transfer program (Medicaid) and devolving another (AFDC). As it turned out, Reagan's "swap and turnback" plan was not even introduced in Congress.

In the 1981 Omnibus Budget Reconciliation Act (OBRA), Reagan won enactment of nine new programs dubbed "block grants" by his administration. Like Nixon's block grants, they extended to operating and capital functions, and *not* to entitlement-type programs. Three were mainly in the health field— for the prevention and treatment of substance abuse and mental health, preventive public health services, and maternal and child health care. None of these programs were especially large, and four of the "blocks" contained only one pre-existing categorical grant. Reagan's reputation as a grant blocker is overrated. However, his block grants have one important point in common with Nixon's. As shown in Table 2-2, these grants lost value over time, both in nominal dollars and in real terms (that is, adjusted for inflation).

Enter the New(t) Federalism

The House Republican majority in the 104th Congress is decidedly not on the fence when it comes to block grants for welfare-type programs. Early on in the "First 100 Days," Speaker Newt Gingrich and his Republican colleagues set about creating block grants for entitlement grant programs with a vengeance. This is in sharp distinction to the policies of Nixon and Reagan. In effect, the new Republican majority in the Congress favors repealing the national "safety net" aspect of grants that provide aid in cash and in kind to poor families and individuals on an open-ended basis.

These devolutionary policies of the new majority in Congress do not stand alone. They are part and parcel of the strong movement in the country towards conservatism and limiting government, which is being played out in the legislative and budget processes. Some cynics see the new devolution as a tactic (even a cover) for conservatism and budget reduction. This doesn't gainsay the point that the new devolution is distinctive historically and likely to cause powerful shifts in the balance of federalism.

Table 2-2 Reagan Block Grant Obligations (millions of dollars)

Block Grant	Year										
	1983	1984	1985	1986	1987	1988	1989	1990	1991	1992	1993
Social Services	$2,675	$2,700	$2,725	$2,584	$2,697	$2,700	$2,700	$2,762	$2,804	$2,800	$2,800
Low-Income Energy Assistance	1,975	2,075	2,100	2,008	1,822	1,532	1,383	1,443	1,610	1,500	1,346
Community Services	373	348	368	352	368	363	319	322	436	360	372
Prevention/Treatment of Substance Abuse[a]	468	462	490	469	509	487	806	1,193	1,269	1,080	1,108
Preventive Health & Human Services	85	87	89	87	89	85	84	83	91	129	143
Maternal and Child Health	478	399	478	457	497	526	554	554	587	650	664
Improving School Programs	462	451	500	477	501	478	400	519	449	446	440
Community Development[b]	2,380	2,380	2,388	2,053	2,059	1,973	2,053	1,972	2,203	2,397	2,790
Job Training and Partnership Act[c]	1,415	1,886	1,886	1,783	1,840	1,809	1,788	1,745	1,778	1,773	1,692

Source: Rockefeller Institute of Government, Center for the Study of the States, *State Fiscal Brief,* January 1995, No. 26.

[a] The prevention and Treatment of Substance Abuse Block Grant included mental health until FY92.

[b] Community Development Block Grant data do not include undistributed allocations, nor do they include spending on the nonentitlement portion of the Block Grant.

[c] The JTPA Block Grant is for the Adult and Youth Training Block Grant portion of the JTPA program.

Essential Questions

James Madison is mis-characterized by conservatives who attribute to him the idea of devolving national programs to the states. Madison's constitutional purpose in 1787 was nation building—in effect, centralization. Indeed, his opening gambit at the Constitutional Convention was a plan that would have given the national government an absolute veto power over state laws. By the same token, classical public finance theory in the modern period assigns redistributional functions to the broadest population group to achieve equal (or close to equal) treatment for the needy and to share this fiscal burden widely. As a nation, we have done this (or at least moved strongly in this direction) since the 1930s. The United States is by no means first among the industrial democracies in centrally providing this safety-net function. However, in our own distinctive, incremental way of making policy, Americans have spent the last six decades building alliances, striking bargains, and forging political compromises that gave the federal government a leading role in setting, administering, and financing a wide range of social policies. Nowhere has this process been more inexorable than in the steady increase in the federal role in social welfare policy. Thus, blocking income-transfer programs to the poor represents a basic change in direction both for American federalism and for social policy.

Issues of Federal-State Relations

This is an exciting, fluid time for American federal-state relations. A recent report by the Advisory Commission on Intergovernmental Relations (ACIR) expressed the view that the U.S. Supreme Court is unlikely to alter its present interpretation of the Tenth Amendment, which reserves the powers not assigned to the national government as reserved to the states or to the people:

> By virtue of the Supreme Court's opinion in *Garcia v. San Antonio Metropolitan Transit Authority*, reversing *National League of Cities v. Usery*, states are virtually powerless to challenge federal action in the courts on Tenth Amendment grounds.[13]

In a similar vein, recent ACIR reports have highlighted legislative preemption by the national government of state and local authority. The commission in 1992 called attention to "an ever widening range" of federal statutes in the commercial, monetary, civil rights, environmental, health, and safety fields.[14] Referring to the number of federal preemptions, the commission said they have

> *increased to the point that over half of all such preemptions in the nation's constitutional history have been enacted by the Congress only since 1969.* These preemptions include prohibitions of economic regulation and other activity by the state and local governments, as well as requirements that states enforce federal laws, conform their own laws to federal standards, and take on new responsibilities. Federal preemptions also may override state and local deci-

sions and prevent states and local governments from pursuing policies preferred by their citizens.[15] (Italics added.)

However, there is now movement towards the states in all three branches of American government on these and other federalism issues. This is reflected in the Court's decision in *United States v. Lopez* and Justice Clarence Thomas's dissent in the term limits decision (*U.S. Term Limits, Inc. v. Thornton*), both of which were handed down in 1995.[16] In the *Lopez* case the Court held that Congress did not have the power to make it a federal crime to possess a gun near a school. Going even further, Justice Thomas's dissenting opinion in the *Term Limits* decision, concurred in by Justices William Rehnquist, Sandra Day O'Connor, and Antonio Scalia, would have strikingly limited the power of the federal government and given the states extensive new authority. The Court found state-imposed term limits for elected members of the House to be unconstitutional since "the power to add qualifications was not within the original powers of the states, and thus was not reserved to the states by the Constitution's Tenth Amendment." The two events—one a decision overturning a federal law and the other a powerful dissent—have renewed the debate in the Court about the relative roles of the enumerated powers of the federal government in Article I of the Constitution and the reserved powers of the Tenth Amendment. The Tenth Amendment states, "The powers not delegated to the United States by the Constitution, nor prohibited by it to the States, are reserved to the States respectively, or to the people."

Indeed, the rhetoric of federal-state relations needs to be reassessed today. This rhetoric has a familiar ring to it. The problem of federal government domination of the states is lambasted as "Leviathan." It is derided as "Mother Knows Best." It is described in terms of intrusion by "pointy-headed" federal bureaucrats in state and local affairs. It is discussed in terms that emphasize mandates without money. It is depicted as the "proliferation" of categorical grants-in-aid. Data provided by the ACIR show an increase from 1993 to 1995 in the number of federal grants-in-aid from 594 to 634.[17] While I have always been skeptical of such raw counts of aid categories, certainly it is fair to say that new block grants will slow such proliferation, although it has to be added that old habits die hard.

Other federal-state issues involve organizational requirements. Federal laws and regulations often tell states how to structure their government, requiring them to set up agencies in certain ways and to create regional and other special bodies that may or may not be the way state and local officials and the public want to operate. On this question, as on others, the situation could change with block grants, but it is unlikely to change the whole picture. In the transportation field, for example, the 1991 Intermodal Surface Transportation Efficiency Act prescribes a regional structure for planning, public participation, and decision making. On the other hand, in the environmental field, a rollback has begun as Congress overhauls laws and changes federal agency roles and staffing, though again it is not clear what the eventual outcome will be. As for federal-aid waivers, they can be thought of in a way suggested by Martha Derthick: "as reversing the historic presumption in inter-governmental relations."[18]

> The historic presumption is that the states are the primary, the bedrock, governments. Domestic functions fall initially to them. Over time, the federal government constrained them by attaching conditions to aid, but it was still up to them in the first instance to decide what to do. The constitutional presumption was in their favor. They were free to do things unless, after the fact, the federal government said they couldn't.
>
> Waivers have reversed the presumption. They assume that power and discretion rest initially with the federal government. It is the primary domestic government. It makes the rules, and if the states want to do something, they must begin by asking its permission.[19]

These are *structural* and *process* issues. We also need to look at issues involving *functions* of government. Increasingly in the twentieth century, particularly in the middle part of the century and continuing up into the 1970s, the national government seemed willing, even eager, to step into any and all functional areas of domestic public affairs. During this century, especially in a response to the Great Depression, with the enactment of welfare-state policies, and under the civil rights revolution and in the environmental movement, a heightened role was assigned to the central government. In the Great Society period, Medicaid was the "400 pound gorilla" in terms of federal intervention in a functional area. State officials often claim Medicaid is not a grant-in-aid; it is a mandate to serve and spend. Maybe it is a good one. Nonetheless, it is portrayed as a federal government initiative that has reduced the fiscal flexibility of the states, growing rapidly in the 1980s, in some years by as much as 19.5 percent. The other side of this argument claims that Medicaid has been used by the states as a way to shift health and health-related activities into the federal aid stream.

In essence what is involved in the debate over changes in Medicaid and AFDC is a tradeoff between *policy goals* and *federalism goals*. Both programs represent mechanisms for aiding needy groups in the society. These programs, as noted, are not an entitlement to individuals or families, because the states set the eligibility rules and benefit amounts. Rather, they require that states serve certain groups along with setting other requirements about the way these functions have to be carried out. People of good will can argue (and many have) that the social purposes encompassed in these two programs are best advanced centrally and that the desirability of advancing them outweighs concerns about the role of states in American federalism.

Some readers may object to the focus on "welfare-type" functions in this analysis. But note the wording. These functions refer to the broad field of social policy. A similarly intense debate is now going on in one other broad functional area—environmental policy. The rollback efforts in environmental policy now underway raise equally profound questions about how states will perform if greater discretion is assigned to them. In other major areas of domestic affairs—for example, transportation and law enforcement and corrections—federalism issues are more settled. The Intermodal Surface Transportation Efficiency Act of 1991 has quieted debate in this field, pending how the new law works, which is not yet known. In the law enforcement and corrections fields, federalism issues that involve the courts are regarded by many state officials as sufficiently serious to require strong remediation. In any event, the issues here are different from those in the arena of social policy. To sum up, there are bound to be differences of view in the body politic that on the one hand reflect a strong concern about some functional area that advocates believe should be centralized and on the other reflect a strong concern that state and local officials may be undercut by such centralization policies. These questions never will be settled for all times. There is no magic arrangement for sorting out responsibilities in American federalism.

Strategies for Strengthening the States

It is useful to consider next different strategies that can be taken to strengthen the role of the states in American federalism. One is legislative and relates to the functional realignment just discussed. A second is constitutional and focuses on structural changes in the basic relationship of the national government and the states. A third is operational.

Functional Realignment

Functional realignment in American federalism is often portrayed as a "sorting-out" process—that is, sorting out functions of government between the national government and the states. Candidates for political office often use this metaphor to indicate their theory of American government. The positions taken in this sorting-out debate involve more than matters of political structure. They involve assumptions about how much money should be spent for particular purposes, how policies should be formed and implemented, and what the results will ultimately be in the lives of citizens. For example, the current debate about welfare block grants can be viewed in terms of federalism and governmental structures, but the more important consideration for many observers involves the amount of money that will be spent on the poor.

There is, as just stated, no one intrinsic way to view the proper alignment of functions in American federalism. Take as an example the function of welfare. It is common among people who write about federalism to argue that welfare should be primarily or exclusively a national government function. The reasons for this appear to be good ones: transferring income should be national because people move from state to state and all eligible people in the country should be treated the same way; also, there are efficiency and equity benefits from sharing the burden of the treatment of the poor across the whole fisc. Indeed, what has come to be known as classical Musgrave public finance theory reflects this position.[20]

Yet, welfare today is hotly debated in terms that suggest it is viewed by the public and most politicians as far more than a check-writing function. Unlike social security retirement benefits, for example, there has been an escalation of the rhetoric about transforming welfare policies from payment systems into *service* systems. The welfare debates of the past ten years have been predominantly about *social-service interventions* to change behavior. This was the aim of the Family Support Act of 1988. The welfare debate currently is not, as it was in the 1970s, about minimum payment levels, benefit disregards, and marginal reduction rates along the lines of arguments for the so-called "negative income tax" approach to welfare reform. More than anything else, the debate today is about how to prevent teenage pregnancy and reduce the number of children born out of wedlock to fathers who are unwilling to take responsibility for them in the kind of traditional family setting that, like it or not, is strongly favored by a sizable majority of the people who participate in elections in America. To a great extent, these welfare debates are about interventions that can prevent dependency on the part of poor parents (mostly single women) through regulatory requirements and remedial services and activities such as job placement and counseling, training, education, and the provision of child care to enable welfare family heads to participate in the labor market.

Whether this behavior-modification function focusing on social services should be assigned to the national government or to the states is not an easy question to answer. Generally speaking, the literature on federalism suggests that income-transfer functions should be centralized, whereas service-type functions should be decentralized. The point is often made that the provision of services (e.g., education, job training, child care) is not a type of activity that can be orchestrated, and even more so that can be managed, by the central government in a nation as vast as the United States. One benefit of federalism is that it allows for the flexibility of state and local action to assess and deal with social service needs in ways that reflect different regions representing a variety of conditions, attitudes and aspirations. One can object to this argument, but it needs to be noted that the main body of writing about federalism has treated this decentralized service attribute of the genre as an advantage of the federal form.

One can also argue that health care for the poor under Medicaid is more of a service function than a check-writing function. Although it is not the aim of this chapter to make a case for a particular way of realigning functions in American federalism, it should be clear that there is no one sorting-out of function in federalism for all times. Ideas and purposes change. Whereas in the 1970s, many people (both experts and non-experts) viewed welfare and health care for the poor as basically an income-transfer function, this is not the case today. In short, the way one views a function has a lot to do with where one puts it.

Structural Change

Another way to change the balance of American federalism is by altering its constitutional structure. Although the framers rejected the idea, the U.S.

Constitution could be amended to institute a state veto of federal laws or a process that would require their reconsideration. There was sentiment to do so on the part of Anti-federalists at the Philadelphia Convention; however, James Madison at the time was in precisely the opposite camp, favoring "a sweeping veto by the national government on all state laws."[21] Madison the politician recanted a decade later, consorting with his fellow Virginian, Thomas Jefferson. He then urged a realignment of American government, ironically in much the same way that today's new majority in the Congress is using the party machinery to devolve responsibilities. In the Kentucky Resolution, which Madison authored (Jefferson authored the Virginia Resolution in the same year, 1798), he asserted that the Constitution (his very own handiwork) created a *compact* of the several states. This interpretation came to haunt Madison's legacy when it was used as an argument for succession by southern states in the middle of the nineteenth century.

Similar to proposals to allow some proportion of the states (usually two-thirds) to veto national laws, recommendations have been advanced to add the word "expressly" to the reference to "delegated" powers assigned to the national government in the Tenth Amendment. It is also possible to follow the lead of other federal countries, for example Canada, Australia, and Germany, where regional governments have a formal role in national government policy making. In Canada and Australia, there are official "Premiers' Conferences" that participate in central government policy making. They meet regularly, share information on common problems with national government officials, and consider and take joint actions. The intergovernmental specialists who staff these bodies have a role in central government decision making on a continuing basis, especially in periods when the Premiers' Conferences are not in session. In Germany, the Länder have strong, explicit administrative responsibilities with less rigorous oversight powers available to the Federal Council than is the case of the national government under U.S. federalism.

Another avenue for structural reform is to change the amendatory process to permit the states to initiate constitutional amendments. Now, the Congress has the power to do this. Indeed, the framers intended that there should be a state route to amendatory reform in crafting the Convention process, which arguably never worked as intended. (The Advisory Commission on Intergovernmental Relations recently recommended that there be a constitutional provision for the call for amendatory conventions that are limited to particular issue areas or proposals.) Still another constitutional avenue for change would add specific constraints to Article I limiting the conditions under which the national government could influence activities of the states. A proposal to do this by legislative action has been advanced by Sen. Hank Brown, R-Colo. and others. Other, less fundamental institutional changes could be accomplished by law, for example, by strengthening the unfunded mandates law enacted in 1995, or by executive action. The unfunded mandate law only applies to future mandates and even then is not high powered.

Using Clout

A third strategy for strengthening the role of the states can be viewed as operational. States already have consequential powers for influencing both the character and execution of domestic programs. Few things demonstrate this more clearly than the emergence in 1995 of the block grant strategy in the House. It was Republican governors who originally pressed for the block grants at a meeting with Speaker Newt Gingrich and Senate Leader Robert Dole at the November 1994 Republican governors conference in Williamsburg, Virginia. Governors as a group—Republicans and Democrats alike—have been pushing since then for these kinds of devolutionary changes in domestic policy. Across the board the organizations representing state governments, such as the National Governors' Association and the National Conference of State Legislatures, have become stronger and smarter. The officials of state government are talented men and women anxious and able to wield strong influence in many areas of domestic public affairs. It used to be assumed that the national government had a monopoly on talented governmental experts and executives. Whether this was ever true, it is not true today. States have won a place at the table, more precisely at the many tables where decisions are made about the character and execution of domestic policy. They are using this clout right now to reshape American federalism.

Conclusion

The jury is out on how the Devolution Revolution will be encompassed in laws that realign functions in American federalism. Some observers have concerns about the functional realignment plans. The essential point here is that this functional realignment may be so great in the final analysis that state government officials may decide that structural and institutional change strategies are no longer as important as they once were seen to be. A major question for federal-state relations is whether to push for constitutional changes to re-balance federalism or to wait and see what happens in the wake of the functional realignment processes currently under way.

In my view, the constitutional route is the wrong road to travel. Devolutionary policy changes and structural and administrative reforms by the states should be the focus of attention for governors, legislators, and other state officials and their partisans. Everyone who cares about the role states play in our governmental system will have an overflowing plate in responding to the new challenges being put to them. In this setting, it would not be wise to devote the time and energy necessary to educate the public and press for constitutional change.

What is more, the constitutional route is not an easy one to take. Opening up the Pandora's box of constitutional change could stimulate efforts that involve divisive, emotional issues that should not be added to the Constitution. The U.S. Constitution is general and short. This is part of its genius. State governments have their moment in the sun right now. They should seize it rather than commit huge amounts of energy and argumentation to constitutional change.

Notes

Author's Note: The author thanks Herb Kaufman and Tom Anton for help in making revisions.

1. Stanley Elkins and Eric McKitrick, *The Age of Federalism: The Early American Republic, 1788–1800* (New York: Oxford University Press, 1993), 43.
2. See Robert D. Putnam, "Bowling Alone: America's Declining Social Capital," *Journal of Democracy* 6 (January 1995): 65–78.
3. Roscoe C. Martin, *The Cities in the Federal System* (New York: Atherton Press, 1965).
4. See Richard P. Nathan, "Defining Modern Federalism," in *North American and Comparative Federalism Essays for the 1990s*, ed. by Harry N. Scheiber (Berkeley, Calif.: Institute of Governmental Studies Press, 1992).
5. Advisory Commission on Intergovernmental Relations, *The Question of State Government Capability* (Washington, D.C.: Advisory Commission on Intergovernmental Relations, January 1985).
6. Martha Derthick, "American Federalism: Madison's 'Middle Ground' in the 1980s," *Public Administration Review* 47 (January/February 1987): 72.
7. See Richard P. Nathan and Fred C. Doolittle, *Consequences of Cuts: The Effects of the Reagan Domestic Program on State and Local Governments* (Princeton, N.J.: Princeton University Press, 1983); and Nathan and Doolittle, *Reagan and the States* (Princeton, N.J.: Princeton University Press, 1987).
8. Steven D. Gold and Corina L. Eckl, "State Budget Actions in 1984," Fiscal Affairs Program, National Conference of State Legislatures, Legislative Paper 45, September 1984. See also Steven D. Gold, "Developments in State Finances, 1983 to 1986," *Public Budgeting and Finance*, 7 (Spring 1987).
9. *New State Ice Co. v. Ernest A. Liebmann*, 285 U.S. 262–311 (1931).
10. Jack L. Walker, "The Diffusion of Innovation among the American States," *American Political Science Review* 63 (September 1969) 880–899. Walker's analysis is for the period 1960–1969; Virginia Gray, "Innovations in the States: A Diffusion Study," *American Political Science Review* 67 (December 1973): 1174–1185.
11. See Nathan and Doolittle, *Consequences of Cuts*, and *Reagan and the States*.
12. Morton Grodzins, "The Federal System," in *Goals for Americans: The Report of the President's Commission on National Goals* (New York: Columbia University Press, 1960), 265.
13. Advisory Commission on Intergovernmental Relations, "Federal Regulation of State and Local Governments: The Mixed Record of the 1980s," A-126, July 1993, iii.
14. Advisory Commission on Intergovernmental Relations, "Federal Statutory Preemption of State and Local Authority: History, Inventory, and Issues," A-121, September 1992. See also "Federal Regulation of State and Local Governments: The Mixed Record of the 1980s," A-126, July 1993; and "Intergovernmental Decisionmaking for Environmental Protection and Public Works," A-122, November 1992.
15. Ibid., 1.
16. *United States v. Lopez* (No. 93-1260) 1995. *U.S. Term Limits, Inc. v. Thornton* (No. 93-1456 and 93-1828) 1995.

17. Advisory Commission on Intergovernmental Relations, "Characteristics of Federal Grant-in-Aid Programs to State and Local Governments: Grants Funded FY 1995," M-195, June 1995.
18. Letter to the author, August 29, 1995.
19. Ibid.
20. Refers to the work of economist Richard A. Musgrave who pioneered public finance theory. See *Public Finance in Theory and Practice*, 3d ed. (New York: McGraw-Hill, 1980), 524.
21. Elkins and McKitrick, *The Age of Federalism*, 83.

3

State Budgeting:
Problems, Choices, and Money

Henry J. Raimondo

Introduction

States are back in style. Not that they were ever completely out of style—certainly state leaders believed state government was innovative and responsive to the people. But now, in the halls of Congress, in the chamber of the Supreme Court, and even in the Oval Office of the White House, states have become the building blocks for re-inventing government operations.

If a single document could tell the story of state government operations, that document would be the state budget. Budgets do not, however, yield their stories easily. They are a thick, overflowing, virtually indecipherable accumulation of numbers, charts, and tables. Yet they contain all the secrets of state government. After all, budgets are about people's problems, political choices, and lots of money.

Budgets determine which programs the governor and legislature agree to support and fund. These programs address the daily problems of the people: safe streets, children's education, the commute to work, medical treatment for ill parents and grandparents, even auto registration.

Budgets are also the playing fields for politicians. Grand political ideas frame the budget debate: taxes versus spending, local control versus state intervention, publicly provided services versus private contracting-out, and, of course, individual choice versus government regulation. Every current in American politics, every public policy fad, and every serious decision to be faced is found in the budget debate.

The glue that holds the budget together is money. States raise and spend a lot of it. While the federal government has the most to spend, states have nothing to be ashamed of when the dollars are added up. States raise money using every tax imaginable. There are taxes—usually more than one—on what you earn, what you spend, and what you save. There are taxes on people, businesses, and even animals. The adage that "two things in life are certain: death and taxes" is true. In fact, even if you are dead, you could pay taxes! States also spend money. Dealing with people's problems does not come cheap. Schools, hospitals, roads, prisons, courts, and more all cost a great deal of money. In this chapter we will look at the public services states provide, how these services have changed over time, what relationships dictate budget decisions, and what emerging public policy issues states will confront in the future.

State Governments' (In)visible Functions

State governments suffer from an image problem. Many people do not know what they do or why they are necessary. The federal government spends money on national defense and transfer programs for individuals (for example, Social Security, Medicare, Medicaid, and food stamps). Local governments educate children, police communities, put out fires, pick up trash, and plow snow-covered streets. What's left for state governments to do?

Public services provided by state governments are seemingly invisible precisely because people have become so accustomed to having them: roadway and rail systems, courts and prisons, welfare payments, subsidized health and nursing home care, moderately priced and accessible public colleges and universities, affordable housing, and financial aid to local governments. A look at the spending habits of state governments will explain what states do, and give some shape to the invisible functions of state government.

Spending Profile

Data from the 1992 *Census of Government Finances* document states' spending patterns. In that year, states spent $611.9 billion on general expenditures. Figure 3-1 shows the distribution of state spending in 1992 grouped under seven categories: elementary, secondary, and higher education; public welfare; health and hospital services; highways; debt service on borrowed money; corrections; and other functions, which include public safety, environment and housing, and government administration among others. For each dollar spent, approximately 34 cents goes for education, 26 cents for public welfare, 8 cents for health and hospitals, 8 cents for highways, 4 cents for debt service, 3 cents for corrections, and 17 cents for the other functions noted above. Unless you or a family member are enrolled in school, receive welfare, are ill, or are in prison, the activities financed by state governments remain out of view.

While this way of looking at spending is useful, it does not relate spending to people. Another perspective is needed. Per capita (person) spending is a measure that tells us how much a state spends on its typical resident. With this calculation a cross-state comparison can be made. The U.S. average for per capita spending in 1992 was $2,404. The five highest spending states were Alaska ($8,157), Hawaii ($4,226), Wyoming ($3,703), New York ($3,359), and Rhode Island ($3,315). The five lowest spending states were Texas ($1,741), Missouri ($1,832), Florida ($1,842), Colorado ($1,871), and Georgia ($1,893). The ratio of spending in the highest state to spending in the lowest state is 4.69 to 1; that is, for every dollar Texas spends, Alaska spends $4.69. When the top five and bottom five states are removed to exclude "unusual" spending behavior, the ratio of spending in the sixth state (Delaware at $3,253) to the forty-fifth state (Tennessee at $1,917) is 1.69, which means that for every dollar Tennessee spends, Delaware spends $1.69.

Figure 3-1   General Expenditures of State Government by Function, 1992

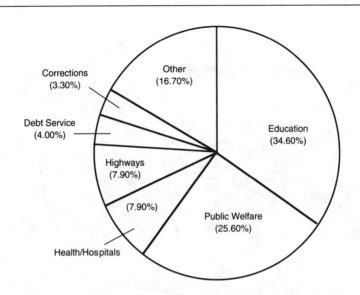

Source: Calculated from U.S. Bureau of the Census, *Census of Government Finances* (Washington, D.C.: Government Printing Office, 1992).

Even without the highest and lowest spending states, broad spending differences across the states remain. These differences reflect variation in costs, choices, quality of services provided, and financial resources among the states. The issue of states' revenue-raising capacity certainly influences states' budgeting practices. So what options do states have to raise money?

Revenue Profile

In 1992 states raised $605.3 billion to finance their general expenditure activities. Revenues came from grants, various taxes (for example, sales, personal income, and corporation income taxes among others), and user charges. Figure 3-2 shows the distribution of these revenue-raising sources: approximately 26 cents from federal grants, 27 cents from sales taxes, 17 cents from individual income taxes, 4 cents from corporation income taxes, 6 cents from other taxes, 9 cents from user charges or fees for a service, and 11 cents from miscellaneous revenue sources. Many of these revenue sources are not progressive revenue systems; that is, they take the same or a greater percentage of income from lower income people than they do from higher income people.

The revenue-raising counterpart to per capita spending is per capita revenues. This measure connects revenue-raising to people and permits interstate comparisons. Taxpayers complain about living in a high-tax state. Or

Figure 3-2   General Revenues of State Government by Source, 1992

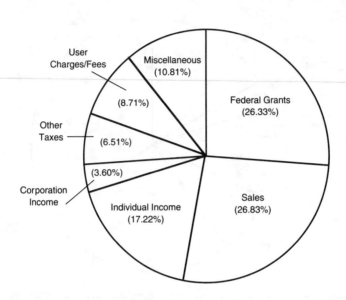

Source: Calculated from U.S. Bureau of the Census, *Census of Government Finances* (Washington, D.C.: Government Printing Office, 1992).

politicians brag to the media that they govern a low-tax state. Per capita revenue is the measure on which such complaints and claims are based. The U.S. average in 1992 was $2,370. The five highest revenue-raising states were Alaska ($9,101), Hawaii ($3,938), Wyoming ($3,697), Delaware ($3,565), and New York ($3,334). The five lowest revenue-raising states were Florida ($1,754), Texas ($1,775), Georgia ($1,833), Missouri ($1,901), and Tennessee ($1,916). The ratio of the highest revenue-raising state to the lowest is 5.19 , meaning Alaska raises $5.19 for every one dollar that Florida raises. When the highs and lows are excluded, the ratio of the sixth highest revenue-raising state (Connecticut at $3,090) to the forty-fifth (Kansas at $1,969) is 1.57, meaning that Connecticut raises $1.57 for every one dollar Kansas raises.

Revenue-raising disparities among the states reflect differences in political willingness and/or economic capacity to raise revenues for public purposes. Some observers of federalism view these disparities, whatever their cause, as a weakness in the federal system that calls for federal government action in the form of mandated policies and/or increased intergovernmental grants. Others see these differences as simply the natural outcome of a decentralized system of decision making.[1]

Budget Process

A budget ties together spending on public services and raising revenues. Twenty-nine states follow a one-year or annual budget cycle; twenty-one states, a two-year or biennial cycle. For forty-six states, the fiscal year extends from July 1st of one year to June 30th of the next year. Four states use different beginning and ending dates: Alabama and Michigan follow the federal government fiscal year (October 1st to September 30th); New York uses April 1st to May 31st; and Texas, September 1st to August 31st.[2]

The typical fiscal year (based on the July 1st to June 30th cycle) is divided into three intervals: preparation, adoption, and implementation.[3] During the preparation interval, from October to December, the executive branch prepares its budget based on accepted economic and fiscal forecasts of state spending and revenue collections. Inaccuracies in the revenue forecast are not uncommon. Democrats and Republicans often make different assumptions regarding revenue estimates to advance an ideological position or justify a fiscal choice involving taxes and spending. For example, Republicans might overestimate revenues to reduce taxes or underestimate revenues to cut spending. Democrats might overestimate revenues to expand human services programs or underestimate revenues to increase taxes. The governor and the legislature resolve such discrepancies later in the fiscal year. The governor presents a budget to the state legislature in January. During the adoption interval, from January to June, the state senate and house or assembly review and rework the governor's budget. In June, the governor signs the budget into law. The implementation interval, which runs the entire fiscal year, refers to the execution of the approved budget resolution.

The governor may veto the entire budget, requiring the legislature to reconsider it, or veto just a portion of the budget. Governors in forty-four states have the line-item veto, which allows disapproval of individual lines in the budget or specific expenditure items. Whether the governor vetoes the entire budget or specific parts, the legislature can vote to override the veto.

In forty-nine states (Vermont is the exception), the state constitution or state statutes require a balanced budget; that is, expenditures must equal revenues. A budget surplus results if expenditures are less than revenues. A budget deficit occurs if expenditures are greater than revenues. When expenditure commitments routinely exceed forecast revenues, the state budget has a built-in deficit, or a structural deficit. Unless expenditures are cut or taxes raised, the structural deficit will persist. Because a budget may be in balance the day it is approved, but in deficit just a month later, thirty-six states prohibit budget deficits being extended into the next fiscal year. Balancing a budget in deficit can be achieved through authorized spending cuts, rainy-day funds, and borrowing.

Most states authorize the executive branch (usually the governor) to take the lead in balancing the budget. Twenty states permit the governor to make selective and across-the-board cuts in spending; thirteen allow the governor to specify only across-the-board cuts; eight empower the governor to decide upon spending cuts up to some maximum (expressed in dollars or percentage); and eight require that the governor consult with the legislature on cutting expenditures.

A financially sound state budget sets aside a percentage of the revenues to be used to make up the shortfall for higher than anticipated expenditures or less than anticipated revenues. This rainy-day fund, formally installed by twenty-nine states, is insurance against a deficit. Some voters and legislators oppose the fund, believing that every dollar of public money should be spent or that the state government should not be holding taxpayers' money as surplus funds. In a recessionary cycle, a rainy-day fund is usually depleted or empty—a dry hole.

Borrowing to close a budget gap entails selling state bonds to raise money to cover the operating budget. However, the debt service on the borrowed money, as well as a repayment schedule to pay back the principle, would appear in subsequent state budgets. To help state executives and legislators maintain fiscal discipline, sixteen states place tight constitutional controls on the use of borrowing to balance state budgets. A recession increases the likelihood of a budget deficit. A budget deficit, in turn, sends bond ratings tumbling. Low bond ratings sour investors on purchasing state debt. As a result, borrowing can be a costly option, if available at all.

These elements—the spending profile, the revenue profile, and the budget process that ties the two together—summarize the activities of state governments in recent years. These activities are the outcome of numerous adjustments over time as states became more assertive in the policy arena.

Changing State Budget Priorities

We have looked at state budgets using financial data for the most recent year for which they are available—1992. We will next look at state budgets as they have changed over time to capture shifting public priorities. Clearly, the combination of people's problems, political choices, and money produces different budgets with each passing fiscal year. In consequence, the scope of our examination widens. In addition to the now familiar spending and revenue dimensions (the operations budget), our investigation will also include states' spending on public infrastructure (the capital budget).

State fiscal policies have changed over time to respond to changes in people's needs. The resources allocated to state financial activities reflect this dynamic behavior. To illustrate this point, data for the 1970s (1970–1979), the 1980s (1980–1989), and the 1990s (1990–1992) have been collected and translated into 1987 dollars to adjust for inflation. This adjustment permits us to view any changes in spending or revenue-raising practices as an indication of new directions in state policy making.

Figure 3-3   Expenditure Profile by Activity and Decade

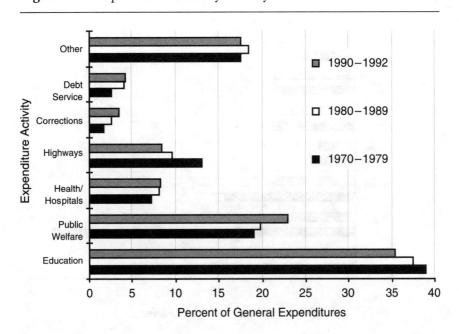

Source: Calculated from U.S. Bureau of the Census, *Census of Government Finances* (Washington, D.C.: Government Printing Office, 1992).

Operations Budget

Figure 3-3 provides an expenditure profile by activity and by decade. The decades have witnessed a reduction in the share of general expenditures allocated to education, highways, and, to a lesser extent, other activities. The gainers have been public welfare, health and hospitals, corrections, and debt service. Generally, investment activities such as education and highways (though still significant) have been gently moved aside by distribution activities such as public welfare and health and hospitals. This switch in emphasis explains state policy makers' interest in recent welfare and health care reforms that promise to save states money. Reductions in these two programs would constrain the growth in state spending and create the opportunity for tax cuts—an outcome that is every governor's fiscal objective.

Figure 3-4 depicts revenues by source and by decade. From the 1970s to the 1990s, the share of general revenues has declined for federal grants (though with some recent gains in the 1990s), sales taxes, corporate income taxes, and other taxes. Shares have increased for individual income taxes, user charges and fees, and miscellaneous revenues. While still heavily dependent on grants and sales taxes, states have generally turned to personal income taxes and away

Figure 3-4   Revenue Profile by Source and Decade

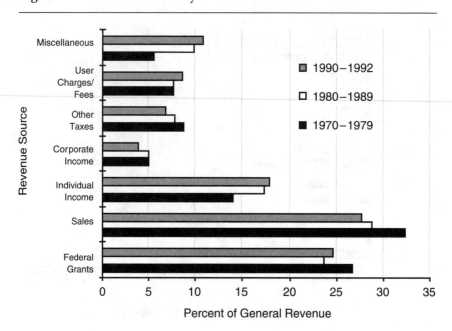

Source: Calculated from U.S. Bureau of the Census, *Census of Government Finances* (Washington, D.C.: Government Printing Office, 1992).

from corporation income taxes, and towards user charges and fees and miscellaneous revenues. This combination has generally made the state revenue-raising system more burdensome for lower- and middle-income people.

Capital Budget

The level of investment in public infrastructure is a critical ingredient in the nation's long-term economic performance. A modern infrastructure allows people, goods, services, and information to move faster and more easily within and through the country. Capital investment also makes the difference in the quality of life. The condition of public buildings, recreational facilities, and air and water treatment systems affects safety, health, education, and leisure activities.[4] If state governments are to maintain the public infrastructure, then the burden on state resources will likely increase. The need for more rather than fewer resources for public infrastructure comes at a time when state budgets are under heightened fiscal stress.

A look at capital spending (adjusted for inflation) by state governments shows that in the 1970s states spent an average of $35.6 billion annually and in the 1980s an average of $29.4 billion annually. If capital spending is broken

Figure 3-5   State Capital Outlay by Function and Decade

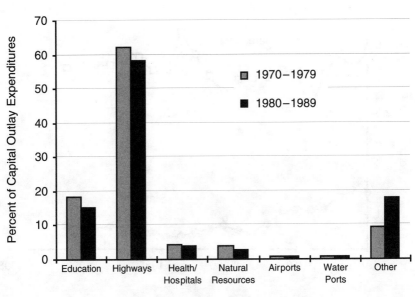

Source: Calculated from U.S. Bureau of the Census, *Census of Government Finances* (Washington, D.C.: Government Printing Office, 1992).

into functional areas, then the investment profile across the decades shown in Figure 3-5 reveals that capital spending on education declined from 18 cents of every dollar spent in the 1970s to 15 cents of every dollar spent in the 1980s; highways declined from 62 cents in the 1970s to 58 cents in the 1980s; health and hospitals remained at 4 cents of every dollar in both decades; natural resources declined from 4 cents in the 1970s to 3 cents in the 1980s; and airports and water ports remained unchanged at almost 1 cent across the two decades. Only the "other" category showed an increase across the decades from 10 cents of every dollar in the 1970s to 18 cents in the 1980s. Much of this increase can be traced to capital spending on correction facilities.

State governments accounted for a declining percent of public infrastructure investment. During the 1970s, the state percentage of public (federal, state, and local) capital spending was 25.6 percent, or $357.7 billion out of a total of $1.4 trillion. That level of investment dropped during the next decade. In the 1980s, the state percentage fell to 19.5 percent, or $333.8 billion out of a total of $1.7 trillion.

A comparison gives more meaning to these absolute dollar amounts. Figure 3-6 displays state capital spending as a percent of gross domestic product (GDP) from 1970 to 1992. As a nation's economy grows, the underlying pub-

Figure 3-6   State Capital Outlay as a Percent of U.S. GDP

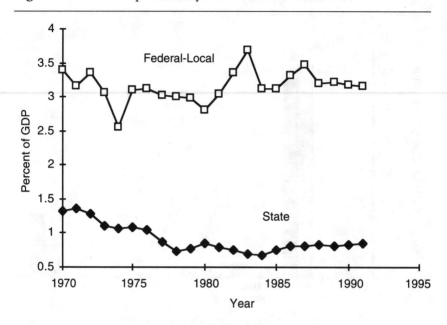

Source: Calculated from U.S. Bureau of the Census, *Census of Government Finances* (Washington, D.C.: Government Printing Office, 1992).

lic infrastructure to support that economic growth should also expand. The benchmark is that spending on infrastructure should increase in the same proportion as GDP increases. Just as a family should save and invest the same percentage when its income increases, a nation should do the same. Figure 3-6 also shows the "Federal-Local" capital spending as a percent of GDP. In 1992, the share of GDP for total federal-local public capital spending was approximately 3.25 percent. For every one dollar of GDP, the federal-local public sector allocated 3.25 cents to infrastructure. Despite the fluctuations over the period 1970–1992, the 1992 share is marginally different from the almost 3.4 percent figure in 1970. The case for state capital spending is more disturbing. In 1992, the state share of GDP for public capital spending ("State") was approximately 0.75 percent. This percent was down from the 1.3 percent in 1970. The decline has been almost constant over the period 1970–1985.

In light of the importance of public infrastructure investment to the states' future economic well-being, this declining trend in the core infrastructure—highways and streets, mass transit, airports, and water ports—requires state policy makers' attention. States might be permitting their public capital stock to deteriorate, which could result in limited potential economic growth.

State Budgets: Economy, Grants, And Population

State government fiscal behavior has obviously changed over the past two and a half decades. While annual changes in spending and revenue raising dominate daily political discourse and media coverage, the economy, federal grants, and population dictate long-term fiscal behavior for state governments. The economy determines the level of productive activity that state governments can tax; the federal grant system establishes the level of external financial support that state governments can expect to receive from Washington; and population trends set the level of demand for public services.

GDP-Revenue Correlation

States live off the performance of the private economy. When the economy grows, revenue-raising capacity is enhanced. Clearly, when the economy stagnates, revenue-raising stalls as well. The simple "GDP-Revenue" correlation is that state general revenues (Revenue) follow the economy, as measured by U.S. gross domestic product (GDP). As the U.S. GDP grows, state general revenues grow. Conversely, as the U.S. GDP declines, state general revenues decline. In fact, a falling GDP clearly depresses state general revenues.

On a state-by-state basis, the GDP-Revenue correlation appears to hold. States with the highest per capita levels of economic activity such as New Jersey, California, New York, and Massachusetts are among the highest revenue-raising states. At the other extreme, states with the lowest per capita level of economic activity such as West Virginia, Mississippi, Alabama, and Kentucky are among the lowest revenue-raising states.

Figure 3-7 traces the U.S. GDP and state general revenues from 1970 to 1992. Generally, the GDP-Revenue relationship holds during years of decline in GDP (e.g., 1974–1975, 1978–1979, 1981–1982, and 1989–1991) and growth in GDP (e.g., 1971–1972, 1975–1976, 1983–1984, and 1991–1992). The most recent national economic recovery (1993 to the present) coupled with the balanced budget news coming out of the nation's statehouses verify the GDP-Revenue correlation.[5]

With projected slow growth (i.e., under 3 percent) in the U.S. economy for the next decade, and with the limited set of revenue-raising systems reviewed earlier, state general revenues should increase only modestly.[6] State policy makers will be under constant economic stress as they strive to meet the demand for public services. The pressure to establish clear priorities, terminate unnecessary programs, and continuously innovate will likely characterize state government operations in the coming years.

Grant-Expenditure Correlation

State governments have routinely looked to the federal government for financial assistance through the intergovernmental grant system. Usually, the

Figure 3-7   GDP-Revenue Correlation

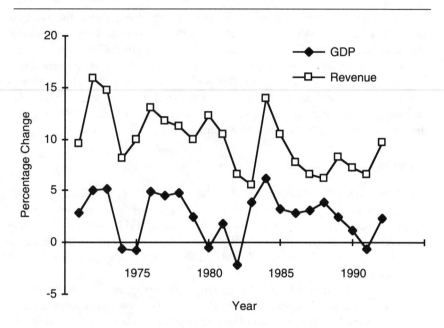

Source: Calculated from U.S. Bureau of the Census, *Census of Government Finances* (Washington, D.C.: Government Printing Office, 1992).

federal government delivered. Federal aid to state governments increased through the 1960s and much of the 1970s. In the 1980s, federal aid began to decline in real terms. The simple "Grant-Expenditure" correlation is that state general expenditures (Expenditure) are closely tied to federal intergovernmental grant (Grant) levels. When grant levels grew significantly, state general expenditures were pulled along. When grant levels grew less dramatically, state general expenditures also grew by less. Figure 3-8 displays this Grant-Expenditure relationship. With few exceptions, the relationship between federal grant levels and general expenditures behave as expected.

The "Grant-Expenditure" correlation plays an important role in state budgeting. As federal budget-balancing initiatives become more popular, the likelihood of little or no growth (even some declines) in federal grant assistance is great. If states cannot or will not raise their own revenues, then they can expect little additional financial assistance from the federal government. Public services and public employment will likely be reduced. Public service dependent populations which include children, the elderly, and the poor, will suffer accordingly. The rest of the decade, then, will be marked by a slow, but steady deterioration in the quality of life for anyone who relies on the state public sector.

Figure 3-8   Grants-Expenditure Correlation

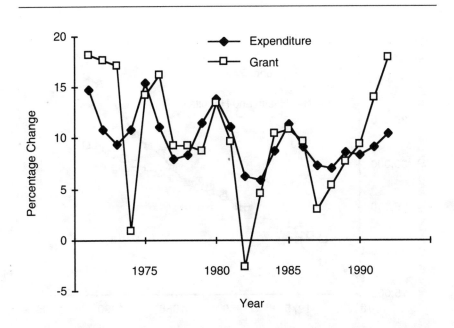

Source: Calculated from U.S. Bureau of the Census, *Census of Government Finances* (Washington, D.C.: Government Printing Office, 1992).

Population-Expenditure Correlation

People demand public services: highways and mass transit to travel to work or move goods, school for their children, health care for their parents or themselves, safe streets, clean air and water, and recreational facilities and parks. The third rule that governs state budgets is the "Population-Expenditure" correlation that says that as the number of people increases, the demand for public service spending increases.

Population and state spending trends confirm the value of this relationship. Population has ranged from 203.3 million in 1970 to 255.2 million in 1992. General expenditures have ranged from $241.9 billion in 1970 to $509.5 billion in 1992. With the exception of 1982 (a recession year), general expenditures grew as population grew. For the period 1970–1992, the average growth rate in population was 1.2 percent and the average real expenditure growth was 5.0 percent. Obviously, general expenditures increased much faster than did population. This outcome is attributable in part to increased cost, enhanced quality, or expanded scope of services provided by the state.

Even more important than the growth of the general population is the growth of certain primary public service users in the population such as those

Figure 3-9   Health Expenditures versus 65 and Over Population

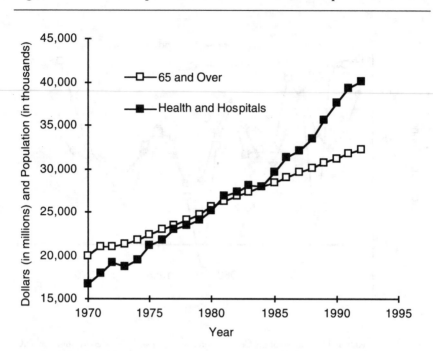

Source: Calculated from U.S. Bureau of the Census, *Census of Government Finances* (Washington, D.C.: Government Printing Office, 1992); and U.S. Bureau of the Census, *Census of Population* (Washington, D.C.: Government Printing Office, 1992).

over 65 years of age. Figure 3-9 shows the growth in the population of those 65 and over for the period 1970–1992. This group of service users ranges from 20 million in 1970 to 32.3 million in 1992. State expenditures for health and hospitals, which include Medicare, are also shown in Figure 3-9. They range from $16.7 billion in 1970 to $40.1 billion in 1992. The average growth rates were 2.8 percent for the 65 and over group and 6.4 percent for health and hospital expenditures.

The growth of the 65 and over population has generally been relatively lower than the growth in health and hospital expenditures. Since 1984, growth in the latter has accelerated and increased the fiscal pressure on state taxpayers. With the baby boom generation (those born between 1947 and 1964) aging, these expenditures will likely explode after 2010 unless cost containment procedures are soon put into place. This face explains in part the governors' interest in some form of health care reform. Governors are all too aware of this demographic time bomb. Health care reform that features cost containment provisions will stay on the public policy agenda for the foreseeable future.

Emerging Policy Issues

These three correlations—economy, grants, and population—largely frame the debates about state budgets. They are permanent features of the budget landscape that budget balancers must juggle year after year. In addition, there are always new objectives that complicate the process. At this time, two emerging policy issues deserve mention: the federal balanced budget amendment, which will likely reduce federal support to state governments, and the re-invention of government that centers around the privatization of public services.

These two emerging issues reflect the new fiscal realities for states in the latter part of the 1990s and beyond—that is, less federal support and the pressure to innovate and cut costs. The problem of passing state budgets that maintain current service levels, anticipate future needs, and strengthen the states' economies will try the skills of public managers and elected officials and the patience of the voters.

Federal Balanced Budget Amendment

Initiatives to balance the federal budget have profound implications for the operations of the federal system of government. The Constitution, Supreme Court rulings, and adequate, available funding are the basis for the states' independent public policy-making powers.[7] Adequate, available funding is dependent in part on sufficient levels of federal grant assistance. Any attempt to balance the federal budget will likely reduce these levels and therefore weaken the foundation for state autonomous decision making. Even so, efforts to balance the federal budget are well under way.

Advocates of a balanced federal budget have initiated a two-pronged attack on the current federal budget deficit. The first part dissolves the structural deficit in the federal budget, a situation where commitments cause expenditures to exceed revenues. The second part is a constitutional amendment to lock-in the balanced budget. The first part took shape in June 1995.

The Republican majorities in the House and the Senate passed plans to balance the federal budget over a seven-year period. Spending would be reduced in the range of $950 billion to $1.4 trillion. The most significant cuts would occur in Medicare (health care for the elderly)—at least $255 billion— Medicaid (health care for the poor)—at least $175 billion—and an assortment of other programs, including several welfare programs.[8] As the earlier discussion of the Grant-Expenditure relationship demonstrated, a reduction in federal grants will likely lead to a cut in state expenditures. Balanced budget enthusiasts, however, are thinking beyond the seven year transition plan. Beginning in 2002, Congress would turn to the blunt instrument of a constitutional amendment to maintain a balanced federal budget. The notion is not new.[9] Since 1980, balanced budget amendments made regular appearances on the congressional agenda. In 1995, an amendment came close to passing.[10]

That amendment read in part: "Total outlays for any fiscal year shall not exceed total receipts for that fiscal year." Further, it stated: "the limit on the debt of the United States held by the public shall not be increased."[11] Any constitutional amendment that requires a balanced federal budget hurts states whose residents receive federally mandated transfer payments and who benefit from direct federal spending and/or federal employment.

Proponents of the balanced budget amendment predict faster economic growth. As the federal government reduces the budget deficit, the competition for borrowing reserves will ease. A decline in interest rates will follow. The national economy will then boom and absorb those workers who were fired with the act of balancing the budget. However, not every analyst sees such an optimistic outcome to a balanced budget amendment.

Some believe that a loss of federal resources will eventually translate into employment losses. Projections for the period 1995–2002 indicate that losses could be in the range of 10 million jobs nationwide. The Middle Atlantic region (especially New York), the South Atlantic (especially Florida), the Pacific region (especially California), the East North Central region (especially Illinois), and the West South Central region (especially Texas) will bear the brunt of any unemployment associated with a balanced budget amendment.[12] Honest differences about how the national economy will react to a balanced budget amendment leads to these two views. Of course, political ideology also plays a role.

Balancing the federal budget may be commendable federal fiscal policy, but its impact on the states will be extreme. A balanced budget amendment will reduce public services, raise taxes, cut public employees, absorb rainy-day funds, or force the sale of state assets. More important, the autonomy of states to fashion their own public policy approaches to solve people's problems will be diminished.

Re-inventing Government

The second emerging issue is the intention to re-invent government. Many voters believe that government has the billions of dollars needed to address the people's problems. Further, there is a nagging feeling that government is not using these billions in the most effective way. Reality still spoils the American Dream, as evidenced by high crime rates, high taxes, low high school graduation rates, high unemployment, low job mobility, low real wages, and so on.

Elected officials are under pressure to be innovative (or at least appear innovative). For many elected officials, re-inventing government or being innovative boils down to one word, privatization. Privatization takes on three different meanings. The first is the sale of a publicly owned asset—for example, a state-owned marina, turnpike, water works, stadium, day-care center, or drug treatment center. The second is the use of a voucher or ticket to purchase goods or services—for example, an education voucher so children may attend the school of their choice. The third is the contracting-out of public services to private vendors—for example, trash pick-up, ambulance service, or school transportation service. In the United States, privatization usually means contracting-out.[13] The appeal of contracting-out is the promise of improved efficiency. Private contractors promise reduced costs for the same level of services through greater efficiency in the production and delivery of the service.

Contracting-out has made some inroads in the provision of educational services, social services (especially health and medical services, ambulance services, homeless shelters, drug and alcohol treatment programs, homeless food programs, and mental health programs), corrections, administrative services, transit services (especially maintenance), construction (especially engineering and inspection services), and recreational and sports facilities management.[14] In each of these cases, public managers have not always privatized the entire function, but rather have divided the function into its components parts and privatized some of these individual components.

Re-inventing government through privatization, especially contracting-out, is fast becoming a preferred approach to public service delivery. The promise of privatization—namely, cost-savings—has not yet materialized in every application. Also, the private provision of public services does not automatically mean better services. Public managers need more experience with contracting-out activities to distinguish the promise of private vendors from their performance.

Conclusion

Prior to the Civil War, "United States" took a plural verb, considered as it was a collection of states. After the Civil War, it became a singular noun, reflecting its status as a unified country. The intergovernmental fiscal arrangements between the states and the federal government in the 1980s and 1990s harkened back to the pre–Civil War mentality—"go-it-alone" federalism dominated policy discussions.

In the 1980s, the federal government gave the states the cold shoulder. Instead of a policy dialogue, it took unilateral policy actions. The signals were unmistakable: a cut in federal grants, an increase in unfunded federal mandates (for example, the American with Disabilities Act and the Clean Air Act, among others), the serious consideration of a balanced budget amendment, and proposed cuts in federal social programs such as welfare and health care. Each action weakened the financial links that bind the federal government and the states together. State governments usually reacted by cutting services and raising taxes.

As the United States approaches the end of the twentieth century, the federal system is not well positioned to expand economic opportunity. The federal government has no coherent domestic agenda to enhance economic competitiveness. The states meanwhile are disinvesting in people, neglecting the public infrastructure, and privatizing public services. Go-it-alone federalism has changed the nature of intergovernmental relations in the United States. The federal government is busy balancing its budget, not deciding how it will meet its financial responsibilities to society as a whole. This financial version of pre–Civil War thinking about federalism will frustrate states as they try to educate their people, rebuild their infrastructure, provide for their homeless, and tend to their elderly and infirm. Thinking of the United States as one country with common problems and shared resources would be a vast improvement.

Notes

1. Henry J. Raimondo, *Economics of State and Local Government* (New York: Praeger, 1992).
2. Advisory Commission on Intergovernmental Relations, *Significant Features of Fiscal Federalism* (Washington, D.C.: Government Printing Office, 1986).
3. Paul Solano and Marvin Brams, "Budgeting," in *Management Policies in Local Government Finance,* ed. J. Richard Aronson and Eli Schwartz (Washington, D.C.: International City Management Association, 1986).
4. Edward M. Gramlich, "Infrastructure Investment: A Review Essay," *Journal of Economic Literature,* 32 (September 1994): 1176–1196.
5. Peter Kilborn, "Economic Growth Leaves States In Best Shape Since Early 80s," *New York Times,* July 16, 1995, 1, 16.
6. "Regional Economies: Booming and Fading," *The Economist,* July 8, 1995, 25–26.
7. Linda Greenhouse, "Justices Step In As Federalism's Referee," *New York Times,* April 28, 1995, A1, A23; and Greenhouse, "Farewell to the Old Order In the Court," *New York Times,* July 2, 1995, Sec. 4, 1 and 4.
8. George Hager, "Daring Budgets Would Create Vastly Smaller Government," *Congressional Quarterly Weekly Report,* May 13, 1995, 1298–1307.
9. Sondra J. Nixon, "Budget Amendments: An Idea That Never Goes Out of Style," *Congressional Quarterly Weekly Report,* January 14, 1995, 142–143.
10. David E. Rosenbaum, "Budget Amendment May Be Short Of Enough States for Ratification," *New York Times,* January 23, 1995, A1, A12.
11. Andrew Taylor, "Budget Amendment's Fate Hinges On a Handful of Democrats," *Congressional Quarterly Weekly Report,* February 5, 1995, 355–358.
12. Wharton Econometric Forecasting Analysis (WEFA Group), "State Impacts of the House and Senate Balanced Budget Amendment," July 1995.
13. David Osborne and Ted Gaebler, *Reinventing Government* (New York: Addison Wesley, 1992).
14. Yolanda Kodrzycki, "Privatization of Local Public Services: Lessons for New England," *New England Economic Review* (May/June 1994): 31–46; and Richard Worsnop, "Privatization," *CQ Researcher,* November 13, 1995.

4

The Transformation of State Electoral Politics

Stephen A. Salmore and Barbara G. Salmore

It is now a commonplace observation that the emergence of candidate-centered campaigns has caused a massive change in presidential and congressional elections. These candidates now use television, radio, and direct mail rather than party organizations to communicate messages about themselves directly to voters. As a result, the candidates' personal qualities and their records in office have become voting cues that rival or surpass the party labels that traditionally determined most voters' decisions. With less visibility and less at stake, candidate-centered voting for state gubernatorial and legislative offices was slower to take hold. The candidates for these offices were less able and had less need to get their message directly to voters. Party labels and organizations remained critical factors in determining these election outcomes.

However, as state government has become more important and visible, it attracts increasingly able and ambitious politicians. More is now at stake in state-level elections, more political players are interested in their outcomes, and more resources are available to wage campaigns. Not surprisingly, therefore, party-line voting is declining and candidate-centered campaigns are also becoming more prevalent at the state level.[1] Throughout the 1980s and early 1990s, these trends, along with the continuing shift of gubernatorial elections out of presidential election years, helped insulate state-level elections from national trends. However, in 1994 powerful national trends had a major influence on election outcomes, as heavy Republican gains were recorded at all levels of government. Strong "out-party" candidates are still better positioned to survive such tidal waves, which are unlikely to occur very often and may not have the same degree of staying power that they once had.

Gubernatorial Campaigns and Elections

Three interrelated developments provide insight into the character of recent gubernatorial contests: the "presidentialization" of gubernatorial elections, the increased decoupling of partisan outcomes in state and national executive races, and trends in the financing of gubernatorial election contests.

Candidate-Centered Campaigns

Over the past three decades, television has transformed the way in which presidents are elected in the United States. Voters, able to see and hear the candidates on the nightly news programs as well as in political advertising, judge candidates on the basis of their character and personal values more than ever before. The personal, even intimate, problems of a Gary Hart, who sought the Democratic presidential nomination in 1984 and 1988, or of a Bill Clinton in 1992 can easily become the focus of voter attention. As a result, presidential candidates' images have become more salient than their party labels and substantive issue positions.[2] The net result is a style of campaigning that focuses almost exclusively on the candidate instead of the party.

Candidate-centered presidential appeals have led to candidate-centered campaign organizations. Presidential candidates increasingly choose to separate their central campaign organizations from the national party organization. The campaign finance laws of the 1970s, which provided for public funding of the general election and partial public funding of individual candidates in the nomination phase—funneled through individual campaign organizations rather than the parties—reinforced this inclination. Many recent candidates not only separated themselves from their national party organizations, but also practically divorced themselves from their fellow partisans running for other offices.

Presidents seeking reelection try to stay above the partisan fray during the actual campaign season. Paid advertising emphasizes their accomplishments in office. Presidents proclaim themselves too busy to debate their opponents, making it difficult for voters to compare the candidates or to get the idea that the challenger might be as accomplished as the current chief executive.

In short, both the presidential campaign and presidential office have become the province of individual entrepreneurs, relying on their own skills and their own resources more than those of their political parties. These developments are mirrored in the campaigns of many governors.

A variety of aggregate data suggests that split-ticket and cross-party voting has become as rampant in recent gubernatorial elections as it is in presidential elections.[3] During the 1950s, the governor's party on average controlled both houses of the state legislature in 68 percent of cases and neither house in only 20 percent of cases. This partisan homogeneity was a consequence of the state electorates' patterns of party identification. Usually, when split control did occur, it resulted from legislative gerrymandering and malapportionment. By the 1970s, although Supreme Court decisions had ended malapportionment and blatant gerrymandering, the governor's party controlled both houses only 53 percent of the time and neither house 35 percent of the time. By 1990, 49 percent of the thirty-five states in which one party controlled both legislative houses had a governor of the other party. The strong Republican trend in 1994 resulted in unified party control in 60 percent of the thirty-eight states in which one party controlled both legislative houses—a percentage still below that of the 1950s.

Another indicator of candidate-centered voting in gubernatorial elections is the increase in partisan turnovers. In the 1950s, 24 percent of elections resulted in partisan turnovers in the governor's office, a figure that rose to more than one-third in the 1970s and 1980s and to 39 percent in 1994. Moreover, party turnovers were much more likely in contests without incumbents. As party identification in the electorate and party organizations in campaigns became less important, candidates of either party had a better shot of winning. The races most likely to be competitive—those for open seats—were much more likely to attract strong contenders.

A popular and seemingly invulnerable incumbent, meanwhile, generally attracts only the weakest of challengers, particularly if the governor is of the majority party, but often even with more balanced party competition. Incumbent governors in such situations seem to barely acknowledge that a campaign is going on. Consider, for example, the 1994 race in Nebraska.

Ordinarily Republicans should be competitive in Nebraska, which has not supported a Democrat for president since 1964. The incumbent governor, Democrat Ben Nelson, had won only narrowly in 1990, defeating a Republican incumbent who had raised taxes. But in 1994, a year in which Republicans made major gains in all regions of the country, Nelson was seen as such a secure incumbent that the Republicans could not field a strong candidate. Running on a record perfectly attuned to the conservative trend of the times—controlling state spending, reforming welfare, starting a state lottery dedicated to funding education projects, and building more prisons—Nelson swamped Republican business executive Gene Spence by almost three to one.[4]

With a Republican tide running in 1994, a number of GOP governors who had won very narrowly in 1990, but who earned public approval by enacting major policy reforms, won reelection by landslide proportions. In overwhelmingly Democratic Massachusetts, William Weld governed as an economic conservative and social liberal, and saw his victory margin go from 3 percent in 1990 to 43 percent in 1994. In Michigan, John Engler defeated a Democratic incumbent by less than 1 percent in 1990. After pushing through major welfare reform, extensive privatization of government services, and entirely shifting the funding of public schools from the local property taxes to the state sales tax, he was reelected with 72 percent of the vote.

In contrast, less secure incumbents of both parties and candidates for open seats must fully engage their opponents. In 1994, with Maine's Republican governor John McKernan finishing his second and constitutionally mandated last term, a three-way race developed that ultimately was won by a former business executive and state public television personality, Angus King, who ran as an independent. The Republican nominee came in third, with just 23 percent of the vote. In the same year, California, Florida, New York, and Texas all featured well-known incumbents who were strongly challenged in races that closely resembled presidential contests. In Texas and Florida, popular Democratic incumbents Ann Richards and Lawton Chiles were each challenged by a son of former President George Bush. In Florida, Jeb Bush, who saw his initial lead wither when his connection to a failed savings and loan association became a campaign issue, lost by less than 2 percent of the vote. In Texas, George Bush, Jr., after running neck and neck with Richards for much of the campaign, went on to a more comfortable than expected 7 percent victory. During the campaign, both Texas candidates spent much time arguing the merits of their successful fights with alcoholism.

New York Democrat Mario Cuomo and California Republican Pete Wilson, incumbents who had won multiple statewide elections and become nationally known political figures, both faced major challenges in 1994. Early on, Cuomo trailed the little-known state senator, George Pataki, then surged to a lead when endorsed by New York City's Republican mayor Rudolph Giuliani in October, only to lose narrowly in November. California's Pete Wilson, opposed by Democrat Kathleen Brown, the state treasurer and sister of former governor Jerry Brown, initially trailed by as much as 23 percent in the polls, but went on to win comfortably as the champion of a statewide referendum to limit illegal immigration. The focus of each of these races was more on the candidates than on their party affiliations. Three of the four challengers were from high-profile political families well known to voters. Both they and the governors they challenged waged very expensive campaigns that featured the thrust and parry of thirty-second television ads that were as likely to feature personal attacks as policy statements. The campaigns went on for much of the year and generated intense press coverage. In sum, they were the equivalent of presidential campaigns fought out at the state level.

The Rise of Direct Primaries

The spread of the direct primary has had the same negative effect on party control of gubernatorial nominations and campaigns that it had on presidential contests. Virtually all gubernatorial candidates have their own campaign organizations and team of personal political consultants. In only sixteen states have provisions been made for pre-primary endorsements by state parties in gubernatorial contests, and there is little evidence that they regularly count for much.[5] Primary elections can be remarkable free-for-alls, with the state party organization helpless to control events.

Minnesota's 1994 gubernatorial race is a good example of the irrelevance of party organizations when nominations can be won in a direct primary by candidates who appeal directly to voters with strong and effective messages. Independent-Republican Arne Carlson was first elected governor in 1990. That year he bypassed the Republican party convention and lost the primary by a wide margin to the convention winner, John Grunseth. However, nine days before the election, Grunseth withdrew from the race in the face of charges of sexual misconduct. Carlson replaced him and went on to win a narrow victory. His relatively liberal record in office did not sit well with the conservative party activists who had originally rejected his candidacy. In 1994, the party convention, by a wide margin, refused to endorse incumbent Carlson, choosing instead a strong abortion opponent favored by the religious right. In the primary election, Carlson defeated the convention's choice by an almost two-to-one margin. In the same primary, the party convention's choice for attorney general was also defeated, by a candidate described by the state's major newspaper as an "eccentric." Similarly, the Minnesota Democratic-Farmer-Labor party convention's designee for governor barely survived a multicandidate primary, winning less than 40 percent of the vote. He went on to lose to Carlson in the general election by almost two to one.[6]

Minnesota was not unique. Rhode Island's 1994 primary voters rejected both party's convention endorsements for the gubernatorial nomination—the Democratic incumbent and a Republican member of Congress. Convention-endorsed candidates also lost in primaries in Colorado, Connecticut, and New Mexico. In fact, the proportion of party-endorsed candidates who go on to win contested primaries has dropped from about 80 percent in the period 1960–1980 to just over 40 percent.[7]

Not all states exhibit such extreme candidate-centered campaigns, and the stronger state party organizations participate in other ways in gubernatorial elections, particularly in encouraging voter mobilization on election day. Republicans often mail absentee ballots to likely Republican voters. Both Democratic and Republican state party organizations make sizable contributions to various statewide races. State Democratic organizations, often in conjunction with Democratic congressional candidates, finance substantial get-out-the-vote efforts in heavily Democratic voting precincts. The Republican National Committee contributes directly to some candidate campaigns. Nevertheless, virtually all campaigns for governor are candidate centered.

The Powers of Incumbency

Part of the advantage of gubernatorial incumbency is related to structural enhancements of the office. The almost universal adoption of the four-year term (now enjoyed by every governor except those of New Hampshire and Vermont, as opposed to only thirty-five in 1964) permits the building of stronger and more visible records. Additionally, more governors are eligible to run for multiple terms—forty-nine currently (Virginia is the sole holdout), up from thirty-five of the forty-eight governors in 1950.

A clear correlation exists between the strengthening of the governor's position and the proportion of incumbents both seeking reelection and gaining it. Between 1900 and 1930, the percentage of governors (who were legally able to do so) seeking reelection ranged from under one-half to less than two-thirds; beginning in the 1960s, it rose steadily to almost four in five by the 1980s. And those who sought to stay in office were more successful. Whereas a third suffered defeat through the 1960s, three-quarters were successful in the 1980s.[8] In 1994, twenty-three of the thirty (77 percent) governors eligible for another term chose to run, and seventeen (74 percent) were successful.

However, executive incumbency, because of its visibility, also can be fraught with dangers. Vincent Breglio, a consultant who worked in many gubernatorial contests, likened voters' views of governors to a microcosm of the presidential race. They see in that chair all the power to make good things happen or bad things happen. . . . For a governor it's meat and potatoes—what's his or her record? If the farmers haven't had rain, the governor's going to get blamed.[9]

Thus, in 1990, when the economy began to sag noticeably, many incumbents chose not to seek reelection. Many of those who decided to face the voters were either defeated or survived very close contests. Only half of the thirty-three governors eligible to run in 1990 were still in office in 1991—ten declined to run and six were defeated in November.

Unlike legislators, who work in relative obscurity and are able to control most of their press coverage and other publicity, governors are in the spotlight. Newspaper statehouse bureaus cover them intensively, as does television, particularly when the state capital is in a major media market. As a political consultant who works in many gubernatorial contests put it:

In Mississippi, say, 50 percent of the people are in the Jackson media market, and they all know about state government. It's the same with Denver and Colorado. New York State is very well covered by TV, but state politics isn't because Albany is a jerkwater town. In a state like West Virginia, only about a quarter of the population lives in that [capital] media market. An incumbent has the opportunity to tell people what his record is during a campaign, whereas in other states they already know.[10]

But governors, like presidents, have learned to use media attention and official resources to their benefit. They are able to obtain extensive media coverage unfiltered by reporters. More and more governors appear in "nonpolitical" tourism ads, often broadcast to their own constituents instead of to vacationers from other states—such ads, featuring incumbent Thomas H. Kean, ran in New Jersey throughout his 1985 reelection campaign. Kean began a New Jersey tradition. His successor, Democrat Jim Florio, also appeared in public service ads that plugged state programs and gave advice on how to deal with health problems. Republican Christine Todd Whitman, who succeeded Florio, put a free enterprise spin on this new gubernatorial habit by appearing in ads declaring that "New Jersey is open for business" that were paid for by the Public Service Electric and Gas Company. Although Whitman argued that proclaiming the state's newly friendly business climate at other than taxpayer expense was desirable, critics saw problems in the ads being financed by a regulated industry that is prohibited from making political contributions.

The Decoupling of Federal and State Elections Outcomes

The ability of governors to run candidate-centered campaigns has also been aided by the growing practice of states holding gubernatorial elections in nonpresidential election years. By 1994, only eleven states held gubernatorial elections in presidential years, as compared with thirty-four that did so in 1932. Two of these states still have two-year gubernatorial terms and are also among the thirty-six states that elect chief executives in midterm years.[11] An additional five states insulate state-level elections from national ones even further by holding their gubernatorial contests in odd-numbered years, when no federal elections take place at all.

The absence of a concurrent presidential election makes it easier for gubernatorial candidates to focus voters' attention on their appeals. Not only is actual coattail voting impossible in the thirty-nine states where presidential and gubernatorial elections never coincide, but the kinds of casual voters that traditionally come out in presidential years and are most prone to engage in coattail voting also are absent from the midterm and odd-year electorates. On average, in the eighteen states that at some point since 1960 have held both midterm and presidential-year gubernatorial elections, turnout is a full 18 percent lower in the former than the latter.[12] However, strong evidence exists that the effect of candidate-centered appeals further transcends the mere structural changes of moving most gubernatorial elections out of the presidential-year cycle. The 1986 elections broke an iron law of midterm gubernatorial elections in place since 1950—that the president's party tallies a net loss in gubernatorial seats in the midterm. Between 1950 and 1982, the president's party lost gubernatorial chairs in every midterm election but 1962 (when no change occurred). The average loss of 6.2 seats was heavier for Republicans (who averaged 7.4) than Democrats (who averaged 4.7).[13] In 1986, however, the president's Republican party gained eight governorships. In 1990, both parties suffered a net loss of one governorship when two independents were elected.

The long-standing pattern of midterm losses for the president's party has been attributed to national trends, particularly the state of the national economy. For their own electoral purposes, presidents attempt to manipulate the economy so that, as much as possible, good news comes in presidential years and bad news, if unavoidable, in the off years, or midterm. Voters attribute the state of the local economy more to the president than to the governor, but they take it out on the governor in the midterm anyway. The Republicans' heavy losses in the recession year of 1982 were widely ascribed to this tendency.[14] However, in 1986 Republican governors did best in some of the places where the economy was in the worst shape. And in 1990 the weak economy took its toll on governors of both parties in almost equal measure—Republicans lost governorships in seven states, Democrats in five, and independents won two, for no net change in partisan balance. The electoral fate of governors is now more closely tied to the economic conditions in their state and their own fiscal performance than to national economic and political trends.

As we have already noted, a major reason for moving most gubernatorial elections to the federal midterm year was to insulate them from the national trends that appear most often in presidential election years. However, in those instances when the midterm congressional elections reflect a strong national trend, governors can get caught in the tide. The Republican gubernatorial debacle of 1982 was similar to the Democrats' problems in 1966, when Republicans gained eight governorships along with forty-seven U.S. House seats, and

1978, when the Republicans picked up eight statehouses to accompany a gain in the U.S. House of fifteen seats. The largest of these pro-Republican mid-term shifts occurred in 1994, when the GOP picked up fifty-three House seats and ten governorships, and achieved their first majority among state chief executives since 1968. However, even this historically noteworthy performance bore the hallmarks of the candidate-centered era: six of the victories were in open-seat contests, and only four Democratic incumbents lost in the general election.

Thus, structural change—moving gubernatorial contests out of the presidential year—also helped to reinforce the increasingly candidate-centered nature of gubernatorial races, and the two together have notably decoupled presidential and gubernatorial partisan outcomes, although incumbents still remain more vulnerable in nationalized midterm elections.

Campaign Finance

The growing advantages of gubernatorial incumbency have generally resulted in more incumbents running, more winning, and more winning bigger victories. Three recent trends in gubernatorial campaign finance have strengthened the incumbent advantage specifically and candidate-centered campaigning generally: dramatically higher campaign expenditures, increasingly heavy campaign contributions from the recipients of official patronage, and public financing in a few states.

The campaign "hyperinflation" (far exceeding increases in the general cost of living) that has struck U.S. Senate races is only too evident in gubernatorial contests as well. As recently as 1978, spending of $3 million by at least one of the gubernatorial candidates occurred in only three states—California, Florida, and Texas. Total expenditures were below $500,000 for both candidates in ten states that year.

In the following two election cycles, expenditures in the same three "leading" states approached or exceeded combined totals of $20 million, and the "$3 million candidate" became the norm in many states. In 1990, four states saw total campaign expenditures for governor exceed $20 million, with two topping $50 million. The average race cost almost $10 million. This figure rose to almost $17 million in the thirteen open-seat contests. Only in Vermont did total expenditures remain below $1 million. But such contests are becoming positively quaint, as other relatively small states saw record multi-million-dollar media contests. Not surprisingly, the most expensive races occur in large states with many media markets and closely contested open seats (such as Texas, California, and Illinois in 1990) or potentially vulnerable incumbents (such as Florida and Alabama in 1990).[15] In 1992, the cost of the average race was just $5 million, but this was still a significant increase over the $3.3 million average for the comparable races in 1988. Open seat races, in Missouri, North Carolina, and Washington, were again the most expensive, with total expenditures in the first two exceeding $10 million. The trend toward higher levels of expenditures was reinforced by the increased number of primary challengers (21 of 24 major-party nominations were contested) as the control over gubernatorial nominations continued to move out of the hands of party conventions and leaders.[16]

The war chests of well-financed incumbents and candidates in hotly contested open seats bulge with the contributions of recipients of official state patronage. Finance reports document massive contributions by those seeking to get or keep state contracts, jobs, or favorable regulatory decisions. Attorneys, contractors, developers and realtors, the financial community, health interests, and unions figure heavily in every state, and agricultural interests are an added concern in some. During New Jersey's midterm legislative elections in 1991, Democratic governor Florio, reeling from a tax revolt that had driven his performance ratings to near historic lows, still was able to raise $2.5 million in one evening at an affair largely attended by lawyers, contractors, builders, and others who had extensive business dealings with the state.

In the wake of the Watergate scandal, which brought taxpayer-funded presidential general election campaigns (and partially funded nomination contests), a number of states made some provision for public funding of state-level races. By 1992, nineteen states had some provision for public funding from either a state income tax checkoff or a small, voluntary add-on, but in only four states did the sums involved approach significance—New Jersey, Michigan, Wisconsin, and Minnesota. All four use the checkoff provision to raise funds that are funneled directly to individual candidates. Gubernatorial elections (both primary and general) in New Jersey and Michigan are largely funded by public money, in systems similar to the federal procedure for presidential contests.[17] In 1995, Kentucky's gubernatorial elections were publicly funded for the first time,[18] and Massachusetts enacted comprehensive campaign finance reform, including public funding of statewide offices, to take effect in 1996.[19]

Experience with public funding in the states reaches back less than twenty years, but two principal effects are discernable: it holds down expenditures and it likely advantages incumbents. When the pioneering New Jersey system was first used in 1977, the sums provided seemed adequate for a state with no commercial television stations of its own and no tradition of media-based campaigns. However, the collapse of the traditional party organizations that year unleashed an escalating spiral of expenditures, which were mostly the result of having to depend on the expensive New York City and Philadelphia media outlets necessary to reach the state's voters. By 1985, gubernatorial candidates in New Jersey spent more than three-quarters of all their funds on television-related expenses.[20] However, the total of about $4.2 million allotted to both gubernatorial candidates in 1985 was less than what any one of the victorious U.S. Senate candidates spent in their three contests between 1982 and 1988. Similarly, Michigan's candidates in 1986 each spent less than $1 million on their contests, as compared with the more than $5 million expended by the two 1984 U.S. Senate candidates.

Unlike presidential campaigns, where major candidates receive extensive news ("free media") coverage for two years preceding the election, challengers in gubernatorial campaigns have had a difficult time running against better-known incumbents. In New Jersey, incumbents Brendan Byrne and Tom Kean won in landslides in the races that took place in 1977 and 1985. Incumbent Jim Florio lost by a narrow margin in 1993, but entered the race with the worst approval ratings of any governor in the history of state polling.[21] In Michigan, incumbents also won three races in landslides, while in 1990 Democratic incumbent James J. Blanchard was narrowly defeated by Republican John Engler.

New Jersey's experience also shows that public funding linked to a limit on total campaign expenditures can eventually create pressures similar to those that have occurred in recent presidential campaigns. In 1989, an increased limit of $5 million, with two-thirds publicly funded, was established. Democratic candidate Jim Florio, however, helped raise an additional $5 million for the state party, which was used to finance a series of generic television ads urging voters to vote Democratic and that featured the same themes and issues that Florio was using in his campaign. In 1993, both Florio and his Republican challenger Christine Todd Whitman raised substantial sums for their respective state parties, which were then used to pay for polling, direct mail, and election day activities as well as generic television ads. The money contributed to the state parties did not come under the nominal contribution and expenditure limits imposed on gubernatorial candidates. In presidential campaigns, money raised for similar state party activities is referred to as "soft money" by some, and "sewer money" by others.

Money is thus a major factor in gubernatorial campaigns, with challengers usually having to spend more than incumbents to offset incumbents' greater recognition levels and electorally useful official resources. In all recent gubernatorial election cycles, the bigger spender has won much more often, and he or she was usually the incumbent. Even in the relatively few cases where incumbents were outspent, they still won more than half the time.

Another sign of the increasingly candidate-centered nature of gubernatorial campaigns is the rise in the number of independent candidates who are able to attract significant numbers of votes. Whereas only a single independent was elected governor from 1960 through 1990—James Longley of Maine in 1974—three have been successful in the 1990s: Walter Hickel in Alaska and Lowell Weicker in Connecticut in 1990, and Angus King in Maine in 1994. Further, in 1994 seven other independent gubernatorial candidates received more than 10 percent of the vote, a percentage that was greater than the winning candidates' margin of victory.

Third-party candidates have perennially been on the ballot, but have rarely attracted many votes. Between 1970 and 1994, the average vote for minor-party candidates running for statewide office has ranged from 1.3 percent to 3.7 percent.[22] The independent candidates who are now attracting votes do so not because of party labels, but because they are sufficiently well known or have enough personal wealth to run modern, high profile, media-driven campaigns. Lowell Weicker was a former U.S. senator and Walter Hickel was a former governor. Other independents in 1994 included a mayor of the state's largest city, a lieutenant governor, and a member of Congress who had previously run for governor. Two were closely associated with already-elected independent governors who chose not to run for reelection. The fact that they were not able to recapture their predecessors' supporters, both finishing distant thirds, underscores the personal nature of independent candidacies. We can expect this trend to continue, and, just as in the presidential contest, ambitious individuals who already have high visibility or the ability to purchase it will become serious contenders for office, with or without a party label.

Thus the presidentialization of gubernatorial contests, the decoupling of state and national politics, and trends in campaign finance have all contributed to the growth of candidate-centered campaigns for state chief executives. Have their compatriots in the state legislatures followed the path of their legislative brethren in the U.S. Congress and also moved down the road to candidate-centered campaigns?

State Legislative Campaigns and Elections

If gubernatorial contests have become "presidentialized," state legislative races are becoming "congressionalized"; that is, they are taking on the attributes that U.S. congressional campaigns have increasingly exhibited.

The Dimensions of Congressionalization

The outcome of most U.S. congressional elections through the 1960s could be explained by a pattern of "surge and decline" related to presidential coattails and performance.[23] Beginning in the 1970s, this pattern substantially broke down, as more voters with weaker identification with the political parties began to do in legislative elections what they already were doing in presidential races—casting their vote more often for the candidate than the party. Because much less information usually was available about challengers to sitting legislators, voters often chose "the devil they knew"—the incumbent. To have any chance of winning, challengers had to become almost as well known and favorably regarded as their opponents.[24] Additionally, challengers found they had to disseminate unfavorable information about their opponents. Otherwise, voters faced with two equally acceptable choices tended to adopt an "If it ain't broke, don't fix it" mentality, resulting in incumbent victories.[25] Three closely interrelated developments contributed to incumbents' advantages and thus increasingly candidate-centered congressional races: more entrepreneurial behavior on the part of incumbents, an expansion of official resources, and changing sources of congressional campaign money.

The entrepreneurial congressional candidate is a product of the decline of the party as vote-cue. When congressional candidates no longer could depend on their party labels to assure victory or the president's coattails to help them in marginal districts, they began to feel electorally insecure no matter how large their previous victories.[26] Thus, they began relying almost exclusively on their own efforts to win reelection. Furthermore, other candidates, who in the past could not expect party organizational support and hence did not run, now saw greater chances of success and were more likely to get into races. As one member of Congress observed in 1983:

> You can look around the floor of the House and see a handful—twenty years ago you saw a lot of them—today you can see just a handful of hacks that were put there by the party organization, and there are very, very few of them left. It is just mostly people that went out and took the election.[27]

"Taking the election" required candidates to make electorally effective use of official resources and to raise their own campaign money.

Informational newsletters and targeted mailings drove up the use and cost of the congressional postal frank. More staff time was detailed to constituency service, and district offices were established or expanded to provide it. A full-time press secretary, previously rare, became a fixture of the staff. Seeking committee assignments for electoral rather than policy reasons became commonplace. The House committee system was reorganized to make acquiring chairmanships and their attendant perks and publicity easier for more members, a reform particularly beneficial to more junior members. More time in session was spent on "position taking" than on legislation.[28]

Federal legislators also acted to change the campaign finance laws in a variety of ways that, intentionally or not, served their electoral ends. Publicly financed presidential elections freed huge sums for contribution to legislative campaigns. The creation of political action committees (PACs) channeled much of this money in distinctive ways. Most came from pragmatic economic interests more interested in access than ideology. Thus legislators on committees overseeing or regulating particular economic sectors could expect large numbers of PAC contributions. Much of the rest of the money came from issue-oriented groups whose support could be had by judicious position-taking.

The limits placed on political party contributions relegated them to third place behind individuals and PACs. Although able to contribute far more heavily than any single individual or PAC, parties were outweighed by a ratio of at least four to one when compared with individual and PAC contributions combined. Furthermore, because nonparty contributions are so much more dispersed and individually are such a small part of the total, incumbents are beholden to no one in particular.

Because PAC money went so overwhelmingly to "properly" placed incumbents to whom party money was not that important, the political parties increasingly targeted their funds to the relatively few open seats and strong challengers. Once the beneficiaries of their largess were elected, they became incumbents, too, and no longer beholden, to the extent they ever were, to their party organizations.[29] The character of "party money" flowing to legislative candidates underwent a related transformation. These candidates increasingly looked for help not to the local, state, or national party committees, but rather to the House and Senate party campaign committees and to "leadership PACs" controlled by senior members. These agents of the "party in government" rather than the "party in the electorate" had only one "special interest:" electing a majority of members with the same partisan label, thus giving that party control of the legislature's organization and leadership positions.

Thus, congressionalization means making congressional incumbents relatively autonomous actors. Official resources build favorable recognition among constituents and give incumbents the ability to raise their own money from grateful individuals and PACs. Challengers rely more on party money but need to demonstrate that they are among the small minority with a realistic chance of winning to get the party's limited resources.

What Encourages Congressionalization?

In the states, three sets of developments are parallel to those at the federal level: Legislative professionalization produces more official resources that can be used for electoral purposes, incumbency is replacing party as a voting cue, and more and more campaign money comes from "special interest" PACs, legislative campaign committees, and leadership PACs. However, campaign finance, the campaign technology that money buys, and the need for that technology differ in important ways from the federal situation.

For much of the twentieth century, as the power and scope of the federal government grew, state government languished. However, the "new federalism" espoused by the Nixon and Reagan administrations (and the cornerstone principle of the Republicans' 1994 congressional victory) has made state government more important, more powerful, and more interesting to competent and ambitious politicians. The "one person, one vote" court decisions that ended blatant malapportionment also changed the nature of representation in the state legislatures, the levels of party competition, and the nature of the contestants.

As in Congress, stronger institutions produced more official resources, at least in the larger states. Staff, particularly partisan staff attached to new or stronger legislative caucus organizations, grew apace. Computers analyzed policy alternatives but also generated newsletters, form letters to constituents, and targeted mailing lists. The number of states holding annual legislative sessions to deal with increased official business grew from nineteen in 1962 to forty-four in 1990. In constant dollars, legislative budgets in the states grew from a total of $236 million in 1972 to $315 million twenty years later.[30]

Larger state budgets and a heavier legislative workload also often produced further official perquisites—higher salaries, increased expense accounts, budgets for legislative aides and district offices, and the chance to gain more visibility (and still more official resources) through leadership positions and committee chairmanships. Not surprisingly, in the face of these developments, more legislators found staying in office attractive, and more people aspired to gain office. From the 1930s to the 1960s, average turnover in state lower houses dropped by half, to about a third, and fell below a third in the 1980s.[31] Even in the face of the Republican juggernaut of 1994, when the GOP gained over 400 state legislative seats across the nation, the turnover rate (20 percent in lower houses, 24 percent in upper houses) was well within the range of previous years. The key to the Republicans' success was not the defeat of incumbents, but rather a lopsided margin in open-seat contests.[32]

Working harder at their jobs and having more interest in keeping them, incumbents not only chose to run for reelection more often, but also were more successful. In the 1960s and 1970s, typically fewer than a fifth of all legislative incumbents were defeated. In the 1980s, this number rarely approached a tenth.[33] Nor do large numbers of incumbents frequently have close races. Half or more of legislators in a sizable number of states run unopposed.[34]

All the things that incumbents do to solidify their positions are reflected, as at the federal level, in the increase in split-ticket voting in legislative elections. Although the heavily candidate-centered contests for governor are more responsible for the sharp rise in split partisan control than are individual legislative races, legislators themselves are responsible for the growing number of instances in which partisan control of the two legislative houses is split.

Between 1961 and 1983, the number of states in which different parties controlled the two legislative houses ranged from four to nine. This number rose to eleven in 1985 and sixteen in 1993. Even in the 1994 cataclysm, when Republican control of both houses in 1995 grew from eight states to nineteen, eleven legislatures remained split. Split-ticket voting is by definition an indication of the waning power of party as a vote cue. Although incumbency and party effects are impossible to entirely disentangle, partisan turnover, as we observed earlier, is more than twice as likely to occur when a legislative race is for an open seat.[35]

The growing role of PAC money in legislative campaigns resembles the role of such monies in U.S. Congressional campaigns. Even in states where professionalization has barely made a dent, turnover (mostly voluntary) still approaches a third, and campaigns are cheap, PACs are growing rapidly as a major source of campaign funds. Typically, about a third of all campaign contributions and a majority of incumbents' war chests come from PACs.

What Limits Congressionalization?

Congressionalization is not complete everywhere or, indeed, almost anywhere. A number of factors limit its development and require adjustments to achieve the same ends in state legislative elections. First, official resources that are useful for individual state legislative contests are fewer. Legislative districts—even those in the upper house—are much smaller than congressional ones. (California state senate districts, which are larger than U.S. House districts, are the only exception.) For example, a U.S. representative in a large state such as Illinois or Ohio serves about 550,000 constituents; the state assembly counterpart serves about 97,000 in Illinois and 110,000 in Ohio, which would be considered large assembly constituencies. Comparable figures are 45,000 in Wisconsin, 23,000 in Connecticut, and a mere 2,500 in New Hampshire—which has the largest lower house in the nation to serve the eighth smallest population.

Although many state legislative budgets have grown, nowhere do they resemble the commitment the federal government makes to the upkeep of its legislature. More than four times as many dollars are behind each member of the federal legislature as are behind those who serve New York State (by far the best financed legislature both absolutely and per capita in the nation), and ten times as many as those supporting the New Jersey legislature, still at the upper end of the national spectrum. California's senate staff allowance is comparable to that of a U.S. House member with a slightly smaller constituency; in the vast majority of states, however, an allowance one-tenth that size— enough to support perhaps one personal aide and a secretary—is extraordinarily generous. A Nevada legislator whose perks consist of $60 for postage and $1,000 for telephone calls over a two-year period or a New Hampshire representative who is paid $100 per year would find the California allowance unimaginable.

Fewer official resources make incumbency less helpful for state legislators than for those in Congress. The effects of coattails on state legislative outcomes diminished by half in the 1970s and 1980s when compared to the 1940s through 1960s, though they are still present to some extent.[36] State legislators also find it harder to achieve the recognition levels of their federal peers. Although systematic data are sparse, in New Jersey, for example, recognition levels of legislators have doubled in recent years but still are half those of members of Congress.[37] In the relatively low-information, low-turnout elections that now take place, party identification doubtless counts for more, too, as fewer of the casual independent voters bother to come out or make their way to the bottom of the ballot when they do.

Individual candidates also do not have the money to tap into the high-cost, high-tech campaign techniques that are so crucial to nurturing candidate-centered voting. Accurate poll samples are no smaller for a legislative race than a congressional one. Media advertising costs depend on the size of a station's market, not the size of a candidate's constituency. Television, the best medium for building recognition quickly, is grossly cost-inefficient for almost all legislative candidates because stations cover so many legislative districts. News coverage is scarce enough for federal legislative candidates, let alone those for the state legislature, and the free "advertising" made possible by the federal frank is not available either.

Furthermore, although an entrepreneurially minded state legislator needs to build personal recognition just as much as a federal legislator does, the payoff is simply not the same in the vast majority of cases. The federal candidate is seeking more prestige, more perquisites, and a higher step on the ladder of political ambition. Despite the longer and more frequent state legislative sessions, most state legislators still will spend less time in the state capital than federal legislators spend in Washington, D.C.

Although campaign costs at the state level are rising steeply,[38] only in the largest states do spending levels even approach those in U.S. House contests. In 1990, U.S. House incumbents spent an average of $693,000 in seeking re-election. In California, the comparable figure for all its state legislative incumbents was $495,000. In other large states such as Ohio, Pennsylvania, New Jersey, and New York, occasional races may cost in excess of $300,000, especially when control of a legislative house depends on the outcome of a few races. However, for the vast majority of state legislative candidates, campaign spending levels are only a fraction of these high-cost races. The much smaller district sizes and much larger numbers of districts ensure that state legislative candidates will never have available the large war chests that most members of Congress routinely possess.

Congressionalization of state legislative elections is far from complete and is significantly less complete than the presidentialization of gubernatorial elections. However, state-level legislative candidates have been creative in devising ways to deal with the shortcomings inherent in running for a legislative seat.

The Role of Political Parties

The key difference between federal and state legislators is that members of Congress are better able to operate as independent entrepreneurs. Their ability to use official resources as campaign resources when party resources failed them led to the description of congressional offices as individual enterprises.[39] Almost all individual state legislators lack the access to such resources.

The obvious solution has been for the state legislators to band together in a larger organization that has the resources they lack: the political party. In the past, incumbents seeking reelection benefited from voters' psychological attachments to the parties more than the work of party organizations. The state organizations were more interested in the governor's office, and county and local organizations were more interested in the mayor or the sheriff. Both the governor and the county officials had what legislators lacked—control of the patronage jobs that are the lifeblood of traditional party organizations.

Some observers believe that revitalized state party organizations, particularly on the Republican side, have a new interest in legislative races. Elaborate studies detail growing state party budgets, larger staffs, and provision of campaign services to legislative candidates. In addition, in both 1980 and 1990, the national Republican party mounted a major effort to aid state parties in capturing more state legislatures to gain greater influence on the decennial process of congressional and legislative redistricting. A closer look casts some doubt on this theory. Although some state parties are performing "service bureau" functions, their budgets actually have decreased over the past few decades once inflation is taken into account. More importantly, no relationship exists between the state parties' organizational strength and either the number or closeness of legislative victories.[40] In fact, it was the weakness of state parties that led many legislative leaders to form campaign committees to help them keep or win their legislative majorities.[41] In addition, as Jeffrey Wice, general counsel to the Democratic State Legislative Leaders Association has observed, "In some states, the state party is the governor's party. It may not always be in the interest of legislative leaders to subordinate their goals to the goals of the governor."[42] The partisan assistance legislators seek has not come from the traditional state party organizations but rather from legislative leaders and their fellow legislators in legislative party caucuses.

California pioneered the initiative and referendum, the use of political consultants, and the election of celebrities to office. California assembly leader Jesse Unruh created almost twenty years ago the first legislative caucus devoted principally to the winning of state legislative elections. Now, legislative caucuses in both houses in more than forty states raise funds to support legislative campaigns, and in many their activities have grown dramatically. For example, in Washington State, contributions to candidates by the legislative campaign committees increased from $223,000 in 1982 to $961,000 in 1992, while in Nevada, such contributions rose from $290,000 in 1990 to $450,000 in 1992. Further, direct contributions are only the tip of the iceberg. The majority of caucus funds are spent on "in-kind" contributions for polling, advertising, and direct mail, whose design is controlled largely by committee professional staff rather than individual candidates. As Harry Meshel, former Ohio senate president, described the activities in his state, the legislative committee "lined up the ad agency, booked the air time, helped make the commercials, and negotiated better rates by arranging for three or four campaigns at the same time. We wanted to make sure the money got used where it counted most."[43]

Although fundraising is carried on by both minority and majority party caucuses, the majority finds attracting contributors easier, particularly the PACs that provide a large portion of such funds. Generally speaking, although state PACs are more willing to contribute to challengers than their federal brethren, and "tend to be more adversarial in their contribution strategies," they also steer contributions heavily toward incumbents and anticipate that challengers will be supported by the large sums they also contribute to legislative caucus campaign committees.[44] With the Democrats in control of about two-thirds of all statehouses throughout the 1980s, an important explanation of their electoral success in that period emerges. On the other hand, the Republicans' success in 1994 in achieving parity of control, and drawing almost even with the Democrats in terms of actual numbers of incumbents, would seem to predict much healthier competition in the years to come.

One advantage to candidates of funds controlled by the legislative leadership is that leaders want nothing more from the recipients than their vote to organize the chamber and reelect the leaders to their positions. As former Wisconsin house leader Tom Loftus explains,

If you are the speaker or the leader of the senate, raising money for targeted seats is as much a part of your job as pounding the gavel to call the house to order. It is your responsibility to keep your party in the majority. The caucus campaign committee is your vehicle. It's your party.[45]

Campaign money is not the only valuable resource the legislative leadership controls. Desirable committee assignments, which provide not only visibility but electorally useful staff and access to individual campaign contributions, also are within the power of the leadership to dispense. California's legendary assembly speaker Willie Brown, who raised almost $5.3 million in the 1992 election cycle and was toppled from office only by term limits, described his use of this power in much the same way as Tom Loftus: "The Speaker in California has an awesome amount of power over House organization, and I don't use it based on party participation or party loyalty; I use it based on Speaker loyalty." [46]

In addition to the interests of the leadership and the rank and file in using campaign funds and organizational resources for mutual benefit, electorally useful government appropriations are available for the leadership to dole out. Besides the normal kinds of "pork barrel" legislation, a few legislatures specifically reserve discretionary funds that members, through the good offices of leaders, can use in their districts. "Worthy legislative projects" have comprised almost 5 percent of Maryland's legislative budget and "special entries" have been awarded to North Carolina senators and assembly members. "Member items" in the New York state legislative budget have run as high as $1.8 million per member. Member items are sums that may be spent on district items entirely at a legislator's discretion.

Just as congressionalization is more or less advanced in various states, so too is the electoral activity of the legislative caucuses. Increasingly, however, legislative leaders share the sentiments of Oregon's House Speaker Larry Campbell. Campbell, whose leadership PAC added $38,000 to the $216,000 the House caucus committee contributed when Republicans finally won control of the lower house in 1990, had observed in 1992 that his party would never succeed "if the caucus didn't get involved in legislative elections."[47]

Varieties of Congressionalization

The shape of legislative politics in a given state is related to the sometimes overlapping factors of state political culture, the level of party competition, and the presence of particularly entrepreneurial leaders.

A state's political culture affects the extent of congressionalization and activity by legislative caucuses. They are almost always advanced in states with a history of strong traditional party organizations.[48] The old "machine" states that stretch in a broad band across the northeast and the industrial midwest are precisely those states—New York, New Jersey, Pennsylvania, Ohio, and Illinois—with strong and active legislative caucuses.

In these states, the legislature has become the repository of many of the patronage jobs once provided elsewhere. In New York, local party officials often are paid staffers on the Albany legislative payroll but work at least part time out of county party offices, in legislative district offices, or in campaign organizations.[49] In New Jersey, the majority and minority partisan staffs provide employment for many campaign staffers in between elections. In Illinois, every professional legislative staff position is partisan, and many of those occupying these positions are deployed by the leadership to work in campaigns. One explains, "By the book partisan staff does campaign work on weekends and during leaves of absence—but everybody violates the rule. . . . There is a token effort made to prevent state resources from being turned into party resources."[50]

A second set of active legislative caucuses are found in the upper Midwest, in states that also traditionally had strong parties, albeit based more on issues than patronage. Wisconsin and Minnesota's legislative caucuses and their fundraising coexist with partially public-financed elections and strict spending limits.

The Wisconsin caucuses are limited to raising only about $150,000 per election cycle and donating a maximum of $3,000 per campaign. Campaign spending is limited if public funds are accepted, and every dollar of PAC money a candidate takes reduces the amount of public money available.[51] Because of the limits on accepting PAC contributions and requirements that candidates raise a minimum on their own and have an opponent, the public money acceptance rate is lower in Wisconsin than in Minnesota, and the per capita expenditures in Minnesota are higher than in Wisconsin.[52] As Dave Travis, majority leader of the Wisconsin Assembly notes, "Candidates in tough races just don't accept public financing when they can raise more than the spending limits. . . . Our public financing system isn't funded well enough to make it attractive to candidates who feel they must spend big bucks."[53] Political scientists confirm Travis's observation. In Minnesota, there is some evidence that public financing has helped make challengers more competitive.[54] In Wisconsin, however, public financing has no effect on competitiveness because the sums involved are too small to convince strong challengers that they are worth accepting.[55]

Caucus activity is less dominant in small or heavily rural states with a tradition of localism and citizen legislatures. In these states with less professionalized legislatures, such as Vermont, Idaho, and Montana, campaign expenditures have increased much more slowly, and direct voter contact by individual candidates remains the dominant mode of campaigning.[56] In a state like New Hampshire, an expensive House campaign directed toward 2,500 constituents might cost $500, principally for lawn signs. Direct mail and radio advertising are unknown, and "the town dump is a good place to campaign."[57] However, even the Granite State is not entirely immune from recent developments. The GOP House caucus committee runs a campaign school and makes small donations to candidates, and in 1990 the Senate Campaign

Committee contributed $48,000 to candidates, making it the largest source of campaign money in the state.[58]

The level of party competition is another factor affecting the extent of congressionalization and caucus activity. A sure recipe for more caucus activity and increased expenditures is a history of close competition or an increase in competition. Ohio and Pennsylvania are examples of the former, while many southern states are examples of the latter. In 1995, Virginia's GOP governor George Allen raised an unheard of $1.2 million for the state legislative races, hoping to give the former capital of the Confederacy the first all-Republican government in a southern state since Reconstruction. Although the effort failed, and the Democrats maintained their five-seat lead in the lower house, the Republicans achieved a tie in the senate.[59]

Summary

State-level campaigns and elections have taken on many of the attributes of executive and legislative contests at the federal level. Certainly, differences remain that seem immutable. Governors do not face the organizational challenges of presidential candidates, do not receive the same degree of national media attention, and are not expected to have the same grasp of foreign policy. But increasingly, like presidents, they run as individuals, succeed or fail because of their retrospective or prospective records as leaders and economic managers, communicate their messages through television, and find party labels and organizations increasingly less important to their endeavors. Also like presidents, their personal popularity is less transferable to their fellow partisans, although they may, if they so choose, raise campaign money for them.

State legislators generally represent smaller constituencies than their federal peers, are less well known to their constituents, and cannot and need not raise the same sums to wage their campaigns. But like U.S. senators and representatives, they rely increasingly less on party labels or executive coattails to bring them victory and more on their own efforts, incumbency, official resources, and candidate-centered campaigns. The costs of modern campaign technology have made legislative campaigns in some of the larger states almost identical in style and form to congressional campaigns and as expensive as well-financed congressional contests were scarcely a decade ago. Even in capitals still populated with "amateur" citizen-legislators, candidates now raise much of whatever funds they need from PACs, as do their federal brethren. And like congressional candidates, that fundraising is much easier for incumbents and leaders.

In the most recent elections, legislative campaign committees in many of the larger states, organized by caucus leaders, have come to resemble the Washington, D.C.-based congressional campaign committees. Instances of targeting resources to open seats, vulnerable incumbents, and strong challengers have grown. The campaign services the committees finance or provide also are similar—polling, direct mail production, strategic planning, and broadcast advertising.

As technology becomes more affordable and available—for example, personal computers, campaign software packages, and greater penetration of cable television—the similarities between contested legislative and congressional contests will grow even further. The major difference is that economies of scale, varying levels of official resources, and fund-raising capacity make most state legislative candidates, even incumbents, more dependent on mutual rather than individual resources than their federal counterparts.

As state politics develops in the same directions as federal politics, the same concerns arise. Campaign finance is an oft-debated topic, particularly the role of special interest PACs and the conversion of public funds to campaign purposes. Newspapers and good government groups often inveigh against "the best legislatures that money can buy." Campaign spending can be regulated in only four ways, listed in the order of their current use and future feasibility: disclosure requirements, contribution limits, spending limits, and public financing.

Disclosure of contribution sources gives the public some information and requires some accountability on the part of candidates. Contribution limits place some check on influence and encourage diversity of funding sources. Spending limits raise both legal and practical objections. In *Buckley v. Valeo*, the Supreme Court ruled that in elections, in the absence of public funding, expenditure limits constitute an abridgment of freedom of speech and are not permissible. Even when public funding is available, candidates may opt not to take it, so long as they observe whatever contribution limits the law specifies. Many politicians argue that both spending limits and public funding discriminate against lesser-known challengers and serve as an "incumbents' protection act." Finally, as a practical matter the public has made clear its disinclination to pay for political campaigns. Public financing has made little headway in recent years, and participation in the tax checkoff that funds gubernatorial races in states like New Jersey and Michigan has dropped steadily since the 1980s— as has the same practice at the federal level for funding of presidential campaigns. Contribution limits have been the preferred "reform" of recent years. Since 1992, Kentucky, Massachussetts, Nebraska, New Jersey, and Ohio have enacted provisions for limiting individual and PAC contributions, often with more generous provisions for contributions to legislative leadership organizations or state parties. Additionally, Missouri, Montana, and Oregon voters have followed California's lead by imposing contribution limits through successful initiative measures. Only Colorado voters have resisted this trend.

A second frequently voiced concern relates to the diminished role of the political parties. From a policy point of view, the argument is made that a collection of entrepreneurially minded officeholders who owe nothing to their parties makes for incoherent policy and lack of accountability. Furthermore, long-term incumbency and "permanent majorities" are said to inspire smugness and arrogance. But others see immobilism and incoherence as a reflection of public opinion and believe that politicians can and do move rapidly and decisively when the public will is clear. As 1994 demonstrated, "permanent majorities" are much less institutionally permanent than were the malapportioned and gerrymandered legislatures that preceded them, when an aroused majority of voters often could not work its will.

Nevertheless, the public is increasingly disposed to seeing the full-time professional legislator as an arrogant and out-of-touch incumbent who uses the perquisites of office to win reelection without effectively dealing with public concerns. The term limits fervor of the early 1990s was a clear reflection of this widespread attitude. In 1990, California, Oklahoma, and Colorado passed initiatives that limited the number of terms legislators could serve. Twelve more states followed their lead at the height of the term limits movement in 1992, and by 1995 the roster of states that had passed some term limitations stood at twenty-one, including nineteen of the twenty-two states with provisions for initiative ballot measures.[60] After 1994, public outrage seemed to subside somewhat. That year, the Massachussetts ballot measure passed only narrowly, and Utah voters declined to tighten the limits passed by the legislature. In 1995, Mississippi voters rejected a term limit measure that would have applied to all offices, local as well as state.

Term limits, however, are unlikely to result in the reemergence of the part-time citizen legislator. The new class of political entrepreneurs that has developed since the 1960s has proven very resourceful.[61] They have succeeded in making politics and elective office a career, and term limitations will be seen as just another change in the rules of the game. The policy role of the states is likely to continue to increase as power and policy initiative continues to flow to them. Governors and state legislators are growing more adept at using the resources at their disposal and acquiring the resources needed to run modern, technologically sophisticated campaigns. In fact, one of the immediate effects of terms limits will be to increase the number of open seats and thus the number of opportunities for ambitious candidates to wage expensive, high visibility campaigns. Multimillion-dollar media campaigns for the state legislature may never take place in New Hampshire or North Dakota, but plenty of room exists for expansion, particularly in a number of the southern states that are now experiencing more competitive partisan politics at the state level. The messages since the Republican triumphs of 1994 have been mixed, and it is difficult to tell if the Republican resurgence will continue, stablilize, or be reversed. In any event, with term limits taking hold, old patterns disrupted, new technologies spreading, and public disenchantment with both major political parties continuing, the prospects for candidate-centered campaigns have grown rather than diminished, as have the prospects for increased volatility.

Notes

1. This argument is elaborated upon in Barbara G. Salmore and Stephen A. Salmore, *Candidates, Parties, and Campaigns*, 2d ed. (Washington, D.C.: CQ Press, 1989).
2. Martin P. Wattenberg, *The Decline of American Political Parties, 1952–1988* (Cambridge, Mass.: Harvard University Press, 1990); and Martin P. Wattenberg, "The Reagan Polarization Phenomenon and the Continued Downward Slide in Presidential Candidate Popularity," *American Politics Quarterly* 14 (1984): 219–246.
3. Much of the aggregate data in this section appears in Larry J. Sabato, *Goodbye to Good-time Charlie: The American Governorship Transformed* (Washington, D.C.: CQ Press, 1983); and Malcolm E. Jewell and David M. Olson, *American State Political Parties and Elections*, 3d ed. (Homewood, Ill.: Dorsey Press, 1988).
4. The discussions of the gubernatorial elections are drawn from Michael Barone and Grant Ujifisa, *The Almanac of American Politics 1996* (Washington, D.C.: National Journal, 1995)
5. Malcolm E. Jewell, *Parties and Primaries: Nominating State Governors* (New York: Praeger, 1984); and Sarah M. Morehouse, "Money versus Party Effort: Nominations for Governor" (Paper delivered at the annual meeting of the American Political Science Association, Chicago, September 3–6, 1987).
6. James Melcher, "Party Endorsements in Minnesota in the Wake of the 1994 Elections: Reform Strikes Out," *Comparative State Politics* 16:6 (December 1995): 1–14.
7. Malcolm Jewell, "State Party Endorsements of Gubernatorial Candidates Declining in Effectiveness," *Comparative State Politics* 16:3 (June 1995): 7–13.
8. J. Stephen Turett, "The Vulnerability of American Governors, 1900–1969," *Midwest Journal of Political Science* 15 (1971): 108–132; and Thad L. Beyle, "Gubernatorial Elections: 1977–1990," *Comparative State Politics* 12:2 (April 1991): 18–21.
9. Barbara G. Salmore and Stephen A. Salmore, *Candidates, Parties, and Campaigns* (Washington, D.C.: CQ Press, 1985), 67.
10. Ibid., 66.
11. Both are in New England—New Hampshire and Vermont. A third New England state, Rhode Island, switched to a four-year term, contested in the midterm, beginning in 1994.
12. Malcolm E. Jewell and David M. Olson, *Political Parties and Elections in American States*, 3d ed. (Homewood, Ill.: Dorsey Press, 1988), 209.
13. John S. Bibby, "Statehouse Elections at Midterm," in *The American Elections of 1982*, ed. Thomas E. Mann and Norman J. Ornstein (Washington, D.C.: American Enterprise Institute for Public Policy Research, 1983), 115.
14. See for example, ibid.; and John E. Chubb, "Institutions, the Economy, and the Dynamics of State Elections," *American Political Science Review* 82 (March 1988): 133–154.
15. Thad L. Beyle, "The Costs of the 1990 Gubernatorial Elections," *Comparative State Politics* 12:5 (October 1991): 3–7.
16. Thad L. Beyle, "The 1992 Gubernatorial Elections," *Comparative State Politics* 15:1 (February 1994): 28–31.
17. The data in this discussion are drawn from Herbert E. Alexander and Michael Eberts, *Public Financing of State Elections* (Los Angeles: Citizens' Research Foundation, 1986).
18. John Charles, "Kentucky's Campaign Finance Laws," *Comparative State Politics* 16:4 (November 1995): 4–8.
19. Lawrence Butler, "Campaign Finance Reform in Massachusetts," *Comparative State Politics* 16:2 (April 1995): 7–15.
20. New Jersey Election Law Enforcement Commission, *New Jersey Public Financing: 1985 Gubernatorial Elections* (Trenton: New Jersey Election Law Enforcement Commission, September 1986).

21. It was widely believed that incumbent Tom Kean intended to opt out of the public finance provisions in 1985 if the race showed any sign of becoming close. (He ultimately won with a record-setting 70 percent of the vote.)

22. Christian Collet and Jerold Hansen, "Minor Parties and Candidates in Sub-Presidential Elections," *Vox Pop: Newsletter of Political Organizations and Parties* 14:2 (December 1995): 1–4.

23. The original statement of the "surge and decline" argument is from Angus Campbell, "Surge and Decline: A Study in Electoral Change," *Public Opinion Quarterly* 29 (1960): 397–418. An application to state elections is made by James E. Campbell, "Presidential Coattails and Midterm Losses in State Legislative Elections," *American Political Science Review* 80 (1986): 45–64.

24. See, for example, Gary C. Jacobson, *The Politics of Congressional Elections* (Boston: Little, Brown, 1987).

25. This explains the recent increase in negative advertising. If negative advertising were to disappear, even fewer challengers would be elected. Because persuasive negative advertising works, finding cases to test this hypothesis empirically is impossible. See Alan Ehrenhalt, "Technology, Strategy Bring New Campaign Era," *Congressional Quarterly Weekly Report,* December 7, 1985, 2559–2565.

26. This argument, advanced by Thomas Mann, got strong empirical confirmation from Gary Jacobson, who demonstrated that incumbents in recent decades have had to increase their victory margins substantially to achieve the same probability of winning the next time. See Thomas Mann, *Unsafe at Any Margin* (Washington, D.C.: American Enterprise Institute for Public Policy Research, 1978); and Gary Jacobson, *The Politics of Congressional Elections,* 2d ed. (Boston: Little, Brown, 1987).

27. Quoted in John F. Bibby, ed., *Congress off the Record* (Washington, D.C.: American Enterprise Institute for Public Policy Research, 1983), 43.

28. Among the most important of the many discussions of these developments are David Mayhew, *Congress: The Electoral Connection* (New Haven, Conn.: Yale University Press, 1974); and Bruce Cain, John Ferejohn, and Morris Fiorina, *The Personal Vote: Constituency Service and Electoral Independence* (Cambridge, Mass.: Harvard University Press, 1987).

29. A point made by David Adamany, "Political Parties in the 1980s," in *Money and Politics,* ed. Michael Malbin (Chatham, N.J.: Chatham House, 1984), 110.

30. "State Stats: The Low Cost of State Legislatures," *State Legislatures* 20 (July 1994): 7.

31. Alan Rosenthal, "And So They Leave: Legislative Turnover in the States," *State Government* 47 (1974): 148–152; and Richard Niemi and L. R. Winsky, "Membership Turnover in State Legislatures: Trends and Effects of Redistricting," *Legislative Studies Quarterly* 12 (1987): 115–124.

32. See Rob Gurwitt, "The Strains of Power," *Governing* 8 (February 1995): 17–23.

33. Rosenthal, "And So They Leave: Legislative Turnover in the States," and Niemi and Winsky, "Membership Turnover in State Legislatures: Trends and Effects of Redistricting."

34. Some examples: In 1986, 75 percent of the candidates for the Massachusetts house, 73 percent of the candidates for the Tennessee senate, 72 percent of the candidates for the Georgia house, and 58 percent of the candidates for the New Hampshire senate ran unopposed. Tidmarch, Lonergan, and Sciortino found fourteen states in which at least one-third of the House seats were uncontested in 1978. See Charles M. Tidmarch, Edward Lonergan, and John Sciortino, "Interparty Competition in the U.S. States: Legislative Elections, 1970–1978," *Legislative Studies Quarterly* 11 (June 1986): 353–374.

35. Jewell and Olson, *Political Parties and Elections,* 3d ed., 216.

36. See Campbell, "Presidential Coattails and Midterm Losses in State Legislative Elections"; Chubb, "Institutions, the Economy, and the Dynamics of State Elections"; and Thomas M. Holbrook-Provow, "National Factors in Gubernatorial Elections," *American Politics Quarterly* 15 (1987): 471–484.

37. Stephen A. Salmore and Barbara G. Salmore, "Congressionalization of State Legislative Politics: The Case of New Jersey" (Paper delivered at the annual meeting of the American Political Science Association, Chicago, September 3–6, 1987).
38. Herbert E. Alexander, *Reform and Reality: The Financing of State and Local Campaigns* (New York: Twentieth Century Fund Press, 1991); Rob Gurwitt, "The Mirage of Campaign Reform," *Governing* 5 (1992): 48–55; Tommy Neal, "The Sky High Cost of Campaigns," *State Legislatures* 18 (1992): 16–23.
39. Robert H. Salisbury and Kenneth A. Shepsle, "U.S. Congressman as Enterprise," *Legislative Studies Quarterly* 6 (1981): 559–576; and Burdett Loomis and Elizabeth H. Paddock, "The Congressional Enterprise as Campaign" (Paper delivered at the annual meeting of the Midwest Political Science Association, Chicago, April 9–11, 1987).
40. The most eminent members of the school arguing that the state parties are more consequential are Cornelius Cotter, John Bibby, Robert Huckshorn, and James Gibson, who have published numerous works on the subject. The fullest explication of their views is Cotter et al., *Party Organizations in American Politics* (New York: Praeger, 1984). The data presented here on party budgets come from this study (39n, 88–89). The other major study of the role of state parties is considerably more restrained in its conclusions. See Advisory Commission on Intergovernmental Relations, *The Transformation of American Politics: Implications for Federalism* (Washington, D.C.: Advisory Commission on Intergovernmental Relations, 1986), chap. 4.
41. Rob Gurwitt, "How to Succeed in Running a Legislature: Pack a Might Wallet," *Governing* 3 (1990): 26–31. See also Cindy Simon Rosenthal, "New Party or Campaign Bank Account? Explaining the Rise of State Legislative Campaign Committees," *Legislative Studies Quarterly* 20 (1985): 249–268.
42. Cindy Simon Rosenthal, "Where's the Party?" *State Legislatures* 20 (June 1994): 33.
43. Ibid.
44. James King and Helanan Robin, "PACs and Campaign Finance in National and State Elections," *Comparative State Politics* 16 (August 1995): 32–44; (quote at 42).
45. Tom Loftus, *The Art of Legislative Politics* (Washington, D.C.: CQ Press, 1995), as quoted in Neil H. Shively, "Portrait of a Politician," *State Legislatures* 21 (March 1995): 17.
46. Quoted in *State Legislatures* 13 (November/December 1981): 26.
47. Quoted in Rosenthal, "Where's the Party?" 31.
48. For a survey of this subject, see David Mayhew, *Placing Parties in American Politics* (Princeton, N.J.: Princeton University Press, 1987).
49. Elizabeth Kolbert and Mark Uhlig, "Albany's Discreet Budget: A Tool for Political Ends," *New York Times*, July 14, 1987; and Ronald Sullivan, "Judge Retains 400 Charges for the Trial of Ohrenstein," *New York Times*, June 16, 1988.
50. Private communication, fall 1987. In the fall of 1987, the student fellows of the Eagleton Institute of Politics at Rutgers University conducted interviews with legislative officeholders, legislative partisan staff, lobbyists, and reporters in several states. This quote and those that follow come from interviews with persons who did not wish to be quoted with attribution.
51. However, in another example of the endless ingenuity of campaign fund raisers, this "PAC problem" can be bypassed. Company employees give donations of less than $20 (the limit for unidentified contributions) to a person designated as a "conduit," who then contributes the pooled money as an individual instead of as a PAC donation.
52. Frank J. Sorauf, *Money in American Politics* (Glenview, Ill.: Scott, Foresman, 1988), 264, 280.
53. Karen Fisher, "A Wobbly Start for Public Campaign Financing," *State Legislatures* 19 (April 1993): 25.
54. Patrick Donnay and Graham Ramsden, "Public Financing of Legislative Elections: Lessons from Minnesota," *Legislative Studies Quarterly* 20 (August 1995): 351–364.

55. Kenneth Mayer and John Wood, "The Impact of Public Financing on Electoral Competitiveness: Evidence from Wisconsin, 1964–90," *Legislative Studies Quarterly* 20 (February 1995): 69–88.
56. Alexander, *Reform and Reality*, 8.
57. Private communication, fall 1987.
58. Rosenthal, "Where's the Party?" 32, 37.
59. Karen Hansen, "Win Is Razor Thin For Dems," *State Legislatures* 21 (December 1995): 11.
60. See Jack Treadway, "Adoption of Term Limits for State Legislators," *Comparative State Politics* 15 (June 1994): 23–30; and Treadway, "Adoption of Term Limits for State Legislators: An Update," *Comparative State Politics* 16 (June 1995): 1–3.
61. See Alan Ehrenhalt, *The United States of Ambition: Politicians, Power, and the Pursuit of Office* (New York: Random House, 1991).

5

Being Governor

Thad L. Beyle

Since the 1960s, state government and politics have been in a state of change. Reform has been most apparent in the governorships of the fifty states. Individually, governors have been strengthened and have become the key political and governmental leaders in their states. As a group, they have worked to solidify their position within the federal system but now find their roles within their states so compelling and difficult, especially with the federal government on retreat from domestic matters, that they have little time to spend on national concerns.

This change in the governorships has had ramifications in other areas of the states' political and governmental policy systems. Conflicts have grown between the governors and certain other actors in the executive branches, as well as between the governors and stronger state legislatures. The state supreme courts have become players in the political process, serving as umpire in some situations and as part of the conflict in others.

A strengthened governorship facing greater challenges has made the position more attractive. The type of politicians that used to seek the office, and the kind of person interested in running for it, have changed. Dollar and consultant politics have replaced party leader and factional politics in many states.

With the political changes in the governorship came a change in the presidential recruitment process. In each of the five presidential elections from 1976 to 1992, at least one of the major party candidates served as governor and three became president. Entrants in the 1996 presidential selection process included former governors and former gubernatorial candidates.

Two basic cycles have a considerable impact on the states in the federal system and on the governors within the states and in the federal system. The first is the cycle of values undergirding the development of American government—representation, neutral competence, and executive leadership. The second is the cycle of leadership, which oscillates between the state and national levels—the shifting locus of activism within the federal system to provide government services.

Tensions between the values of representation, neutral competence, and executive leadership affect governors within their own state governmental systems. Shifting policy activism affects the governors within the federal system as responsibilities for various governmental services are transferred, in subtle and not so subtle ways, from states to the national government and, more recently, back to the states. These two cycles provide the setting in which states and governors function.

Governors as Chief Executive Officers

The office of governor has developed significantly since the establishment of colonial governments in America. After an initial period of imposed executive dominance, the new state constitutions promoted the value of representation. Legislatures reigned supreme, with governors often serving as mere figureheads. By 1800, the situation began to change as the power and prestige of governors gradually increased. However, the direct election of a number of other state administrative officers was an important legacy of the pursuit of representation.

Following the Civil War, and in reaction to the excesses of achieving representation, the value of neutral competence gained in stature. The goal was to remove favoritism and patronage from government, substituting neutrality or the concept of "not who you know, but what you know." This movement fostered the establishment of independent boards and commissions that diluted gubernatorial power. During this period, the drive for a civil service or merit system was launched. Thus, the goal of attaining neutral competence in government was added to the goal of representation. Thousands of state merit service employees were not only insulated from the winds of politics, but also from management by the governor.

In the twentieth century, the need for strong executive leadership emerged. New Jersey governor Woodrow Wilson (D, 1911–1913) championed the cause, along with several other strong governors—Charles Evans Hughes (R, 1907–1910) in New York, Robert La Follette (R, 1901–1906) in Wisconsin, Hiram Johnson (R, Prog., 1911–1917) in California, and Frank Lowden (R, 1917–1921) in Illinois.

The stature of governors has increased greatly across the states and in the federal system over the last few decades because of historic reforms, the type of individuals holding office, the actions taken under their direction, and an increased capacity in the office. Governors now are compared with private sector corporate leaders; they are public sector, state-level chief executive officers (CEOs). Expectations for gubernatorial performance have increased, perhaps beyond realistic levels.

Enhanced Capacity

Governors are responsible for running large enterprises that are similar in scope to Fortune 500 companies. For example, when the 1993 total expenditures of the states are compared with the 1993 sales of the nation's largest companies, twenty-three states rank with the top fifty corporations and thirty-four had expenditures equal to or greater than the top one hundred.[1]

The magnitude of the dollar decisions made by the California governor, administrators, and legislators is comparable to those made by executives at EXXON and IBM, the third and fourth largest companies; those by New York State leaders to executives of Mobil and Philip Morris, the sixth and seventh largest companies; those by Florida and Texas governmental leaders, to management at Chrysler, Texaco and DuPont, the eighth, ninth, and tenth largest companies. Other states in range of the top fifty corporations are Alabama, Connecticut, Georgia, Illinois, Indiana, Kentucky, Louisiana, Maryland, Massachusetts, Michigan, Minnesota, New Jersey, North Carolina, Ohio, Pennsylvania, Tennessee, Virginia, Washington, and Wisconsin.

Do the governors have adequate executive tools to manage such large enterprises? Are they as prepared to be the CEOs of their states as their private sector counterparts are to run businesses? Do the offices of the governors have the necessary capacity to assist the governors in managing their enterprises in state government?[2] Certainly, progress has been made. Since the early 1960s, no shortage of reforms has taken place throughout the states. The agenda for these reforms was drawn from changes at the national level initiated by the president and from a series of reports calling for reform in state governments.[3]

The general goals of government reforms have been to enhance gubernatorial and legislative abilities to lead the states in more progressive directions. In 1967, former North Carolina governor Terry Sanford called upon the states "to make the chief executive of the state the chief executive in fact"; a decade later political scientist Larry Sabato declared that executive branch reforms had made the governors "truly the masters" of state government.[4]

One common reform has been to lengthen the term of office. Since 1955, the number of governors eligible for four-year terms instead of two-year terms has increased from twenty-nine to forty-eight. This change allows governors to spend more time on policy and administrative concerns and less on reelection campaigns.[5] By 1995, only New Hampshire and Vermont still restricted their governors to a two-year term.

Another reform has increased opportunities for succession. Since 1955, the number of states precluding their governors from serving successive terms has declined from seventeen to just one—Virginia. The number of states allowing a governor to serve two consecutive terms has increased from six to twenty-eight. Eighteen states in 1995 had no restrictions on the number of terms a governor could serve, despite a growing movement to impose term limits. Changes in succession ability allow a governor more time to spend on policy and administrative concerns, that is, if the voters return the governor to office. Lifting term limitations also allows voters to retain a governor who is doing a good job.[6]

Yet another reform shortens the ballot, but the numbers indicate more modifications are needed to reduce the still large number of separately elected officials. In 1955, 514 separately elected state level officials, beside the governor, headed 337 state agencies. In 1994, 511 separately elected officials, other than the governor, headed 260 state agencies in the 50 states.[7] In terms of 12 major state offices, in 1992 there were 304 separately elected officials compared to 306 in 1972.[8] Fewer elective offices, and thus more appointed offices, would give the governor a broader policy and administrative reach and the citizens a governor with greater control of the executive branch of state government.

The final reform is the veto. Between 1955 and 1995, the number of governors who could veto all legislation only rose from forty-seven to forty-nine. Only the governor of North Carolina lacks the veto power. Until recently, attempts to change this have been stalled by partisan and separation-of-powers fights. The voters of the state will finally get their opportunity to adopt an amendment to the state's constitution giving the governor the veto in the 1995 elections. The number of governors with an item veto rose from thirty-nine to forty-four. Ten governors now have the power to cut specific spending items; twenty-six others have the power to veto substantial language in appropriations bills.[9]

Governors' offices have expanded rapidly over the past decades. In 1956, political scientist Coleman B. Ransone, Jr., reported that governors' offices averaged 11 staff members, with a range from 3 to 43 among the states.[10] In 1976, the National Governors' Association (NGA) found an average of 29 staff members, with a much broader range from 7 to 245.[11] A 1994 survey indicated that there were nearly 54 staff members per governor's office, with a range from 8 (Wyoming) to 216 (New York).[12] Thus, over a four-decade period the average number of gubernatorial staff members grew about fivefold. Increased staff means more flexibility and greater support for the governor in his or her many roles. Growth also creates more patronage positions—and more opportunity for confusion.

The configurations of gubernatorial staffs can be classified from the very personal to the very institutional. Their makeup correlates closely with the size of the state. Larger states have larger and more institutionalized offices and processes, with adequate and specialized staff resources to assist the governor. Smaller states have smaller and more personalized offices that often lack the breadth and depth possessed by those in larger states. In these offices, the governor must rely on a small pool of individuals to cover all the variety of responsibilities. In between are the growing, mid-size states. Here, a governor may feel the need for an institutionalized office but actually have only a small, personalized staffing structure and process at his or her disposal.[13]

A critical expression of gubernatorial authority is the budget process. A chief executive must be able to control the development and execution of the state's budget. Governors have consolidated their power over the budget process by placing state budget offices under their direct control.[14] In so doing, they have refocused the budgetary process from an earlier preoccupation "with the custodial functions of auditing and accounting" to emphasizing "new and conceptually rich systems of management decision making."[15] The budget and the budgetary process remain mechanisms by which a governor controls a state's finances, but as the budget process has been opened to include planning and policy analysis approaches, the management capability of governors has been greatly enhanced. The budget can now more nearly be "the ultimate statement of any government's (and governor's) policy choices."[16]

The policy planning process is also critical. Initially seen as part of the economic development function of state government, and thus located in those departments, state planning agencies have been migrating closer to the governor. In 1960, only three of the thirty-seven state planning agencies were located in the governor's office; two others were housed in departments of administration and finance. A decade later all fifty states had state planning agencies. Twenty-nine were in the governor's office and seven were in departments of administration or finance.[17]

Many of these agencies became policy planning offices, taking on a broad set of activities and responsibilities. By 1988, all but five states had policy planning offices to assist the governor. These offices are usually located either in the governor's office or within the budget office or in the department of administration or finance. Policy planning agencies that stand free of the budget agency and process are generally reflective of strong governorships. Their close ties to the state's chief executive are indicative of their importance within the state's governmental system.[18]

What do these offices accomplish? A 1985 Council of State Planning Agencies survey indicated that they have two major responsibilities, varying in emphasis from state to state—policy development and administration.[19] The goal of policy planning offices is to see to it that factors other than narrow agency perspectives and purely budgetary or political concerns be brought to bear in the policy process.

But in the late 1980s and early 1990s, the nation's economic woes forced sophisticated policy analysis to take a back seat. The governors' budgetary powers were the engines of gubernatorial policy politics. In almost every state, the impact of the recession, changes in the economy, and a declining federal government presence in domestic affairs caused severe budgetary turmoil as state revenues fell and a need for state governmental action rose. While hard to quantify, most decisions made by state leaders had at their base the realities of state budgetary shortfalls; other issues and perspectives were set aside as the need to balance state budgets and keep necessary programs and services going became paramount. Raising taxes and cutting back governmental programs were the main agenda items for most governors. Sophisticated policy analyses were eclipsed by the continual need for massive and quick changes in state budgets.

The mid-1990s has seen a more conservative mood settle across both the federal and state governments. Sophisticated policy analysis remains dormant in the face of a continuing drive to cut back or redirect government programs. Voter insistence that taxes not be increased but cut has extended the fiscal and policy malaise of the recession years and helped transform it into a new type of fiscal and policy malaise based on conservative ideology and goals.

The ability to reorganize government is a powerful tool. In 1956, only two governors had the power to initiate state government reorganization by executive order, subject to legislative confirmation; by 1994, twenty-two governors had this power.[20] During the 1960s many reformers argued that the residue of past trends and decisions left state governments unmanageable and unresponsive to gubernatorial direction. Such criticism spurred the executive branches of nearly two dozen state governments to undertake comprehensive reorganization, and nearly all states engaged in partial reorganizations. In comprehensive reorganizations, the executive branch is consolidated to various degrees under the control of the governor. Most partial reorganizations bring many programs and agencies working in the same functional area under one departmental roof. These reforms have been most prevalent in economic development, environmental protection, transportation, and human services.[21]

Reorganization enables a governor to reshape the executive branch for a variety of reasons. These include providing a clearer focus on particular problems and delivering governmental services efficiently. There are additional steps that can be taken to allow governors to make state governments more focused and responsive, for example, a decrease in the numbers of separately elected officials. There are several states today that would benefit from giving their governors the ability to initiate reorganization, subject to confirmation by the legislature.

Appointing and Removing Personnel

Chief executive officers, whether in the private or public sector, must be free to choose those who will serve in their administration. The power of appointment is a dual power, for it also includes the power to remove.

Many governors are constrained by the number and types of positions to which they can make appointments. First, governors cannot appoint any of the members of the thirty-three separately elected boards and commissions in twenty-three states. These boards are charged with responsibilities in public education, public utilities, higher education, and various regulatory activities.[22]

Second, governors cannot appoint separately elected officials to office, unless they fill a vacancy created by death or resignation. These officials have their own constitutional base of authority and their own constituency of supporters. In effect, most states operate under a plural executive model rather than the presidential model we see at the national level where the president and vice president are the only elected executive branch officials and they are elected as a team. The number of statewide elected officials ranges from one—the governor in Maine and New Jersey—to ten in North Carolina and North Dakota.[23]

Third, governors cannot appoint officials who by constitutional authority are to be appointed by some other officer or by the legislature. Some argue that this constraint is less than it seems, as those making such appointments are the governor's own appointees. While this may be true in some states, in Texas, for example, boards and commissions in effect run most of state government. Because of the staggered terms of the officials appointed to these boards and commissions, a Texas governor may be well into a second term before gaining some control, and then only indirectly through the newly appointed members.[24] However, in 1991 former governor Ann Richards (1991–1995) was able to get the legislature to provide her with more executive power by adding some important appointments to the governorship and giving it effective control over several others.[25]

Practical political concerns affect a governor's appointment choices.[26]

- The sheer number of appointments to be made can so overwhelm a governor that he or she may fail to focus sufficiently on key appointments. Replacing too many people can draw a governor too deeply into the bureaucracy, obviating any policy or administrative benefits.
- Patronage appointments serve as rewards, but many individuals and groups feel they should be rewarded. Appointments are evaluated with a jealous eye, and jealousy is not a positive basis on which to build a working relationship.
- Conflicting expectations over how an appointive office should be conducted can lead to struggles within the governor's coalition.

Coupled with the power of appointment is the power of removal. If changes in policy are needed, incumbent officeholders often must be replaced with those who will carry out the proposed reforms. In most situations, key officeholders resign as a new administration comes in. But conflicts arise when resignations are not forthcoming or when a change in priorities elevates previously minor positions to importance, creating the need to appoint new officials to them.

Only twenty-three state constitutions provide governors with the power to remove individuals from positions in the state executive branch, and all but six of these put varying degrees of restrictions on this power. The power of removal is contained in the original constitutions of just five states. However, as more constitutions are being revised, the power of removal is being built in. Eleven of the fourteen states that revised their constitutions after 1945 included this power for the governor. Other states provide statutory removal powers for their governors.

Governors can still experience problems exercising their right to remove personnel. Joseph Schlesinger noted that "even when a governor can remove an official, he is constrained by the wrangle which would result."[27] It is a power, therefore, that tends to be used only as a last resort. Moreover, a series of federal court decisions placed potentially severe restrictions on the removal power. In a 1976 case, *Elrod v. Burns*, the U.S. Supreme Court decided (5 to 4) that a patronage firing violates an individual's political liberties under the First Amendment. The ruling said that "political belief and association constitute the core of those activities protected by the First Amendment of the U.S. Constitution."[28]

This strict standard was relaxed in two subsequent decisions. In a 1980 case, *Branti v. Finkel*, the Court reaffirmed (6 to 3) its 1976 decision but also ruled that "if the employee's private political beliefs would interfere with the discharge of his public duties, the First Amendment rights may be required to yield to the state's vital interest in maintaining governmental effectiveness and efficiency." The burden of proof would be on the employer.[29] In a 1983 case,

Connick v. Myers, the Court decided (5 to 4) to add another restriction on the employee's right by holding "that the First Amendment does not protect from dismissal public employees who complain about their working conditions or their supervisor."[30] In these cases, the Court indicated a balance was needed between an individual's rights and the administration's needs, and it was the Court's role to weigh those conflicts.

Although none of these cases involved them, governors were aware of the problems the decisions could cause. At the 1982 "New Governors' Seminar," sponsored by the National Governors' Association, the newly elected governors were cautioned:

> Know the *Elrod v. Burns* case, the 1976 five-to-four Supreme Court decision regarding the firing of personnel. You cannot fire for a political reason, and you are personally liable. It even destroys the privacy privilege of counsel.
>
> The *Elrod v. Burns* decision requires an indemnification statute, and be sure that it covers the unpaid boards and commissions as well as full-time state officials."[31]

In 1990, the Court handed down a 5 to 4 ruling in *Rutan et al. v. Republican Party of Illinois* that directly affected the removal powers of governors. The decision, which focused on the patronage process of the Illinois governor's office in the James R. Thompson administration (R, 1977–1991), said that state and local governments violate an individual's "First Amendment rights when they refuse to hire, promote or transfer . . . [an employee] on the basis of their political affiliation or party activity."[32]

The decision on how Thompson handled so-called blue-collar patronage—"the conventional doling out of state jobs to the party faithful"—struck down the "hiring freezes Thompson imposed, more or less continuously throughout his tenure . . . [as] merely patronage tools used to ensure that worthy Republicans got available state jobs." Thompson found the decision ironic as he had been chided by Republican party leaders in the state for not being "grateful enough to those who labored in the GOP vineyards." Thompson, at the end of his tenure in office, said "the Supreme Court of the United States certifies what these Republican chairmen refused to believe all along—that I had the best patronage machine in the nation, that it was a Republican machine."[33]

Gubernatorial Powers

Political scientists have often attempted to compare the powers of the fifty state governorships. Research results have been presented in a series of comparative indices and analyses, which have then been followed by critiques of the indices and rejoinders to these critiques. The first such comparative gubernatorial power index was published by Joseph Schlesinger in 1965; it has served as the foundation of subsequent academic efforts. At its base are the governor's appointment power, budget-making power, tenure potential, and veto power.[34]

A question persists as to whether these academic pursuits and counter suits have any meaning in the real world of governors. An answer to this question may not exist, but in 1987 the NGA Office of State Services issued a State Management Note in which the same questions pertaining to the comparative institutional powers of the governors were addressed.

The NGA concluded that "the framework in which a Governor performs his or her job can be an important factor in a successful governorship." It noted that the indices were used only as a suggestion of the framework and that some "governors have proven to be vital and strong leaders in many areas despite institutional shortcomings that may hamper their success," while others "have failed to provide strong leadership to their states even where formal provisions indicate an authoritative office."[35]

The NGA analysis included the four items in the Schlesinger index—appointment powers, budget-making power, tenure potential, veto power—and added two additional measures: the governor's political strength in the legislature and the legislature's ability to change gubernatorial budgets. The first three indices primarily concern the governor's power within the executive branch; the second three concern the governor's power vis-à-vis the legislature.[36]

A comparison of these two sets of indices is contained in Table 5-1. According to the Schlesinger indices, based on a total score of 20 points the governorships grew in strength from an average of 13 points in 1960 to 16.2 points in 1994. Governors gained considerably in their veto power, more moderately in their budget power and tenure potential. The 1994 average of 16.15 came down a bit from the 1989 average of 16.6 due to the success of the term limit movement in a number of states, which reduced some governors' tenure potential.[37]

According to the NGA indices, governorships have experienced minimal growth in strength. Between 1965 and 1994, out of a total of 32 points, the average score rose from 20.9 to just 21.8. Most indicators held at about the same level, though tenure potential increased while party control of the legislature decreased. This latter decline was due primarily to the effects of an increasing number of states with a "powersplit" in the control of the governorship and the state legislature (discussed below).[38]

In 1994, the most powerful governorships according to the NGA 32-point-scale index were in Maryland (28.2), West Virginia (28), New York (25.5), and Nebraska (25). The least powerful governorships were in South Carolina (17), Vermont (17.5), New Hampshire (18.3), and Maine (18.5).

These findings demonstrate what many have suggested: Reforms have been made on both sides of the separation-of-powers relationship, and while governors may now have more institutionalized powers at their disposal (budget-making, tenure potential, veto), state legislatures possess powers that are often used at the expense of the executive (budget-changing authority, party control).

How have the formal/institutional powers of the governors of individual states fared from 1965, at the beginning of the era of state government reform,

Table 5-1   Gubernatorial Powers, 1960–1994

Formal powers (range)	Political Scientists				
	1960	1968	1981	1989	1994
Appointments (1–5)	2.9	3.0	3.2	3.2[a]	2.8
Budget making (1–5)	4.0	3.6	4.7	4.8	4.8
Tenure potential (1–5)	3.3	3.7	4.1	4.2	4.1
Veto (0–5)	2.8	2.6	4.1	4.4	4.4
Average score	13.0	12.9	16.1	16.6	16.15
Possible range	3–20	3–20	3–20	3–20	3–20
Actual range	7–19	8–20	10–20	12–20	12–19

Institutional powers (range)	National Governors' Association			
	1965	1985	1990[b]	1994[b]
Appointments (0–7)	3.8 est.[c]	4.0 est.[c]	4.2	4.0
Budget making (1–5)	4.5 est.[c]	4.8 est.[c]	4.8	4.8
Tenure potential (1–5)	3.3	4.1	4.2	4.1
Veto (1–5)	4.2	3.6	4.4	4.4
Legislative budget-changing power (1–5)	1.3	1.2	1.3	1.3
Party control (1–5)	3.8	3.4	3.1	3.2
Average score	20.9	21.1	22.0	21.8
Possible range	5–32	5–32	5–32	5–32
Actual range	14–29	16–27	15–29	17–28

Sources: Schlesinger index: (1960) Joseph A. Schlesinger, "The Politics of the Executive," in *Politics in the American States,* ed. Herbert Jacob and Kenneth N. Vines (Boston: Little, Brown, 1965), 229; (1968) Schlesinger, "The Politics of the Executive," in *Politics in the American States,* 2d ed. (1971); (1981) Thad L. Beyle, "Governors," in *Politics in the American States,* 4th ed. Virginia Gray, Herbert Jacob, and Kenneth N. Vines (1983), 458–459; (1989) Beyle, "Governors," in *Politics in the American States,* 5th ed., ed. Virginia Gray, Herbert Jacob, and Robert Albritton (Glenview, Ill.: Scott, Foresman, 1990), 574; (1994) Beyle, "Governors," in *Politics in the American States,* 6th ed., ed. Virginia Gray and Herbert Jacob (Washington, D.C.: CQ Press, 1996), 237. National Governors' Association: (1965, 1985) Office of State Services, "The Institutionalized Powers of the Governorship: 1965–1985," *Management Note* (Washington, D.C.: National Governors' Association, June 1987), 12–13; (1990, 1994) Author's Calculations.

[a] Adjusted to make one-to-six point score into a one-to-five point score by dropping each state's score by one point.

[b] Author updates of original NGA indices.

[c] Estimates based on information in NGA report.

to 1994? To determine this we can total the NGA index scores of each state for 1965 and 1994 and then find the difference between the two. These differences range from +10 for West Virginia to -5.3 for California, a spread of 15.3 points. In fact, the governorships of eight states increased their strength by more than 25 percent (West Virginia, North Dakota, Iowa, Indiana, Rhode Island, Arkansas, Mississippi, and Arizona), while four states saw their governorships weaken by more than 25 percent (California, Virginia, Maine, and Massachusetts). The remaining thirty-eight states saw rather modest changes in their governors' powers.

Governorships in the Midwest gained the most power over the period (+3.1 points on average), followed by southern states (+1.4 points). Northeastern state governorships gained little on average (+0.4 points), while western state governorships actually lost some power (-0.7 points).

The sixteen states with 38 percent or greater rural populations gained 2.5 points on average while the thirty-four states with 37 percent or less rural population gained only 0.5 points on average. However, those states with larger urban populations had already provided their governors with greater institutionalized power by 1965, which indicates that the more rural states were playing catch-up in providing their governors with additional power.

A major cause of the decline in gubernatorial power indices vis-à-vis the legislature is the increasing number of divided governments in the states. Since World War II, the power of the political parties in the states has declined.[39] Nowhere is this more apparent than in the increasing number of states faced with a "powersplit"—a situation in which the governor faces a legislature controlled either totally or in part by the opposition party.[40]

In 1954, nine of the then forty-eight states (19 percent) had a politically divided state government, mainly in states outside the South. By 1966, when these comparative measures of gubernatorial power were first published, only thirteen of the fifty states (26 percent) were divided politically, again mainly outside the South. Since the mid-1980s, about three-fifths of the states had powersplits—twenty-seven states following the 1994 elections. The three independent candidates elected governor in Alaska (1990), Connecticut (1990), and Maine (1994) are the most extreme examples of this trend.

The irony of a powersplit is that as reformers successfully change or enhance institutions at the state level, a growing malaise in the political parties undermines the abilities of certain key, state-level actors to follow through on those reforms. While some decry this situation as detrimental to effective government, at least one observer suggests that it may actually lead to better policy through necessary compromises that take in many points of view.[41]

Gubernatorial Conflict with Other State Government Actors

Political reforms do not always achieve their intended purposes. Some create unanticipated consequences that then generate additional reforms; others create conflict with previous reforms. And politics may render some reforms unworkable.

Conflicts within the Executive Branch

Governors often face their greatest conflicts within the executive branch itself. Several governors have had serious problems with the lieutenant governor's power while the governor was out of the state. For example, conflict has arisen over calling special legislative sessions, appointments to administrative and judicial positions, pardons, the governor's salary, and control of the national guard. Other problems have come about when the governor and the lieutenant governor were of different parties or different factions within the same party. Also, difficulties have emerged when the lieutenant governor had constitutional leadership responsibilities in the legislature that provided a separate power base.

Governors have at times found themselves at odds with the state's attorney general when legal issues took on a political cast. An attorney general may challenge a gubernatorial action in court on constitutional grounds. Who is to serve as the governor's legal adviser in such a case? Alternatively, who is to lead the prosecution of a governor when he or she has been accused of wrongdoing? This problem arose during the impeachment of Arizona governor Evan Mecham (R, 1987–1988).

Finally, governors must face other statewide elected officials intent on seeking the governorship. In the 255 gubernatorial elections from 1977 to 1995, lieutenant governors were candidates in 73 of the races (29 percent) and won 20 of them (27 percent). In the same period, attorneys general were candidates in 57 of the races (22 percent) and won 14 of them (24 percent). Over these nineteen years state treasurers were candidates in 11 of the races (4 percent), winning 2 of them (18 percent).[42] Under such circumstances, conflict instead of cooperation is often the rule.

Conflicts with Other Branches of Government

With the concept of separation of powers built into most state constitutions and the American constitutional system, conflict between the executive and the legislative branches is inevitable. Conflicts may occur over setting state government policy, raising and spending money, administering policy, appointing officials to executive and judicial positions, controlling the legislative process, and calling special sessions.

When the governor and the legislature are of opposite parties, conflict can take on a divisive partisan tone. If gubernatorial and legislative leaders have conflicting political ambitions, strife may result between the branches. In the 252 gubernatorial races between 1977 and 1994, state house speakers were candidates in 26 of the races (10 percent) and won 9 of them (35 percent).[43]

Gubernatorial-legislative tensions are greatest in most states at budget time, when the money and policy decisions must be made. It is the "governor's budget," but the legislature has to pass it; it also must be balanced. Dollar decisions became particularly difficult to make in the harsh economic times of the early 1990s. Budget makers faced declining resources coupled with increasing demands for services. Skeptics aside, however, some states have risen to the challenge of getting a workable budget passed and signed into law by elevating the level of cooperation between the two branches.

California governor Pete Wilson (R, 1991–) received high marks from both the media and the Democratic leadership of the state legislature for his efforts to reconcile the $14 billion deficit the state faced in 1991.[44] Massachusetts governor William F. Weld (R, 1991–) was likewise commended for his role in dealing with the state's dire fiscal situation.[45] And, despite his use of the veto to keep the Connecticut legislature "on task" for a state income tax, Gov. Lowell P. Weicker, Jr. (I, 1991–1995) was able to achieve his goal without any members of his A Connecticut Party in the legislature (not counting the lieutenant governor, who presided over the state senate).[46]

The execution of the budget by the governor leads to a second area of potential conflict—the legislature's interest in how its actions are administered. Legislatures have tried several ways to make sure legislative intent is followed. Governors often read these efforts as legislative intrusion into executive branch responsibilities. For example, some executive branch positions are appointments that constitutionally must be confirmed by the legislature. However, in some states legislatures have either constitutional or statutory authority to make appointments. In certain cases, they can appoint legislators to boards, commissions, or councils in the executive branch. If these bodies maintain an advisory role, problems may not arise. However, if they exercise management responsibilities, as twenty states allowed in the mid-1980s, charges of legislative intrusion may be lodged and challenged in state courts as a violation of separation of powers.[47]

Another area of conflict concerns vetoes, both gubernatorial and legislative. In 1947, governors vetoed about 5 percent of the bills presented to them. These vetoes were overridden by a legislative vote in only 1.8 percent of the cases.[48] In the 1992–1993 legislative years, 5.6 percent of the bills presented to governors were vetoed; 3.2 percent of these vetoes were overridden. However, in these averages there were some interesting extremes: Gov. Ned McWherter (D, Tenn.) did not veto a single bill presented to him, while Gov. Pete Wilson vetoed 21 percent of the bills presented to him, none of which were overridden.[49]

As the ability of governors to use the item and amendatory vetoes grows, conflicts with the legislative branch escalate. A governor can veto special policy provisions in budget bills that have not run the full course of legislative review, thereby forcing the legislature to consider the issues in open debate.[50]

State legislatures have turned to the legislative veto—a procedure that permits them "to review proposed executive branch regulations or actions and to block or modify those with which they disagree."[51] The legislative veto became increasingly popular in the 1970s and into the 1980s, with forty-one states adopting it by mid-1982. However, both federal and state courts have called it an unconstitutional violation of the separation-of-powers concept.[52] Voters in New Jersey (1985), Alaska and Michigan (1986), and Nevada (1988) rejected giving this power to their legislatures.

Conflicts between the executive and legislative branches of state governments have increasingly gone before state courts. These courts usually decide in favor of the governor and the executive branch, citing the separation-of-powers clause in the state's constitution.[53] However, they sometimes rule against the executive when separation of powers is not in question, as in policy and civil rights issues.

Governors and judges are often at odds over specific decisions, such as the death penalty or the selection and appointment of judges. In 1986, three states—California, North Carolina, and Ohio—had highly contested, negative, policy-related contests for the chief judgeship of the state's supreme court. In all of these races the incumbent governors were actively involved in judicial politics.

A new area of contention is brewing between governors and legislatures on one side and the courts on the other. As governors propose, and legislatures adopt, state budgets with severe cuts in appropriations, the courts, like all parts of state government, find themselves unable to fulfill their responsibilities with the reduced amounts of available funds. Can the courts force the other two branches to take the necessary monetary actions, including raising taxes, to ensure that the courts receive enough money to operate? According to experiences in fourteen states, yes, they can. In September 1991, the chief judge of New York's State Court of Appeals, that state's highest appellate court, filed suit charging that the governor and the legislature failed to provide the courts with adequate funds—a violation of the state constitution. A decision in favor of the courts is possible, as all the earlier suits consistently favored the judiciary.[54]

As governors seek to carry out their responsibilities conflicts arise—conflicts that are built into the charters of state government and exacerbated by political and policy differences.

Measuring Gubernatorial Performance

There are several ways by which gubernatorial performance can be rated. The first and most obvious way is by the voters when they decide whether or not to reelect an incumbent governor. Table 5-2 provides a picture of gubernatorial elections since 1970 and indicates just how well incumbent governors have fared in their reelection bids.

During the period 1970–1995, there were 365 separate gubernatorial elections in the fifty states. In 80 of these contests (22 percent), the incumbent governor was term limited and could not seek reelection; 68 others (19 percent) decided against seeking another term. Reasons for not seeking reelection could include a decision to retire from public life, a desire to return to the more lucrative private sector, a bid to seek a higher office—usually a U.S. Senate seat—or simply an acceptance of the futility of attempting reelection in the face of negative media and dissatisfied voters.

Of the 217 incumbent governors who did seek reelection, 157 of them (72 percent) won another term in office. Thus nearly three-quarters of the incumbent governors facing the electorate passed the "gubernatorial performance test."

Table 5-2   Gubernatorial Elections, 1970–1995

			Number of Incumbent Governors				
							Lost
							In
		Number of				In	general
	Number	Democratic	Eligible			In	general
Year	of Races	winners	to run	Ran	Won	primary	election
1970	35	22 (63%)	29 (83%)	24 (83%)	16 (64%)	1	7
1971	3	3 (100)	0	—	—	—	—
1972	18	11 (61)	15 (83)	11 (73)	7 (64)	2	2
1973	2	1 (50)	1 (50)	1 (100)	—	1	—
1974	35	28 (80)[a]	29 (83)	22 (76)	17 (77)	1	4
1975	3	3 (100)	2 (66)	2 (100)	2 (100)	—	—
1976	14	9 (64)	12 (86)	8 (67)	5 (63)	1	2
1977	2	1 (50)	1 (50)	1 (100)	1 (100)	—	—
1978	36	21 (58)	29 (81)	22 (76)	16 (73)	1	5
1979	3	2 (67)	0	—	—	—	—
1980	13	6 (46)	12 (92)	12 (100)	7 (58)	2	3
1981	2	1 (50)	0	—	—	—	—
1982	36	27 (75)	33 (92)	25 (76)	19 (76)	1	5
1983	3	3 (100)	0	—	—	—	—
1984	13	5 (38)	9 (69)	6 (67)	4 (67)	—	2
1985	2	1 (50)	1 (50)	1 (100)	1 (100)	—	—
1986	36	19 (53)	24 (67)	18 (75)	15 (83)	1	2
1987	3	3 (100)	2 (67)	1 (50)	0	1	—
1988	12	5 (42)	9 (75)	9 (100)	8 (89)	—	1
1989	2	2 (100)	0	—	—	—	—
1990	36	19 (53)[b]	33 (92)	23 (70)	17 (74)	—	6
1991	3	2 (67)	2 (67)	2 (100)	0	1	1
1992	12	8 (67)	9 (75)	4 (44)	4 (100)	—	—
1993	2	0	1 (50)	1 (100)	0	—	1
1994	36	11 (31)[a]	30 (83)	23 (77)	17 (74)	2	4
1995	3	1 (33)	2 (67)	1 (50)	1 (100)	—	—
Totals	365	285 (78%)	217 (76%)	157 (72%)	60 (28%)	15	45

Sources: Council of State Governments, *The Book of the States, 1994–1995* (Lexington, Ky.: Council of State Governments, 1994), 37; and selected issues of *Congressional Quarterly Weekly Report.*

[a] One Independent candidate won.

[b] Two Independent candidates won.

Of the 60 incumbent governors defeated in their bids for reelection, 45 (75 percent) lost in the general election while 15 (25 percent) failed to receive their own party's renomination in the primary. These defeated incumbents came from all parts of the country, though there was a slightly higher tendency for them to be from the Midwest (19) and South (17) than from the Northeast (14) or West (10). The hardest state on incumbents is Texas where four incumbents have been defeated for reelection since 1970.

Table 5-3   Approval Ratings of Current Governors, 1995

Class and governor	Highest/lowest rating	Most recent rating (date)
Class of 1994		
Frank Keating, R-Okla.	74	74 (7/95)
Jim Gehringer, R-Wyo.	72	72 (9/95)
Angus King, I-Maine	68	68 (10/95)
Bill Graves, R-Kan.	68	68 (6/95)
Tom Ridge, R-Pennsylvania	61	61 (9/95)
George W. Bush, R-Texas	58/49	57 (10/95)
John Kitzhaber, D-Ore.	57	57 (11/95)
Don Sundquist, R-Tenn.	54	54 (5/95)
Gary Johnson, R-N.M.	48	48 (2/95)
David Beasley, R-S.C.	46	46 (5/95)
George Pataki, R-N.Y.	49/34	46 (12/95)
Fob James, R-Alabama	45/41	45 (9/95)
Ben Cayetano, D-Hawaii	44	44 (2/95)
John Rowland, R-Conn.	51/34	43 (12/95)
Lincoln Almond, R-R.I.	44/33	34 (9/95)
Parris Glendening, D-Md.	34/18	34 (10/95)
Class of 1993		
Christine Todd Whitman, R-N.J.	63/37	52 (11/95)
George Allen, R-Va.	68/48	49 (10/95)
Class of 1992		
Mike Leavitt, R-Utah	85/75	85 (9/94)
Marc Racicot, R-Mont.	79/54	74 (12/95)
Jim Hunt, D-N.C.[a]	74/40	74 (11/95)
Steve Merrill, R-N.H.	79/60	62 (12/95)
Tom Carper, D-Del.	62	62 (10/94)
Ed Schafer, R-N.D.	68/59	59 (3/95)
Mel Carnahan, D-Mo.	50	50 (10/94)
Jim Guy Tucker, D-Ark.	54/39	39 (5/95)
Mike Lowry, D-Wash.	37/21	32 (12/95)
Class of 1991		
Howard Dean, D-Vt.	80/63	71 (2/95)
Kirk Fordice, R-Miss.	60/37	60 (6/95)
Brereton Jones, D-Ky.	64/35	40 (4/95)
Fife Symington, R-Ariz.	64/16	37 (10/95)
Edwin Edwards, D-La.	32/21	28 (2/95)
Class of 1990		
Ben Nelson, D-Neb.	55/79	72 (5/95)
Zell Miller, D-Georgia	65/44	65 (11/95)
John Engler, R-Mich.	64/42	62 (12/95)
George Voinovich, R-Ohio	62/45	61 (10/95)
Arne Carlson, R-Minn.	63/29	57 (9/95)
Lawton Chiles, D-Fla.	58/22	51 (9/95)

Table 5-3 *(continued)*

Class and Governor	Highest/lowest rating	Most recent rating (date)
Class of 1990 *(continued)*		
William Weld, R-Mass.	67/41	50 (11/95)
Jim Edgar, R-Ill.	71/37	46 (11/94)
Pete Wilson, R-Calif.	52/15	23 (12/95)
Class of 1989		
Bob Miller, D-Nev.	58/48	58 (11/95)
Class of 1988		
Evan Bayh, D-Ind.	73/40	62 (12/95)
Gaston Caperton, D-W.Va.	35/14	26 (8/94)
Class of 1986		
Roy Romer, D-Col.	75/45	70 (10/95)
Tommy Thompson, R-Wis.	81/57	63 (10/95)
Class of 1982		
Terry Branstad, R-Iowa	69/37	49 (5/95)

Source: Compiled by the author.

[a] Initially served in the governorship from 1977 to 1983; Hunt was reelected to the office in 1992 after a ten-year absence and is listed here as part of the class of 1992.

The unsuccessful incumbents were evenly split between Democrats and Republicans, with primary losers more likely to be Democrats and general election losers slightly more likely to be Republicans. Republican incumbent losses were more pronounced in the 1970s; Democratic losses have been spread fairly equally over the three decades.

A second way to measure gubernatorial performance is through use of the rapidly growing number of statewide opinion polls that ask respondents how well they feel their governor is performing his or her job. These statewide polls are conducted by an array of individuals and organizations ranging from university institutes, to the media, to political parties, to political candidates, to professional pollsters. Questions are asked of samples of adults, of registered voters, and of likely voters. The results of these polls are disseminated through the media and become a political fact of some importance to those serving as governors.

Table 5-3 presents gubernatorial performance ratings taking the 1995 incumbent governors by "class"—that is, the year the governor was first elected to office for his or her current tenure. Overall, these governors had an average job approval rating of 54 percent. This average masks a considerable range of approval ratings—from 85 percent for Mike Leavitt (R, Utah) and 81 percent for Tommy Thompson (R, Wis.) to 21 percent for Mike Lowry (D, Wash.). Twenty-seven of the governors received positive ratings, in excess of 50 percent. On average, Republican governors had higher job approval ratings: 55 percent versus the Democrats' 52 percent.

One striking aspect of these ratings is their diversity within the classes. For example, in the Class of 1992 there is a sixty-four-point difference between the highest-rated governor (Leavitt of Utah at 85 percent) and the lowest-rated governor (Mike Lowry of Washington at 21 percent). In the Class of 1994, there is a forty-point difference in the approval ratings of the top-rated governor (Frank Keating of Oklahoma at 74 percent) and the lowest-rated governor (Glendening of Maryland at 34 percent).

A third way to measure gubernatorial performance is to ask a sample of interested observers to rate them. In the summer of 1994, I asked some 388 political scientists, members of the media, and additional knowledgeable individuals how they felt their governors were doing.[55] This reading of the incumbent governors of 1994 found considerable consistency between how the public sized up their governor's performance and how these interested observers did.

Where there were differences, the public was more volatile in their views on gubernatorial performance. Interested observers were neither as negative nor as positive as the public.

One interesting finding of this survey was the correlation between how well governors interacted with the media, the executive branch, and the state legislature and how highly they were rated.[56] Governors who maintained solid relationships with the media generally received higher ratings. This should come as no surprise as public knowledge and feelings toward a governor are most readily shaped by the nature of media coverage, be it negative or positive.

The Shift of Activism in the Federal System

Over the past two decades, activism in the federal system has shifted from the national level to the state and local governments. The states were rocked by what John Shannon, former director of the Advisory Commission on Intergovernmental Relations (ACIR), called the three R's: revolt, recession, and reduction. The late 1970s saw the revolt of the taxpayers in the forms of tax-reducing propositions 13 and 2½ in California and Massachusetts, respectively. The recession or economic downturn of the early 1980s was felt for a lengthy period of time in some parts of the country. And the reduction in federal grant-in-aid funds accelerated throughout the Reagan administration.[57]

In the face of this economic tumult state and local governments took steps to pick up part of the slack, raising additional funds to meet their commitments. For local governments, the decline in federal aid was partially compensated by increases in state aid and by their own money-raising efforts. By the mid-1980s, the economy had healed in most parts of the country and budgetary decisions had eased for the states. However, this turned out to be the calm before the storm.

As the decade of the 1980s was closing, recession reemerged, hitting hard. As the recession deepened, tax revenues in the states fell; at the same time the needs of those affected by the downturn increased. Governors and state legislatures were faced with some damning options: raise taxes, cut services, or both. Policy makers anguished over the tough tax "enhancement" decisions that had to be made.[58] What's more, the added revenues that additional taxes brought in only served to keep state government going, often at a much-reduced level—they did nothing to enhance the role or impact of state government.[59]

Such decisions, however warranted, can carry a heavy price. For policy makers, this meant defeat at the polls. In 1990, three of the six eligible incumbent governors in New England decided not to seek reelection because of their low standings with the public over tax issues; a fourth was defeated in the general election, in good part because of the state's poor economic conditions.[60] New Jersey governor James J. Florio (D, 1990–1994), faced with the need to increase taxes, joined the ranks of "tax-loss" governors in a narrow defeat in his 1993 bid for reelection.[61]

For these governors feeling the white hot political heat generated by raising taxes, there was some solace in watching what was happening to the national administration. After a 1988 presidential campaign built on reading lips and never raising taxes, the president had to bite the same bullet and acquiesce to a tax hike at the national level. But while doing so, the national administration never acknowledged what the governors already knew—there was a serious recession abroad and a pervasive need to provide assistance to those being affected. President Bush joined that list of these tax-loss governors with his 1992 reelection loss to Gov. Bill Clinton (D-Ark., 1979–1981, 1983–1992).

Not all governors in office during this time felt the negative wrath of the voters. A prime example is Gov. Pete Wilson of California. Wilson faced what most would agree were monster deficits during his first term. He and the California legislature had to make some very difficult tax and spending decisions in dealing with an annual budget deficit that was greater than the total budgets of all but a few states. While his approval ratings sank precipitously into the teens, he still won reelection in 1994.[62]

This same 1994 election brought another "R" into play: the massive shift in the U.S. Congress to Republican control. The Republicans' "Contract with America" called for both tax cuts and program cuts at the national level. If adopted intact, a major restructuring of the responsibilities in our federal system would most certainly ensue *(see Chapter 2)*.

Even as improving national and state economies were adding to the tax coffers, this so-called political recession was hitting the states with an as yet unknown impact on state budgets and programs. Governors and other state and local leaders became fearful of seeing national-level decisions to reduce the national deficit shift the economic burden to the states—in effect, balancing the national budget on the backs of the states.

Governors in Association

Governors have taken significant steps to revitalize and redirect multi-state organizations during the last two decades. Foremost among these organizations is the National Governors' Association (NGA). The NGA's precursor emerged in 1908 after a call by President Theodore Roosevelt to the governors to meet with him to discuss conservation issues.

Getting Organized

For many years, the governors met regularly as the Governors' Conference to discuss a broad agenda, with the Council of State Governments (CSG) serving as secretary. During the mid-1960s, as federal grant-in-aid programs proliferated and the federal government intruded further into the states in the form of Lyndon Johnson's Great Society programs, the governors felt the need for a more permanent organization. They set up an office in Washington, D.C. to press their views, interests, and needs upon the federal government. State legislative and local government leaders were taking similar steps.

The strong showing of state executive and legislative organizations in the nation's capital was significant. Distrusting the efficacy of their U.S. congressional members, state leaders felt that a strong and independent state presence in Washington was one of several steps that had to be taken for adequate representation in the national policy process.[63]

Growth of the National Governors' Association

Under the leadership of a series of strong governors, the Governors' Conference began to broaden its agenda and approach.[64] In 1966, it changed its name to the National Governors' Conference (NGC) "to distinguish it clearly from the regional conferences which had sprung up."[65] In 1967, NGC switched from an ad hoc committee structure to a system of eleven standing committees. The NGC began advocating a body of policy positions that were agreed to at annual meetings.[66] In 1977, the NGC became the National Governors' Association "to signify the broad scope and ongoing nature of the organization."[67]

During the 1970s, the NGA began a series of activities to enhance the performance of governors within their own states. "The New Governors' Seminar," held within two weeks after general elections in even-numbered years, used incumbent governors as faculty. Subjects covered included organizing the governor's office, press and public relations, management of the executive branch, executive-legislative relations, intergovernmental relations, the governorship as a partnership involving one's spouse, and the transition period from campaigning to governing.[68] In addition, printed materials and guidebooks were prepared for governors to take back to their home states, and transition assistance was made available.[69]

A growing emphasis on the states and governors as innovators appeared in a series of surveys and publications.[70] These surveys and reports helped disseminate ideas across the states on how to solve problems through innovative programs. What had been known as a governor's "show-and tell" now became more systematic and analytical. Two national organizations of gubernatorial staff—the Council of State Planning Agencies and the National Association of State Budget Officers—became NGA affiliates, providing it with needed policy and budget-planning capabilities.[71]

In 1983, Carol Weissert concluded that the NGA

> has gone from serving primarily as a social event to providing information, technical assistance and research needed for responsible state leadership; from shying away from taking issue stands to assuming in charting a national policy course; and from having no Washington presence to spearheading a strong Washington lobbying effort.[72]

Larry Sabato argued that the governors used the NGA as a vehicle to assert themselves at the

> national level in an unprecedented and surprisingly effective manner . . . revolutionized from the hollow shell of yore to a bustling, professional lobby that can achieve results (and overcome serious handicaps to effectiveness inherent in a high-powered constituency such as the governors).[73]

Regional governors' associations also became more active in policy concerns. Some of this interest flowed naturally from the region itself, for example, energy and natural resources in the West, agriculture in the Midwest, and race and economic development in the South. Some stemmed from the allocation of federal grant-in-aid funds or other federal decisions. In some instances states in a particular region banded together to provide improved higher education or to seek a "pork barrel" project.

Although the results of these activities varied, the governors of the fifty states, by joining together, became more a part of the national policy-making process. They took new and innovative steps to provide their states with enhanced representation at the national level.

National Policy Leadership

Beginning with the chairmanship of Gov. Lamar Alexander of Tennessee (1985–1986), the NGA took a further step toward shaping public policy. The governors conducted a fifty-state assessment of the status of American education, in which seven issue areas were addressed. At the 1986 NGA annual meeting, a report developed in response to this assessment was presented that set an agenda for each governor to follow to improve education.[74] Over the next five years, the governors were to give an account at the NGA annual meeting of the specific steps they were taking to achieve educational reform in their individual states.

Following the Alexander example, succeeding NGA chairs oversaw yearlong initiatives on a variety of policy concerns. In 1986–1987, Gov. Bill Clinton of Arkansas had the governors focus on economic development and job creation. Out of this effort was the adoption of a welfare reform concept calling for "a mandatory education and training program for able-bodied welfare recipients . . . [making] work more attractive than welfare,"[75] an NGA report,[76] and the first of the annual reports on educational reform in the states.

In 1987–1988, New Hampshire governor John Sununu had the NGA address the changing balance in the federal system.[77] This was followed in 1988–1989 by Virginia governor Gerald Baliles's initiative studying the states and the international economy. During the 1989–1990 chairmanship of Iowa governor Terry Branstad education was revisited. In 1990–1991, Gov. Booth Gardner of Washington led the NGA in addressing health care reform.[78] The NGA in 1991–1992 took a third look at education under the chairmanship of Missouri governor John Ashcroft. Other initiatives have included redesigning state government[79] and a Campaign for Children under Governor Howard Dean of Vermont (1994–1995).

Even as the governors addressed this variety of issues, their abiding interest in education and health policies were evidenced through annual reports.[80] The high point in their efforts at educational reform occurred in 1989 when the NGA hosted President George Bush at an educational summit held in Charlottesville, Virginia. Out of this and subsequent interactions with the national administration, President Bush endorsed a series of objectives established by the NGA Task Force on Education.[81] With the 1992 election of former NGA chair Bill Clinton to the presidency, the governors seemed poised at the point of maximum possible impact on domestic policy concerns.

A Governor Moves into the White House

The Clinton Administration took up some of those issues of greatest concern to the states and their elected officials. An economic stimulus plan and health reform were major agenda items for the first two years of Clinton's term. When economic plans include efforts to stimulate local economies, there is hardly a state or local official who will reject the possibility of accepting federal funds and programs that translate into jobs. But Clinton's economic stimulus plan coupled such programs with cutbacks elsewhere and with some tax increases. While there was support for new programs and spending, there was no support for the proposed cutbacks and tax increases.[82]

Some NGA leaders also worried that continuing such "business-as-usual" federal programs was being done at the expense of deficit reduction. The NGA suggested that any such plan be based on a $2.75 spending cut for every $1.00 in tax increases, not the nearly one-to-one ratio of cuts to taxes they saw in the Clinton plan. The vice chairman of the NGA, South Carolina governor Carroll Campbell (R, 1987–1995), argued, "there's nothing new about that, nothing bold and nothing that offers long-term solutions."[83]

The Clinton administration's focus on health care reform was an extension of what he and his fellow governors had been addressing in the states. Governors and other state leaders had long been carrying the burden of health care reform in their individual states from the perspective of trying to keep their budgets in balance. Some of these leaders felt they knew what was best for their states and despaired over the president and Congress ever agreeing on a solution. Others, such as Florida governor Lawton Chiles (D, 1991–   ), argued, "There's got to be a federal role. Without a federal plan, we can't get . . . to universal coverage."[84]

If there was one item in the health care reform package that the governors needed to have addressed, it was Medicaid. Even though 57 percent of the program was funded with federal money, it was the increasing costs of health care and unfunded mandates that prompted Indiana governor Evan Bayh (D, 1989–) to lament, "money for education and infrastructure . . . [is] all gobbled up by sky-rocketing health care." Even President Clinton indicated that "the most frustrating part of the job [of governor] was simply writing bigger checks every year for the same Medicaid program" at the expense of "education and economic development and the other important issues before us."[85]

Yet the health care reform proposals began to highlight problems developing in the NGA. While there was little question on the nature of the problems involved, there was disagreement on how to solve those problems and especially on how to pay for the solutions. These differences began to split the governors along partisan lines, which threatened "to disrupt the NGA's bipartisan spirit—and any hope of bipartisanship on Capitol Hill."[86] Ultimately, as theoretical approaches began to take on specifics, the decline of bipartisanship killed the health care effort. A caveat in an NGA press release was most telling: "Governors may differ considerably on critical issues such as mandates, financing and enforceable budgets."[87]

The governors have kept at it, though, trying to sell a bipartisan "Call to Action" at their early 1994 meeting in Washington, D.C. But the differences remain over the goals, the hows, and the finances. Their threat to move forward on their own if Washington's policy makers didn't make headway turned out to be less a threat than an announcement of what they will have to do anyway.[88]

The Impact of Elections

The 1994 elections and the shift of power in the U.S. Congress from the Democrats to the Republicans fueled the bipartisan decline. President Clinton became another weakened Democratic president facing an ascendant Republican Congress, and his prospects for winning reelection in 1996 dimmed. The upcoming presidential election began to drive the actions of those in Congress as well as in the White House—that is, when Speaker Newt Gingrich's "Contract with America" wasn't doing the driving.

The 1994 elections in the states were profitable for Republicans running for governor as well. Going into the elections there were 29 Democratic governors, 19 Republicans, and 2 Independents. Following the elections, there were 30 Republican governors, 19 Democrats, and 1 Independent. A Republican governor could be found in eight of the nine largest states, Florida being the single exception.[89] And, importantly for the 1996 presidential election, they also held the governor's chair in Iowa and New Hampshire, the two states in which the earliest caucus and primary action will occur. The NGA's bipartisan spirit of the 1985–1992 period will be further rent by its ambitious Republican governors, several of whom harbor presidential aspirations. While only Pete Wilson of California stepped across the line to be a candidate for the GOP nomination, others, such as Wisconsin's Tommy Thompson, Michigan's John Engler, and Massachusetts' William Weld, were mentioned as possibilities. Once they have reached this heady level, governors with such ambitions begin to tailor their words and actions toward achieving that goal.

At a secondary level, several of the Republican governors have been pegged as possible running mates for the ultimate GOP presidential candidate. New Jersey governor Christine Todd Whitman can be added to those mentioned above in this category. Depending on who the presidential nominee is, the need to balance the ticket, for example, regionally or, in the case of Whitman, with a woman, may make a governor a very desirable choice, especially if he or she is from a state with a sizable number of electoral votes.

Some GOP governors likely have ambitions to become members of a Republican president's cabinet. After the 1988 elections, President Bush selected New Hampshire governor John Sununu as his chief of staff. Sununu's support in helping Bush win the New Hampshire presidential primary—the first in the nation—was well-rewarded.

Several of President Clinton's cabinet appointments came from among his gubernatorial peers: former Arizona governor Bruce Babbitt (D, 1978–1987) at Interior, former South Carolina governor Richard Riley (D, 1979–1987) at Education, former Vermont governor Madeleine Kunin (D, 1985–1991) as undersecretary at Education, and former Michigan governor John Blanchard (D, 1983–1991) as ambassador to Canada. A new Republican president might be expected to fill cabinet appointments from the pool of governors as well. GOP governors may start preparing their resumes and aligning their support with certain candidates with just such an appointment in mind.

The 1994 elections also had an impact on governors' access to national policy makers. The NGA and individual governors had now to work with the new Republican congressional leaders and committee chairs. Who had better access than Republican governors? The fruits of the 1994 election victories opened up the policy process to GOP governors. In particular, John Engler of Michigan and Tommy Thompson of Wisconsin took advantage of their unique access to press their policy agendas. (In fact, some observers suggested Engler was spending more time in Washington with Congress than he was in Michigan with the state legislature.)

The governors, Democrats and Republicans alike, remained worried about the drive to balance the federal budget and erase the federal deficit. What they saw coming down the tracks were serious cutbacks in domestic programs at the federal level. States would then be forced to pick up the slack and assume the financial burden of these cutbacks. More plainly, they would have to raise taxes to fund what the federal government would no longer cover. Their organizing phrase was "don't balance the federal budget on the backs of the states," and the governors and state legislatures held a serious trump card—if congressional leaders wanted to pass a balanced budget amendment, they would have to have the support of thirty-eight state legislatures. An early face-off on this conflict occurred shortly after the 1994 elections when the Republican Governors' Association (RGA) met for their annual meeting in Williamsburg, Virginia.

The Republican governors told the new Republican congressional leaders that they could go along with the drive to balance the federal budget through federal domestic program fund cutbacks only if the many unfunded mandates requiring state and local officials to provide public programs without federal aid were removed. As Governor-elect John Rowland of Connecticut indicated, "If you don't get rid of the mandates, it's not going to happen."[90] Governor-elect Tom Ridge of Pennsylvania echoed this sentiment: "If they're going to reduce the dollars and continue to tell me how to spend them, I'm not interested in that."[91]

The RGA governors also warned the new congressional leaders not to get diverted on divisive social issues such as school prayer. They emphasized that the major issues surrounding the budget deficit—health and welfare reform and correcting Medicaid—were paramount. They pressed the leaders to be fully aware of the governors' goals, which, in Utah governor Mike Leavitt's words, were: "give us the ball and then get out of the way."[92]

While the NGA had been instrumental in helping Congress develop and pass a welfare reform bill in the late 1980s, by mid-1995 the bipartisan divisions in the NGA effectively put it outside the welfare reform debate. The chairman of the NGA, Democratic governor Howard Dean of Vermont, stated the situation this way: "The NGA has been paralyzed, and I think it will continue to be paralyzed for the foreseeable future."[93] Republican governor Tommy Thompson of Wisconsin, the 1995–1996 chairman-elect of the NGA, agreed. In his words, the "NGA [had] been iced out of the negotiations."[94]

Even as the NGA as a group remained outside the debate, some governors were still involved in the welfare reform effort of 1995, notably Tommy Thompson, and John Engler of Michigan. These two governors could have "touted their track records in reducing welfare dependence" as their entree to the issue and to the congressional leadership. This working marriage between gubernatorial and congressional Republicans has been at work developing extensive change in welfare legislation.[95]

After three decades of enhancing power, governors as an organization have now lost their hold on national policy shaping, while individual governors of the appropriate partisan stripe have gained considerably. With the 1996 presidential elections drawing nearer, and with both governors and congressional leaders seeking or helping others to seek the GOP presidential nomination, it is not likely that this situation will change appreciably in the near future. Unhappily, when there is so much basic agreement on the need to restructure the responsibilities within the federal system, the lack of involvement of coalescing organizations such as the NGA can only reduce the opportunities for such change to come about.

Conclusion

The last several decades have seen considerable growth in the ability of America's governors to fulfill their responsibilities. The governorship has been enhanced within the states and the governors have increased their voice in national affairs outside their states' boundaries. And the governorship has become one of the major springboards to national office, including the presidency.

Now, in the mid-1990s, there are storm clouds on the horizon for governors, within their own states and as a group seeking better policies for all states. The impact on the states of the recession of the late 1980s and early 1990s may seem tame when compared to the potential impact of major policy shifts now being considered within our federal system. If some of these changes are adopted and states are placed in the position of becoming the "courts of last resort" for a series of programmatic cutbacks or terminations, state budgets will be put at considerable risk.

That the NGA, the vehicle of joint action in recent years, has been supplanted by the actions of just a few governors in seeking solutions for a wide array of problems also bodes ill for the governors. We may be entering a new phase in a "go it alone" federalism where the rewards are hard to find and the blame easier to fix on those running state governments. Governors and state legislators will agonize over budgets, programs, and political futures as many of those living within the states over which they preside find themselves at a greater disadvantage in this new American federalism.

Epilogue

In the early months of 1996 some unforseen changes occurred in the federal system involving the governors of the fifty states.

At first blush, the 1995 policy and budget standoff between Democratic President Clinton and the Republican leadership of the House (Speaker Gingrich) and Senate (Majority Leader Dole) looked to be a bitter, ideological battle over who is to gain the upper hand in running the federal government in Washington, D.C. That the 1996 presidential election was looming larger and closer as each day passed seemed to drive the point home that the real goal was power.

But what was supposed to happen did not. The Republicans were not able to get their promised legislation into law due to the veto pen held by the president. And the president held firm to his positions, coopted some of the Republicans' ideas and positions, and gave a strong State of the Union address, all of which put the Republicans on the defensive.

However, in February 1996, as the primary season began, it was the governors working together as the NGA who may have started the process of breaking up the power jam in Washington. After a year of "freelance" Republican gubernatorial involvement with the Republican congressional leadership in developing legislation, when the Republicans lost their strategic position vis-à-vis the president, these governors lost their strategic role.

The 1996 Annual Winter Meeting of the NGA held in Washington may have sparked a rebirth of the bipartisan strength for which the NGA had been known in the past. After a tough round of negotiations, the forty-seven governors attending the meeting presented to the Washington protagonists their suggested plans for solving the Medicaid and Welfare reform components of the D.C. standoff. This sort of bipartisan pressure, and suggestions from all across the country, may be the leverage needed to bring some closure to the issues involved.

Why did the NGA do this? In a year that started with one major state's Republican governor confiding to a journalist that the NGA's days may be numbered, these governors were faced with an insolvable set of problems based on one fact: they could not move forward on their own state budgets until they knew what was going to happen at the national level.

These governors, some of the "doers" in the federal system, were being hamstrung by some of the "talkers" in the system in Washington. The governors, and the state legislators, have to know what the fiscal commitment of the federal government will be in addition to what policy changes in federal-state programs will be passed before they can pass their own state budgets. So they came together as an organization of the fifty governors through the NGA and presented the national leaders with a state-based road map out of the current stalemate. This not only bodes well for the states and the NGA, but for the national government and the American people as well.

Notes

1. "The Fortune 500," *Fortune*, April 18, 1994, 220–222; and NASBO, *State Expenditure Report* (Washington, D.C.: National Association of State Budget Officers, 1995), 9.
2. Regina Brough, "Powers of the Gubernatorial CEOs: Variations among the States," *Journal of State Government* 59 (1986): 58–63.
3. Among these were Advisory Commission on Intergovernmental Relations (ACIR), various reports; Committee for Economic Development, *Modernizing State Government* (New York: Committee for Economic Development, 1967); Terry Sanford, *Storm over the States* (New York: McGraw-Hill, 1967); National Municipal League, *Model State Constitution*, rev. ed. (New York: National Municipal League, 1968); and Citizens Conference on State Legislatures, various publications between 1967 and 1971.
4. Sanford, *Storm over the States*, 188; and Larry J. Sabato, *Goodbye to Good-time Charlie: The American Governor Transformed, 1950–1975* (Lexington, Mass.: Lexington Books, 1978), 63.
5. Advisory Commission on Intergovernmental Relations, *The Question of State Government Capability* (Washington, D.C.: ACIR, 1985), 129.
6. Thad L. Beyle, "Term Limits in the State Executive Branch," in *Limiting Legislative Terms*, ed. Gerald Benjamin and Michael J. Malbin (Washington, D.C.: CQ Press, 1992), 159–180; Council of State Governments, *The Book of the States, 1994–1995* (Lexington, Ky.: Council of State Governments, 1994), 28–33.
7. Council of State Governments, *The Book of the States, 1994–1995*, 55–56.
8. Keon S. Chi, "State Executive Branch Reorganization: Options for the Future," *State Trends & Forecasts* 1:1 (December 1992): 8.

9. ACIR, *The Question of State Government Capability*, 129; Council of State Governments, *The Book of the States, 1994–1995*, 141–142; and Ronald C. Moe, *Prospects for the Item Veto at the Federal Level: Lessons from the States* (Washington, D.C.: National Academy of Public Administration, 1988), 3–50.

10. Coleman B. Ransone, Jr., *The Office of Governor in the United States* (University: University of Alabama Press, 1956), 44.

11. Center for Policy Research, National Governors' Association, unpublished data from a 1976 survey of thirty-eight governors' offices. The adjusted averages exclude the one or two largest states, as their size would skew the overall averages.

12. Council of State Governments, *The Book of the States, 1994–1995*, 53.

13. Thad L. Beyle, "Governors Views on Being Governor," *State Government* 52 (Summer 1979): 108–110.

14. Council of State Governments, *The Book of the States, 1994–1995*, 55–56, 317–321.

15. Lynn Muchmore, "Planning and Budgeting Offices: On Their Relevance to Gubernatorial Decisions," in *Being Governor: The View from the Office*, ed. Thad L. Beyle and Lynn Muchmore (Durham, N.C.: Duke University Press, 1983), 174.

16. Carl W. Stenberg, "States under the Spotlight: An Intergovernmental View," *Public Administration Review* 45 (March/April 1985): 321.

17. Thad L. Beyle and Deil S. Wright, "The Governor, Planning, and Governmental Activity," in *The American Governor in Behavioral Perspective*, ed. Thad L. Beyle and J. Oliver Williams (New York: Harper and Row, 1972), 194–195.

18. Thad L. Beyle, "The Governor as Innovator in the Federal System," *Publius* 18 (Summer 1988): 133–154.

19. Under policy development were policy analysis and new initiatives (thirty-four states), briefing the governor on policy concerns (twenty-eight states), assisting on major gubernatorial initiatives (fifteen states), and impact analysis (seven states). Under administrative were coordinating and providing service to the governor's cabinet and subcabinet councils (seventeen states) and to interagency commissions, task forces, and working groups (twenty-four states) and programmatic responsibilities in specific functional areas (sixteen states) and in the regulatory areas of state government (ten states).

20. Council of State Governments, *The Book of the States*, 1994–1995, 55–56.

21. Council of State Governments, *The Book of the States, 1982–1983* (1982), 145–147; *The Book of the States, 1984–1985* (1984), 44–45; *The Book of the States, 1986–1987* (1986), 45–47; *The Book of the States, 1988–1989* (1988), 47–48; and *The Book of the States, 1990–1991* (1990), 75–78. See also James K. Conant, "In the Shadow of Wilson and Brownlow: Executive Branch Reorganization in the States, 1965 to 1987," *Public Administration Review* 48:5 (September/October 1988): 892–902.

22. Council of State Governments, *The Book of the States, 1994–1995*, 70–71, 483.

23. Ibid., 70–71.

24. Jack Brizius, of Brizius and Foster, Management Consultants, telephone conversation with author, September 11, 1987.

25. Richard Murray and Gregory R. Weiher, "Texas: Ann Richards, Taking on the Challenge," in *Governors and Hard Times*, ed. Thad L. Beyle (Washington, D.C.: CQ Press, 1992), 179–188.

26. Diane Kincaid Blair, "The Gubernatorial Appointment Power: Too Much of a Good Thing?" in *Being Governor: The View from the Office*, 118–121.

27. Joseph A. Schlesinger, "The Politics of the Executive," in *Politics in the American States*, ed. Herbert Jacob and Kenneth N. Vines (Boston: Little, Brown, 1965), 225.

28. Elder Witt, "Patronage Firings," *Congressional Quarterly Weekly Report*, July 3, 1976, 1726.

29. Elder Witt, "Supreme Court Deals Blow to Public Employee Firings for Solely Political Reasons," *Congressional Quarterly Weekly Report*, April 6, 1980, 889–890.

30. Elder Witt, "Employee Rights," *Congressional Quarterly Weekly Report*, April 6, 1983, 791–792.

31. Thad L. Beyle and Robert Huefner, *Evaluation of the 1982 Seminar for New Governors*, report submitted to the National Governors' Association, February 23, 1983.

32. Cheri Collis, "Cleaning Up the Spoils System," *State Government News* 33:9 (September 1990): 6.

33. Charles N. Wheeler III, "Gov. James R. Thompson, 1977–1991: The Complete Campaigner, the Pragmatic Centrist," *Illinois Issues* 16:12 (December 1990).

34. Schlesinger, "The Politics of the Executive," in *Politics in the American States* (1965); Schlesinger, "The Politics of the Executive," in *Politics in the American States*, 2d ed. (1971), 210–237; Thad L. Beyle, "Governors," in *Politics in the American States*, 4th ed., ed. Virginia Gray, Herbert Jacob, and Kenneth N. Vines (1983), 180–221; and Beyle, "Governors," in *Politics in the American States*, 5th ed., ed. Gray, Jacob, and Robert B. Albritton (Glenview, Ill.: Scott, Foresman, 1990), 201–251.

35. Office of State Services, *The Institutionalized Powers of the Governorship, 1965–1985* (Washington, D.C.: National Governors' Association, 1987).

36. Some differences exist between the NGA index and those based on Schlesinger's study: (1) The NGA indices were called institutional and not formal, which allowed a broader interpretation of what could be brought into the presentation and analysis. (2) The added measures—the legislative budget-changing ability and the governor's political strength in the legislature—probably reflected a real world view of the constraints on governors not captured in previous efforts. Including the governor's political strength in the legislature could lead to more varied results as each election could change this score, especially as so many states are now experiencing a political party powersplit between the governor and the legislature. (3) Only six offices were used to develop the appointment power index. The range of potential appointment power was greater (up to seven) than for the indicators (up to five), reflecting the importance of this single indicator where a large effect can be felt. (4) A twenty-year comparison of these indices showed just how far the American governorship has come during the most recent era of state government reform.

37. Council of State Governments, *The Book of the States, 1994–1995*, 28–33.

38. Sharon Sherman, "Powersplit: When Legislatures and Governors Are of Opposing Parties," *State Legislatures* 10:5 (May/June 1984): 9–12.

39. Morris P. Fiorina, "Divided Government in the States," *PS: Political Science and Politics* 24:4 (December 1991): 646.

40. Sherman, "Powersplit."

41. Alan Ehrenhalt, "The Political Virtue of Partisan Deadlock," *Governing* 8:4 (January 1995): 7–8.

42. Thad Beyle, "The Speaker's Office as a Political Stepping Stone?" *North Carolina Insight* 15:1 (January 1994): 30–31, updated.

43. Ibid.

44. Richard W. Gable, "California: Pete Wilson, a Centrist in Trouble," in *Governors and Hard Times*, 43–59.

45. Dennis Hale, "Massachusetts: William F. Weld and the End of Business as Usual," in *Governors and Hard Times*, 127–150.

46. Russell D. Murphy, "Connecticut: Lowell P. Weicker Jr., a Maverick in the 'Land of Steady Habits,' " in *Governors and Hard Times*, 61–75.

47. National Conference of State Legislatures, "Legislators Serving on Boards and Commissions," in *State Legislative Report* (Denver: National Conference of State Legislatures, 1983), 4–5; and North Carolina Center for Public Policy Research, *Boards, Commissions, and Councils in the Executive Branch of North Carolina State Government* (Raleigh: North Carolina Center for Public Policy Research, 1984).

48. Charles W. Wiggins, "Executive Vetoes and Legislative Overrides in the American States," *Journal of Politics* 42 (1980): 1112–1113.

49. Council of State Governments, *The Book of the States, 1994–1995*, 148–150.

50. Ran Coble, *Special Provisions in Budget Bills: A Pandora's Box for North Carolina Citizens, A Special Report* (Raleigh: North Carolina Center for Public Policy Research, 1986), 9–12.
51. Walter J. Oleszek, *Congressional Procedures and the Policy Process*, 4th ed. (Washington, D.C.: CQ Press, 1995), 340.
52. The federal case was *Immigration and Naturalization Services v. Jagdish Rai Chada* 462 U.S. 919 (1983).
53. Jody George and Lacy Maddox, "Separation of Powers Provisions in State Constitutions," in *Boards, Commissions, and Councils in the Executive Branch of North Carolina State Government*, 51, 52. Joseph F. Zimmerman, "New York Updates," *Comparative State Politics* 12:6 (December 1991): 32–34.
54. For more on this see Thad Beyle, "Gubernatorial Report Cards: Summer 1994," *Spectrum: The Journal of State Government* 68:2 (Spring 1995): 14–20.
55. Thad L. Beyle, "Enhancing Executive Leadership in the States," *State and Local Government Review* 27:1 (Winter 1995): 26–28.
56. Beyle, "Enhancing Executive Leadership in the States," 32–33.
57. John Shannon, "The Return to Fend-for-Yourself Federalism: The Reagan Mark," *Intergovernmental Perspective* 13 (Summer/Fall 1987): 35.
58. For a series of case studies on the problems state leaders faced in the early 1990s, see *Governors and Hard Times*, 59.
59. Several political scientists have argued that advocating tax increases is not necessarily a risk for governors. See Gerald M. Pomper, "Governors, Money, and Votes," in *Elections in America*, ed. Gerald M. Pomper (New York: Dodd, Mead, 1968), 126–148; Theodore Eismeier, "Budgets and Ballots: The Political Consequences of Fiscal Choice," in *Public Policy and Public Choice*, ed. D. Rae and Theodore Eismeier (Beverly Hills, Calif.: Sage, 1979), 121–150; and Richard T. Winters, "Governors and Electoral Retribution" (Paper delivered at the annual meeting of the American Political Science Association, Chicago, September 3–6, 1987).
60. Those New England governors declining to seek reelection were Michael S. Dukakis (D-Mass., 1975–1979, 1983–1991), Madeleine M. Kunin (D-Vt., 1985–1991), and William A. O'Neill (D-Conn., 1980–1991). The defeated governor was Edward DiPrete (R-R.I., 1985–1991).
61. For more on the Florio governorship and the 1993 election, see Janice Ballou, "Whitman vs. The Comeback Kid," *The Polling Report* (November 29, 1993): 1, 6–7; and Neil Upmeyer, "The Polls Weren't Wrong," *New Jersey Reporter* 23:4 (November/December 1993): 38.
62. For more on the Wilson governorship, see Richard W. Gable, "California: Pete Wilson, a Centrist in Trouble," in *Governors and Hard Times*, 43–59.
63. Jacqueline Calmes, "444 North Capitol Street: Where State Lobbyists Are Learning Coalition Politics," *Governing* (February 1988): 17–18, 20–21.
64. Among these governors were John Volpe (R-Mass., 1965–1969), Marvin Mandel (D-Md., 1969–1977), Daniel Evans (R-Wash., 1965–1977), Calvin Rampton (D-Utah, 1965–1977), Robert Ray (R-Iowa, 1969–1983), Scott Matheson (D-Utah, 1977–1985), and Lamar Alexander (R-Tenn., 1979–1987).
65. Carol Weissert, "The National Governors' Association," *State Government* 56 (1983): 49.
66. Ibid., 50.
67. Ibid., 49.
68. Thad L. Beyle, "Gubernatorial Transitions: Lessons from the 1982–1983 Experience," *Publius* 14 (Summer 1984), 13.
69. Publications on the transition by the National Governors' Association include *The Critical Hundred Days: A Handbook for New Governors* (1975), *The Governor's Office* (1976), *Governing the American States: A Handbook for New Governors* (1978), *Transi-*

tion and New Governors: A Critical Overview (1982), *The Transition: A View from Academia* (1986), *The Departing Governor: Transition Out of Office* (1986), *Gubernatorial Perspectives on Transition* (1988), *The Governor's Final Year: Challenges and Strategies* (1990), and *Organizing the Transition Team* (1990).

70. Publications on innovations by the National Governors' Conference and Association include *Innovations in State Government* (1974), *Governors' Policy Initiatives: Meeting the Challenges of the 1980s* (1980). The 1982 survey was conducted by the NGA, the Council of State Planning Agencies (CSPA), and The Governors' Center at Duke University; the 1983 survey was conducted by the CSPA.

71. Scott Matheson, *Out of Balance* (Salt Lake City, Utah: Peregrine Smith Books, 1986), 240.

72. Weissert, "The National Governors' Association," 52.

73. Larry Sabato, *Goodbye to Goodtime Charlie: The American Governorship Transformed*, 2d ed. (Washington, D.C.: CQ Press, 1983), 180.

74. National Governors' Association, *Time for Results: The Governors' 1991 Report on Education* (Washington, D.C.: National Governors' Association, 1986).

75. Julie Rovner, "Governors Jump-Start Welfare Reform Drive," *Congressional Quarterly Weekly Report*, February 28, 1987, 376.

76. National Governors' Association, *Making America Work: Productive People, Productive Policies* (Washington, D.C.: National Governors' Association, 1987).

77. National Governors' Association, *Restoring the Balance: State Leadership for America's Future* (Washington, D.C.: National Governors' Association, 1988).

78. National Governors' Association, *A Healthy America: The Challenge for the States* (Washington, D.C.: National Governors' Association, 1991).

79. National Governors' Association, *An Action Agenda to Redesign State Government* (Washington, D.C.: National Governors' Association, 1993).

80. See, for example, National Governors' Association, *Educating America: State Strategies for Achieving the National Educational Goals* (1990), *Results in Education* (1991), *State Progress in Health Care Reform* (1992), and *Transforming Education: Overcoming Barriers and a Guide to Building Public Support for Educational Reform* (1993).

81. "Education: Consensus on Goals Reached by Bush, NGA Task Force," *Governors' Weekly Bulletin* 24:5 (February 2, 1990): 1–2.

82. Jeffrey L. Katz, "Self-Interested Cities, States Cozy Up to Clinton's Plan," *Congressional Quarterly Weekly Report*, March 6, 1993, 517–518.

83. Ibid., 518.

84. Ceci Connolly, "If Governors Are Harbingers, Clinton Faces Tough Road," *Congressional Quarterly Weekly Report*, August 21, 1993, 2261.

85. Ibid., 2261–2262.

86. Ibid., 2262.

87. Ceci Connolly, "As Clinton Inches Toward Reform . . . Governors Tiptoe Around the Issue," *Congressional Quarterly Weekly Report*, October 9, 1993, 2736.

88. Ceci Connolly, "Governors Agree System Ailing, Disagree With Clinton on Cure," *Congressional Quarterly Weekly Report*, February 5, 1994, 249.

89. Thad L. Beyle, "Pete Wilson for President?," *Spectrum: The Journal of State Government* 68:1 (Winter 1995): 11.

90. Andrew Taylor, "Governors: Don't Balance Budget Without Ending Mandates," *Congressional Quarterly Weekly Report*, November 26, 1994, 3403.

91. Ibid.

92. *The Hotline* 8:47 (November 21, 1994): 12.

93. Jeffrey L. Katz, "Governors Group Sidelined In Welfare Debate," *Congressional Quarterly Weekly Report*, May 20, 1995, 1423.

94. Ibid.

95. Ibid.

6

The Legislature: Unraveling of Institutional Fabric

Alan Rosenthal

Legislatures are probably the principal political institutions in the states—the guts of democracy. They have managed to survive, and on occasion even prosper, over the course of more than a two-hundred-year lifetime. Their standing with the public has rarely been high, but in recent years it has been perilously low. Ironically, legislatures since the 1960s have made considerable progress and today are more representative and democratic than at any time in the past. Yet, indications are that the legislature, as an institution, may be in serious jeopardy.

Prior to their revitalization, which began in the mid-1960s, legislatures were unrepresentative, malapportioned, and dominated by rural areas of the states. The legislative process was, in many instances, a sham; power within the institution was narrowly held and not democratically exercised. Major issues were sidestepped, and initiatives for state policy were left to the governor. The legislature's role in the most important business of government, that of allocating funds, was minimal. Whatever the positive outcomes, and however well served the people of a state might have been, relatively little was attributable to the performance of the legislature.

Legislative Development

The reapportionment revolution, precipitated by the Supreme Court decisions in *Baker v. Carr* (1962) and *Reynolds v. Sims* (1964), was the first stage in the transformation of American state legislatures. A new generation of members—led by a number of outstanding leaders and supported by allies drawn from the ranks of citizens, businesses, foundations, and universities—went to work to reshape legislative institutions.[1]

The decade from about 1965 to 1975 can appropriately be termed the period of "the rise of the legislative institution." Traditional assemblies modernized; reformed legislatures emerged. Probably the clearest and most enduring consequence of reform was the strengthening of the institutional capacity of legislatures. Capacity can be defined in terms of space, time, and information. The improvement of legislative facilities, with the renovation of capitol buildings and the construction of legislative office buildings, provided space for standing committees, legislative staff, and members.

Legislators began spending more time on the job, both in and out of session. All but seven states changed their constitutions so that their legislatures could meet annually rather than biennially. Legislatures in California, Pennsylvania, Illinois, Massachusetts, Ohio, Wisconsin, Michigan, and New York are now in session practically year round. Even those that have limited sessions of shorter lengths schedule committee meetings three or four days per month during the interim period. The extra time has enabled legislatures to become more involved in making policy, in shaping the budget, and even in running government itself. In one form or another, the legislature has become a constant presence that cannot be ignored.

The single greatest boost to legislative capacity came as an outgrowth of professional staffing. An increase in the number of people employed and their broad distribution within legislatures meant that everyone was served to some extent. Legislative leaders acquired greater support. Standing committees received the assistance they needed to delve more deeply into their policy domains. Fiscal staffs afforded the appropriations and finance committees the wherewithal to play larger roles in the budget process. Caucus and partisan staff buttressed the legislative parties, both in lawmaking and on the campaign trail. Audit and evaluation staffs enabled legislatures to try their hands at oversight, inquiring into the efficiency of executive agencies and assessing the effectiveness of governmental programs. Finally, individual members benefitted, most often from pooled staff resources. In the larger states, members were granted their own legislative and district aides.

One of the goals of the reform movement was the coequality of the legislative and executive branches of state government. Just as the rhetoric of reform instilled the idea of independence in many legislative bodies, the activity of reform reinforced the separation of legislative and gubernatorial power. With time on their hands, staff at their call, and resources at their disposal, legislatures began to assert themselves. In some places—Arizona, Colorado, Mississippi, and South Carolina, for example—the legislature traditionally had been the dominant branch. Florida, too, could be categorized as a "legislative state." However, in many more places governors dominated or had a substantial edge. Reform allowed the legislatures to narrow the gap. While governors still set the agenda, at least when it comes to the major issues, they are no longer the sole source of major policy, nor do they always get what they want.

As a result, state legislatures are in better shape now than they were twenty-five years ago. They are active participants in the process of making public policy, allocating public funds, and overseeing the administration of state government. Legislatures are more representative. Periodic reapportionment, the emergence of women and minorities in legislative ranks, and the close relationship forged by members with their districts have changed the composition and behavior of legislative bodies. Legislatures are responding to public demands and needs. They duck fewer issues, wrestling even the most contentious problems. They have adopted noteworthy measures in the areas of the environment, education, and social welfare. And they have been willing to raise taxes when additional revenues were necessary. Not every legislative policy succeeds. The gap between policy pronouncement on the one hand and levels of funding and administrative follow-through on the other can short-circuit any policy drive. Substantial room for improvement does exist. But progress has been made, even in the area of implementation.

Legislative Professionalization

Along with reform and modernization have come not only the professionalization of state legislatures, but also the professionalization of legislators themselves. Twenty-five years ago, almost all members of state legislative bodies, with the exception of a few in California, identified themselves by their occupation outside the legislature—attorney, businessperson, insurance broker, farmer, rancher, and so forth. Not anymore. Significant proportions of members now cite their occupation as legislator. Most are full-time or virtually full-time legislators who have made politics their career. Nowadays "citizens" and "professionals" constitute the two principal breeds within the legislator species. The former, or old breed, generally has another occupation or substantial interests outside the legislature. The latter, or new breed, usually has no other *significant* occupation and little time or interest for anything other than politics. This new breed is on the rise. Indeed, within individual states professional legislators are setting the pace, pressuring the part-time, citizen legislators to keep up, or even driving them out.[2]

Not all states have proceeded in the careerist direction. Neither have they proceeded at the same rate. The larger states have the greatest proportions of members pursuing wholly political careers. At least two-thirds of the members in Michigan, Pennsylvania, and Wisconsin are career politicians, although a number of them practice law or engage in additional activities that provide income. Half or more of those in Illinois, Massachusetts, and New York are full time, or practically so. Slightly fewer are full-time legislators in Arizona, Iowa, Missouri, and Ohio, and about one-quarter are full time in Connecticut, Florida, and Minnesota.[3] Only 15 percent are full time in Maryland.[4] Legislatures also exist at the other end of the spectrum, where nearly all members are part time. Indiana, Kentucky, Nevada, New Hampshire, North Dakota, Vermont, and Wyoming are examples. At present, about one-fifth of the nation's legislatures are largely in the hands of professional legislators, and one-fifth are moving gradually, but inexorably, toward the professional model. Another two-fifths may or may not go that way in the years ahead. The remaining fifth are likely to remain firmly in the hands of citizen legislators for some time to come.[5]

What Promotes Careerism

The professionalization of legislative careers is attributable to a number of factors. Among the most potent are the increasing demands on members' time, the greater resources available to members, and the rising levels of compensation.

Time. The amount of time that legislatures are in session is two or three times greater today than in earlier years. Although most state constitutions set limits on the length of legislative sessions, about one-quarter do not, including California, Illinois, Massachusetts, Michigan, New York, Ohio, Pennsylvania, and Wisconsin. In California, for example, voters in 1966 approved Proposition 1-A, which eliminated constitutional limits on session length (as well as limits on legislative pay). This measure allowed members to devote more time to the legislature. The length of sessions increased from 107 days in 1965 to 143 in 1967. By the 1993–1994 biennium, the California legislature was in session for eight months of each year.

Even when annual sessions are limited, as in Florida (sixty days) or Maryland (ninety days), the time legislators spend on their jobs has increased dramatically. In addition to regular and special sessions, legislators attend meetings of standing committees and special committees during the interim period when the senate and house are not convened. Probably the greatest increase in time spent on the job results from members' attention to constituency affairs. In many states, legislators now politick throughout their districts year round, appearing before local groups and organizations and dealing with constituent demands in district offices. Fundraising is also an ongoing enterprise.

Whether identified as full time or part time, whether part of a highly professionalized legislature or a less professionalized legislature, the demands on members' time have increased substantially. Even in Kentucky, which has a part-time, citizen legislature that meets only biennially, members devote half of their time to various aspects of legislative work.[6] New Mexico's legislature feels that it has to maintain its "citizen" status to please the public. Nonetheless, members who are retired from outside occupations spend almost all of their time on legislative concerns, and most of those who maintain some type of outside commitments devote at least half of their time to legislative affairs. Fewer than one-fourth of New Mexico's legislators can afford to keep their time commitment much below half.

Resources. Staff and facilities encourage service. The resources now available to legislators enable them to do their jobs more effectively and efficiently. They also provide them with invaluable support during reelection bids. On average, legislative staffs grew by a quarter between 1979 and 1988, by which time the number of full-time legislative staff exceeded fifty in all but twelve states. The average number of staff per member has been as high as 23.9 in California, 17.0 in New York, 9.9 in Florida, 8.7 in Michigan, 8.1 in Texas, 7.8 in Pennsylvania, 6.5 in New Jersey, and 6.0 in Illinois. By contrast, in Idaho, New Hampshire, New Mexico, North Dakota, Vermont, and Wyoming, one staffer on average served three, four, or five members.[7] The most recent trend in staffing patterns is to have a staffer assigned to an individual legislator, working out of his or her statehouse or district office. Currently, seventeen states provide staff or staff allowances to individual members.

Compensation. With the professionalization of legislators came a marked rise in legislative salaries. Higher salaries made it possible for members to derive a substantial portion of their income from legislative service. Currently, California's legislators are paid $72,000 per year, as well as $101 per diem. All told, California legislators realize about $93,000 in compensation per year. The speaker of the assembly and the president pro tempore receive an additional $14,400, and the floor leaders of the two houses an extra $7,200. Most members have no need for outside income and can devote all their energies to the legislature. The yearly salary of New York legislators is $57,500 per year. This sum is supplemented by per diems of $89 and leadership stipends, known as "lulus," of between $6,500 and $30,000. These are so liberally dispensed that every member of the senate and 114 of 115 assembly members receive them.[8]

By contrast, in a number of states salaries lag far behind. Unless they are independently wealthy or supported by a spouse's income, legislators find it financially difficult to abandon outside occupations when their yearly compensation is $15,000 or less, as it is in about half the states. Although some make the sacrifice, how many can be expected to spend half or two-thirds of their time on the legislature if their salary is $65 per day for forty-five calendar days, as it is in Utah? Most would not be able to serve for long if the salary was just $100 a year, with no per diem, as it is in New Hampshire. There is little danger of being overrun by professional law makers in either Utah or New Hampshire!

Some states have even held salaries down to preserve their citizen legislatures. In Florida, for instance, the salary had been kept at $12,000 a year since 1969 (when it was raised from $1,200), partly out of fear that more money would attract different types of people and the legislature then would lose its citizen status. In 1985, however, Florida legislators voted themselves a pay raise to $18,000 a year and provided that their salaries would increase automatically every year by the same percentage that the average salary of state employees rose in the preceding year. In view of this improved remuneration, coupled with increasing time demands, chances are that the number of full-time, professional members in the Florida legislature will grow in the years ahead.

Only the smaller states, where the level of compensation is limited by the constitution or strong tradition, may be immune to the trend toward the full-time, careerist legislature. But nothing can be taken for granted. In Vermont, for instance, legislative leaders are trying to devise a response to increased pressure—one that does not include a full-time, professional legislature. Survival of the current system is doubtful, however. Laments one senate leader, "I'm not optimistic that two decades from now you're going to find a citizen legislature in Vermont."[9] In fact, as members spend more time on the job, the legislature can easily engage their energies full time and become their main line of work. The natural tendency is for legislators "to identify with the position" and become firmly rooted in the legislative way of life.[10]

Not all legislators have responded equally to the lure of political professionalism. Democrats have been more likely than Republicans to identify as full-time legislators and to pursue careers in politics. Alan Ehrenhalt explains the Democratic proclivity in terms of the difference in party attitudes toward government, which results in legislative office having a greater attraction for Democrats than for Republicans. In his view, this is the age of entrepreneurial candidates, who effectively nominate themselves for office. People like this "tend not only to enjoy politics but to believe in government as an institution." Democrats fit this mold, Republicans do not. "It is not easy to find conservatives," Ehrenhalt writes, "willing year after year to put up with long hours and low pay for the privilege of being part of a government they essentially distrust."[11] Morris Fiorina agrees that the Democrats gain from professionalization, but he argues that this results from a difference in opportunity costs, rather than a difference in beliefs. According to him, amateur legislatures favor Republicans; more professionalized legislatures favor Democrats. While professionalization may advantage incumbents of both parties, it is more likely to encourage Democrats to seek office in the first place. The reason is that in amateur legislatures Republicans have more flexibility to combine legislative service with outside careers, whereas Democrats, with less outside income to lose, are more willing to sacrifice outside careers to pursue service in a professional legislature.[12]

Ehrenhalt's conclusions are based, in part, on his thoughtful observations contrasting Democrats and Republicans in the highly professionalized Wisconsin legislature. However, recent elections tend to qualify his findings. In 1992, Wisconsin Republicans won control of the senate and in 1994 they added control of the assembly. Republican efforts to recruit and fund better candidates, and the willingness of Republican candidates and incumbents to work as hard as Democrats at their legislative jobs, were largely responsible for this shift. The new Republican breed may not like government as much as Democrats like it, but they still want to have an impact on its policies.

Fiorina's findings, based on indirect evidence, are also qualified by recent Republican electoral gains in states such as California, Illinois, Michigan, New Jersey, Ohio, and Pennsylvania, where both salaries and legislative professionalization are high. Intensive recruitment efforts and the allocation of funds and other campaign resources by legislative party leaders have had an impact, diminishing the effects of differences in orientations toward government or differences in opportunity costs. Furthermore, the boost given Republicans everywhere by their congressional and state gubernatorial and legislative electoral gains in 1994, followed by the adoption of more conservative policies by the U.S. Congress and in the states, will likely further erode such effects.

One of the objectives of the term limits movement, which began in 1990, is to reverse the trend toward the professional legislator. In the twenty-one states that have imposed on its legislators term limits of six, eight, or twelve years, it is possible that careerism will be contained, if not eliminated. But early signs from California give little indication that political ambition is much diminished. Of the twenty-seven legislators who did not seek reelection in 1994, only five retired from public office—the rest ran for another office.

Ambition for Public Office

The new professionals are people who enjoy politics and "prefer it to any other line of work."[13] They differ from those who populated legislatures in former days. There are fewer males, fewer lawyers, and somewhat fewer whites.

Most notable is the increase in the number of women in the nation's statehouses. They accounted for 4 percent of the nation's legislators in 1969; by 1995, women accounted for 20.6 percent of the total. In Washington, 39.5 percent of senators and representatives were women, in Nevada 34.9 percent, and in Colorado, 32.0 percent. African-Americans have also made gains, up from 2.2 percent in 1970 to about 7 percent in 1995. Hispanics, too, have picked up seats. While they hold just 2 percent of the total nationwide, Hispanics number more than 10 percent in Arizona, Colorado, New Mexico, and Texas and more than 5 percent in California and Florida.[14]

The occupational composition of state legislatures has changed dramatically as well. The numbers of businesspersons, farmers, and professionals have diminished. The decline in attorneys is especially noticeable. Attorneys, particularly those in larger firms, cannot afford the necessary time, and they refuse to jeopardize their practices by disclosing the names of clients, as required by regulations to reduce conflicts of interests. Nationally, the proportion of attorneys serving as legislators declined from 30 percent in 1960 to 20 percent in 1979; by 1993 it was down to about 16 percent.[15]

These former mainstays of state legislatures are being replaced by career politicians who come from the ranks of unseasoned lawyers, teachers, preachers, spouses of professionals, single people who can live on a legislative salary, public organizers, and others. This new breed has either more disposable time or fewer outside pursuits. Teachers in elementary and secondary schools can spend the fall semester in the classroom and take leave during the spring to attend the legislative session. Recent years have seen teachers, frequently sponsored by local educational associations, become the largest growing occupational grouping in state legislatures. Their numbers are particularly strong in Alabama; in a number of other states they account for almost one out of five members. In Washington, police officers and fire fighters are likewise attempting to flex their political muscle by getting their members to run for the legislature to represent their interests.

By the time the professional legislator arrives in the senate or house, he or she most likely has already held some other office. In New Jersey roughly three out of five legislators have been mayors, council members, or elected county officials before arriving at the statehouse in Trenton. In Ohio, 73 percent of the representatives and 83 percent of the senators had held party or elective office prior to their election to the legislature. In Alaska's 1993–1994 legislature, fifteen of the sixty members had either been elected mayor or been elected to the borough assembly or school board. More than a fifth had had prior governmental experience upon entering the legislature.[16] According to one review of the literature, previous experience in elective positions ranges from 30 percent in Oregon, Utah, Minnesota, and Washington to 50 percent in Massachusetts, North Carolina, and Connecticut.[17]

Only a few states thus far have seen legislative staff become elected representatives or senators. In California, one out of every four or five members has previously served as a personal aide to a member or as a consultant to a committee. In Alaska one out of every four members and in Wisconsin one out of every six members served as either a congressional or legislative staffer before being elected to the statehouse.

The Appeal of Public Office

What distinguishes full-time, professional politicians from part-time citizens is not only where they have come from but also where they are going. Fewer old timers harbored career ambitions in politics. They intended to serve awhile and return to private careers. By contrast, many of the new breed want to spend their careers in government or politics. They find public office appealing and the game of politics exhilarating. They take pleasure in their status, delight in the exercise of power, and have policies they want to advance. There can be no doubt that the legislature is seductive. This is demonstrated by the fact that few members voluntarily depart from it.

The small proportion of those elected who are truly citizen legislators follow their original game plan and leave within a short span of time. Others become frustrated and decide not to run again. Some, like a former member of the South Carolina house, burn out: "I got tired [she said], lost my energy. It was time. I lost my support group, which peeled off. And I didn't want to go through the same issues again."[18] A number have to leave to provide for growing families or for children approaching college age. Some leave when their pensions vest. Some are scared off by unfavorable redistricting after a decennial reapportionment or by changes in the demographic and political compositions of their districts that diminish their chances for reelection. Some exit for health reasons. And a few die while in office.[19]

A number of legislators depart as soon as they have a shot—even a long shot—at higher office. Members of the house tend to run for the senate when a seat becomes open; members of both bodies often jump at a chance to run for a congressional seat or for statewide office. A number of presiding officers, who feel that there is a danger of overstaying their welcome (such as Tom Loftus, speaker of the Wisconsin assembly) or whose terms as top leader are limited by tradition (such as Alan Karcher, William Hamilton, and Chuck Hardwick, all speakers of the New Jersey assembly) choose to run for governor as their way out.

Despite all of these reasons for departure, the fact remains that relatively few people leave of their own volition, except in pursuit of a higher office. For example, the Florida legislature has been able to hold its members despite a low level of compensation. In the 120-member Florida house, from 1972 through 1990, the number of those running for reelection or for another office ranged from 86.6 percent to 97.5 percent. In the Florida senate, the pattern is similar. From 1974 through 1990, the number of members running for reelection or for another office ranged from 80 percent to 100 percent. This pattern is repeated in state after state. California and Illinois have been losing only about 5 percent of their members voluntarily at any single election. In Michigan, Wisconsin, and Ohio, the percentage has been only slightly higher. Between 1958 and 1984, Indiana's voluntary turnover declined to about 7 percent. In states such as Connecticut and Maryland, which claim to have citizen legislatures, the departure rates have been about 10 percent. Even Kentucky and Tennessee have moved along a similar path. There are, of course, exceptions. New Hampshire, where a third of the members voluntarily leave the legislature at term's end, is one of them. Montana is another. There, from 1966 to 1992, an average of one out of five members in the house and one out of four in the senate left voluntarily because of lack of pay, lack of support, or too much competition at the polls.[20]

Why do so many choose to stay? There are almost as many reasons for serving as there are legislators who serve. Some are drawn to the legislature and then remain there because they desire to serve their community and its people. Some are committed to a certain policy domain or a specific issue. Some want to promote a particular ideology. Many relish the excitement of the political process and the influence of the office. A few view legislative service as a way to promote their outside occupations (such as building a clientele for a law practice). Some like the income, as modest as it may be in places, and a number delight in the life-style. Usually one's motives are mixed. For example, a study of Arkansas legislators found their motivations comprised of "some combination of altruism and ambition, of public-regardingness and private desire."[21] However great the frustrations and hardships legislators have to endure, they are obviously outweighed by the rewards of legislative life.

Even in those states where professionalism has made only modest headway, most legislative members have political careers in mind—at least in the back, if not the very front. In his book on the Colorado legislature, which is still regarded as a citizen legislature, John Straayer writes that members "are rarely apolitical citizens who just come to Denver to do a good-hearted and brief public service stint for the benefit of their fellow citizens." They want to advance in politics, aspiring to seats in Congress or statewide office.[22] A survey of Ohio legislators found that one-third of the representatives and two-fifths of the senators were definitely interested in running for other offices, and another one-quarter of each house expressed a tentative interest.[23] How many others harbored such an interest, but chose not to express it? Many individuals are willing to remain in the legislature until they find a better political alternative. And if such an opportunity never arises, they simply content themselves with where they are. Indeed, in a few places, such as New York, legislators are reluctant to give up their seats and salaries even when they can run for an open seat in the U.S. House.

Among those who do enter the legislature with no thought of pursuing a long-term career, a number get hooked. One Florida senate leader characterizes the legislature as composed of "citizens" like himself, but these citizens have been in office for years. He himself never anticipated a lengthy career, but explained: "I got good at it, I liked it, I got satisfaction; every time I thought about quitting, I was promoted." Nineteen years later, and after holding several leadership positions, he was still in service. A former California assemblyman explained that he did not start out to become a career politician. But legislative life for him was intriguing, and reasonably secure. His own service evolved into a career. In his opinion, "you become a career politician when you're in the legislature," regardless of prior aspirations. In California, as in twenty other states, term limits make a political career more difficult, but by no means impossible.

Legislative Politicization

The state legislature has always been a political body; electoral considerations have always been salient, especially to the representatives in forty-five states and the senators in eleven states who have to run every two years. But the rise of professionalization has brought with it a marked increase in politicization. Legislatures have become attractive places for politicians of any type. Here, members can ply their political trade, exercise influence, and await opportunities to run for something even better.

State legislatures are becoming more like the U.S. House of Representatives, where most members view politics as a career and care a great deal about retaining their office. "As politics has become a profession, and service in the House a realistic and attractive career, job security has become as important for the professional representative as for any other professional—but more problematic."[24] State legislative office is prized as well; thus, as in the U.S. Congress, incumbents seek to solidify their hold on it.

This concern with retaining one's job is not surprising. For careerists, a defeat means not only a loss of status, but of livelihood. "After all," as two scholars write, "for the old breed electoral defeat was a disappointment; for the new breed it may be the end of a career."[25] To reduce occupational risk, therefore, many legislators today make electoral concerns paramount. "They start running the day they take their oath of office" one observer noted of New Jersey legislators. "Everything they do is geared toward the election," said another in Illinois. "The thought of re-election may not occur to a first term legislator within the first five minutes after winning the election, but I would not count on that," noted a Michigan legislator.[26] A recent nationwide survey of 304 state legislators who had served fifteen years or more found that 67 percent of them agreed with the proposition that legislators were more likely today than formerly to give priority to their reelection.[27]

The Reelection Drive

In view of the advantages that incumbents are thought to possess nowadays, this overriding concern with reelection may seem exaggerated. The reelection rates of incumbent legislators, while not as high as that for members of the U.S. House, have been impressive by any standard.[28] In the professionalized legislatures of the large states—California, Illinois, Michigan, New York, and Pennsylvania—nine out of ten incumbents have been returned. The same proportions have met with success in Wisconsin, a somewhat smaller state with a professionalized legislature, and in Indiana, Maryland, Minnesota, and Ohio, where career professionalization has not gone quite as far. The advantages of incumbency can be seen in Florida, too. The success rate for incumbents running for the house from 1972 through 1990 ranged from 82 percent to 97 percent, and for the senate from 1974 through 1990, from 71 percent to 95 percent.

Most districts are relatively safe, not only for incumbents but for a particular party as well. Natural demographic patterns are the reason for this. Even decennial reapportionments tend to leave most incumbents reasonably secure. Over time, the demography of a district may change, so that an incumbent's partisan advantage within a specific district may diminish. But one or the other party is still likely to maintain a partisan advantage even a decade after redistricting. During this time the incumbent has had multiple resources to help him or her secure a clear advantage.

Incumbents are more likely than challengers to be known by the district's voters. They have the media edge that goes with holding public office. In addition, they have devoted some of their own time, and most of their staff's (in states where legislators enjoy a personal staff), responding to constituent problems, intervening on their behalf with administrative agencies of government, and "bringing home the bacon" to their districts in the form of public works and other projects.

One study of the lower houses of twenty state legislatures found a decline over the period 1950–1986 in the proportions of marginal seats; in less than half the states examined were more than 50 percent of the seats competitive. In Tennessee, only one out of five house seats was competitive, in Massachusetts, one out of four, and in California and New York, one out of three.[29]

Yet, subjective—not objective—standards are what count for candidates. In the incumbent's mind, there is no such thing as a safe district. Whatever their margins of victory in prior elections, however "safe" their district may appear to the analyst, incumbents know that lightning can strike. They have seen colleagues relax their efforts and subsequently lose their seats. They live in perpetual danger of casting a roll-call vote that upsets their constituency or mobilizes a key interest group to seek their defeat. And they worry lest national trends, an unpopular candidate at the top of their ticket, or scandal blindside them. Those in the large states, where media campaigns count for so much, are alert to their opponents' war chests and to the possibility that last-minute contributions to them will allow a stealth attack at the very end, when the damage can be irreparable and it is too late to respond effectively.

The Cost of Political Campaigns

Given their preoccupation with reelection, for many contemporary legislators the campaign never ends. A candidate's initial election to office is quickly followed by the first stages of the next campaign—planning, positioning, and fundraising. Only those who feel inviolable or who are on their way out anyway (voluntarily or because of a term limit) can take much of a vacation from the perpetual quest for votes.

The scope, nature, and conduct of legislative campaigns vary tremendously. The population of a district and its size and geography affect how a campaign is conducted. So do the urban, suburban, or rural nature of the district and its demographic makeup. Wherever possible, candidates will go door to door, making personal contact with voters. Even in larger districts, ambitious candidates can reach a good number of people personally.

Today's candidates supplement door-to-door techniques with media campaigns. In large states with heavily populated legislative districts, candidates tend to rely on media campaigns almost exclusively. Modern technologies enable legislators to publicize their names, convey their chosen images, and disseminate their messages to the public. Radio is a popular medium, because the cost is reasonable. Television, while more expensive, is also a common medium of campaigning, especially in the larger and more competitive districts of the big states. Direct mail is another technique that is widely used.

Funding campaigns has become a much larger part of legislative life lately. "Money," in the words of the late Jesse Unruh, former speaker of the California assembly, "is the mother's milk of politics." If this was true thirty years ago when Unruh reigned, it is even truer now. It is difficult to imagine many modern legislative campaigns being run without firm financial support. California leads when it comes to levels of spending on legislative campaigns. Tom Hayden spent a record $2 million on an assembly seat and Cecil Green spent $1.4 million in a special election for a senate seat. In 1994, legislative campaign fundraising totaled $78.4 million, up by 9 percent from 1992. In nine of twenty senate races and nine of eighty assembly races, the amount of money raised by both candidates exceeded one million dollars. In assembly open-seat contests, the median amount raised by winners was $289,000. In Washington, five campaigns in 1990 topped the $237,283 record of 1988, and seven other races exceeded $200,000. That same year in Oregon the campaigns of fourteen candidates ran above $120,000. However, not all campaigns run so high. In Colorado, senate races can cost from $30,000 to $40,000, while $20,000 is about par for a house seat. And in New Hampshire and Wyoming, only a few thousand dollars are spent on most races.

Across the states, the amount of money expended has been growing. One study, comparing 1978 campaign expenses to those of 1986, showed a 144.8 percent increase in spending on California assembly races, a 111.1 percent increase on Colorado house races, a 154.2 percent increase on Oregon house races, a 285.9 percent increase on the California senate, an 80.6 percent increase on the Colorado senate, a 379.1 percent increase on the Oregon senate, and a 149.8 percent increase on the Washington house and senate.[30] By 1990, instead of costing hundreds of dollars, a candidate for a house seat in Maine typically spent between $4,000 and $5,000, while a senate candidate spent between $20,000 and $35,000.[31] Even in Vermont, where "successful election campaigns get waged with less money than it takes to buy a good used car," the costs have been going up. In 1990, one candidate for a senate seat set a record by spending $25,000, sending the state into momentary shock.[32]

Unless provision is made for public financing of legislative elections, as in Minnesota and Wisconsin, candidates have little reason to skimp on fundraising. No one wants to take any extra chances. In the larger states, particularly in California, elections have taken on the aspect of a nuclear arms race, with costs escalating even higher. Elsewhere, too, the incentive is to raise as much money as possible. Incumbents believe, with some justification, that raising large amounts will discourage serious opponents. And, in any event, stockpiled funds can be used for future reelection races or runs for higher office. Furthermore, there is some danger in slackening one's efforts. Fundraising, to alter Unruh's metaphor, can be compared to milking a cow: If you stop milking a cow, the milk will dry up.

Legislative Campaign Management

Individual legislators are more absorbed in campaign fundraising than ever before. Four out of five veteran legislators surveyed agreed that more time is now spent raising campaign funds.[33] Not only is the individual legislator heavily involved in this enterprise, but the legislative party and the legislative leadership have also come to play major roles in the contemporary candidate-oriented campaign.

Leadership and caucus campaign committees, which began developing in the 1970s and now exist in forty states, are marvelously effective in raising funds. It is much more difficult for a lobbyist or an interest group PAC to turn down a legislative leader than to turn down a rank-and-file member. Willie Brown, as speaker of the California assembly, was renowned for his fundraising abilities.[34] So was Vern Riffe, speaker of the Ohio house, whose annual birthday party routinely grossed close to $1 million. Leadership and caucus campaign committees are also effective in distributing funds. Since their overriding objective is to win or maintain a legislative majority (garnering as many seats as possible along the way), their money goes to candidates who can put it to best use—that is, challengers running for marginal or open seats and incumbents from marginal districts who are targeted by the opposition.

Legislative leaders and legislative party committees not only play a part in raising and allocating monies, they also have a role in the general management of campaigns. A growing number have become active in the recruitment of candidates.[35] Some help run campaign schools. Some are involved in the bulk purchase of campaign technologies—consultants, polling, media production—that are offered to candidates. And some spend money on behalf of candidates for mailings, brochures, and advertising in print and electronic media.[36]

There is evidence that legislative party efforts have been paying off. One study suggests that focusing party resources has resulted in increasing margins for members of the New York Senate.[37] It is generally believed that Democrats took the Vermont house in 1992 largely because Speaker Ralph Wright spent several years recruiting and coaching candidates and kept watch over his party's campaigns. In 1992, Republicans in Kansas managed well enough to take control of the house and make gains in the senate. While Kansas Democrats had always been organized and aggressive, the Republicans began to match them blow for blow. "It's almost scary how this is evolving," said the chief of staff to the senate president, "we're a part-time legislature, but running for office is becoming a near full-time job."[38]

The Campaign in the Legislature

In view of the increasing involvement of legislative leaders and legislative parties, it is unlikely that the campaign could have been kept out of the legislature. But competition, too, has played a role. The campaign pervades the legislative system and process today in part because of the competition between the two major parties in an increasing number of states. Nowadays, either party can win control of the senate or house in about three-fourths of the states, while the rest still are relatively safe for one party or the other.

For three decades the Republicans were the minority party in the states. The Democrats habitually won about 60 percent of the fifty governors' races and held roughly 60 percent of the 7,424 seats in the fifty legislatures. Yet, Republican strength progressively increased, particularly in the southern states where voters were already voting for GOP candidates in presidential and gubernatorial elections. The breakthrough occurred in the elections of 1994, when Republicans took control of the U.S. Senate and the U.S. House, the latter for the first time in almost forty years. The modern history of party control of state legislatures is portrayed in Table 6-1. The 1994 upheaval left Republicans in control of almost half of the total seats in state legislatures. Prior to this election, the Democrats controlled sixty-four chambers and the Republicans controlled thirty-one. Afterwards, the Republicans controlled forty-eight and the Democrats fifty.

Legislatures are much more partisan than they used to be, with Democrats vigorously contesting Republicans over control of the legislative chamber as well as over policy. But party as a unifying force on matters of policy is less salient than party as an organization for electoral combat. If the next election requires that party members rally round an issue to keep their majority, that is quite a different matter.

Legislators do not conceive of party as having much influence on how they vote on bills. Nor are they willing as individuals to go along with a party

Table 6-1   Party Control of State Legislatures (number of states)

Year	Democratic Control	Republican Control	Split Control
1960	27	15	6
1962	25	17	6
1964	32	6	10
1966	23	16	9
1968	20	20	8
1970	23	16	9
1972	26	16	7
1974	37	4	8
1976	35	4	10
1978	31	11	7
1980	29	15	5
1982	34	11	4
1984	26	11	12
1986	28	9	12
1988	29	8	12
1990	30	6	13
1992	25	8	16
1994	18	19	12

Source: Compiled by the author.

position that puts them at risk of losing support in their district.[39] Disciplined caucuses are few and far between. Diversity can be found within each party, since members' constituencies have different interests and members themselves diverge in their beliefs. When veteran legislators were surveyed about what they perceived to be changes in the nature of the job, 52 percent of them cited an increase in ideological conflict in the caucus; only 11 percent felt it had decreased.[40]

Republicans today are likely to be ideologically tighter than Democrats. This is because the GOP spread is from moderate to conservative while the Democratic spread is from liberal to conservative. Moreover, Republicans in a number of states have united under the banner of U.S. House Speaker Newt Gingrich. Republican legislative candidates have signed the "Contract with Ohio," the "Contract with Maryland," and so forth. In contrast, Democrats, stung by defeat, suffered demoralization. One member of the Ohio house described the "humiliating anger" felt in the caucus as a result of losing the majority. In Wisconsin's assembly, Democrats are "divided and resentful, pointing fingers at one another." In Florida, Republicans' steady progress toward their goal of majority status in both chambers (they won control of the Senate in 1994) has stricken house Democrats with fear.

If party members agree on anything, it is the importance of party control. Legislative leaders act as campaign managers, legislative parties function as campaign organizations, and legislatures themselves serve as electoral battlegrounds. Each party attempts to position itself and its members in the best possible light in anticipation of the ever-impending election. Political self-promotion is the order of the day. In New York, for example, television cameras and studios and direct mail are supported by public funds. Elsewhere, resources are more limited, but mailings to constituents by members clearly have political, as well as legislative, purposes.

Legislative party leaders, especially if in the majority, can see to it that their newer and more vulnerable members are given assignments on key standing committees—positions that enable them to raise campaign funds from affected interest groups or bring more than a rasher of bacon home to their constituencies. The majority can also ensure that threatened party members have popular bills to carry or items for their districts in the appropriation act, providing them with accomplishments to tout to their constituents.

In struggles on the floor, each party attempts to put the other on the wrong side of a vote on a popular issue. The minority will introduce amendments designed to embarrass the majority, rather than really accomplish a legislative purpose. The majority party does whatever is within its power to protect against being put on the down side of an issue. It appreciates that its marginal members feel that they cannot afford to cast even one very unpopular vote. For example, a vote for a tax increase can be used against them for years in the future and a thirty-second commercial can help unseat them at any time. One defense of the majority is to refuse to recognize the minority for amendments that may be mischievous. Kansas Republicans, angry after the 1988 campaigns that resulted in Democratic gains, pushed through a rules change that made it almost impossible for the minority to force a role-call vote on amendments, thus saving themselves the substantial embarrassment that could accompany a recorded position on a controversial issue.[41] In a legislative body up for grabs, members want to avoid having to cast tough votes. Legislative leaders do whatever they can to take their partisans off the hook. By enabling members to vote *for* something through the use of substitute amendments rather than *against* something, leaders can help to cushion the shock. This may be "slight comfort," according to a legislative leader in Florida, "but it prevents a head-on vote against a popular issue."

What has been happening is that the function of the legislature has become that of crystallizing partisan views, not reconciling them (except in the most formal sense of bringing them to a vote). Electoral objectives are being advanced at the expense of the legislative processes of deliberation and legitimation.[42]

Over the years the legislative parties in many states have hired staff to support their cause. Partisan staffing was relatively unknown thirty years ago. It is now a mainstay of legislatures in the large, two-party states. Illinois, Pennsylvania, Michigan, and New Jersey are among the nation's leaders in this respect.

Connecticut exemplifies one way in which partisan staff can mushroom. Until the early 1970s, the Connecticut general assembly had little professional

staffing. At that time, its nonpartisan central staff—research, fiscal, bill draft-
ing, and program review—became firmly established. Somewhat later, the
party caucuses added their own professionals. When the Republicans took
control of the legislature in 1984, the Democrats regained their majorities in
1986, and additional space was made available by a new legislative office building, the staffing pattern in Connecticut changed dramatically. In 1987, another
one hundred partisan staff positions were created, added to the fewer than
three dozen already in existence, and divided up among the four legislative
parties for allocation to their members. In the early 1980s, Connecticut's small
caucus staffs were oriented mainly toward legislation; the orientation of larger
caucus staffs is now focused on constituencies and campaigns.

In California, the politicization of staff has spread beyond the caucuses to
standing committees. Committee staff were once completely nonpartisan.
Today, partisan professionals staff all the assembly committees, as well as the
senate fiscal committees. In the words of a long-time observer of the California scene, "the policy experts have been replaced by political hired guns whose
main job is to get their bosses elected."[43]

The campaign activities of legislative staff have been challenged in several
states. In 1987, the Manhattan district attorney brought an indictment for
grand larceny and conspiracy against the New York senate minority leader and
one of his colleagues. Public funds were being used for campaigns, with eight
Democratic candidates, six of whom were challengers, receiving the services of
workers on the senate minority's payroll. The minority leader was ultimately
acquitted, but only after a period of painful publicity. A few years later, New
Jersey endured its own staff-campaigning scandal. Called into question (but
not ruled to be illegal) were the incidental campaign activities of partisan staff
on legislative time and the use of public resources, such as office computers and
telephones, for campaign purposes. Perhaps the most dramatic case of illegal
staff involvement in political campaigns occurred in Washington in 1992.
After a lengthy investigation there, the state Public Disclosure Commission
found that the four party caucuses had used state equipment, time, and
personnel to plan and run campaigns. The caucuses admitted responsibility,
agreed to desist from such practices, and paid fines for having violated the law.
But public resentment ran high and the legislature suffered scars as a result.

Officially, partisan staff will not get involved in campaigns (unless individual staff members take leaves of absence). Unofficially, one of their jobs is
to advance the party's electoral fortunes. As one New Jersey staffer described
the electoral connection: "We don't do anything on a campaign, but everything we do is for the campaign." However much they may or may not be directly involved in campaigns, there is little doubt that it is in the nature of the
job for partisan staff to approach issues in a partisan way, emphasize partisan
differences, and seize opportunities to score partisan points.

Partisanship is on the rise as the minority threat grows and new members
with little stake in past arrangements take their places in the legislature. Vir-

ginia and Maryland provide examples of legislatures that have recently been confronted with this new partisanship. The Virginia General Assembly used to be known as a bastion of southern civility. No longer. Its 1995 session has been called the "ugliest, meanest and most partisan" in decades. Traditionally, each session day the legislature would begin with the "Morning Hour," a custom that afforded law makers a chance to introduce hometown guests and schoolchildren sitting in the gallery. In a recent session, however, nearly every day for six weeks Democrats and Republicans alike took to the floor of the house and invoked personal privilege to attack one another in angry speeches.[44] The change in Virginia can be attributed in large part to increasing party competition. The so-called "Virginia way" of bipartisanship began eroding when Republicans started to capture seats in the house and senate. With the legislative elections of 1995, the GOP had gained a tie in the senate, although they were still five seats short of control in the house.

Maryland has never been a very partisan state, mainly because there have been too few Republican members to make a difference. When Ellen Sauerbrey became minority leader, the Republicans in the Maryland house were the third weakest minority in the country. But Sauerbrey had a different game plan than her predecessors. She led her party in a more partisan direction in an effort to increase its membership. "How will Maryland ever become a two-party system if Republicans are content to sit back and do our little individual things and feel good when we get a bill passed?" was the way she put it.[45] She made a conscious decision to fume, fuss, and toss bombs to throw the Democrats off stride and make them sit up and take notice of the Republican caucus. Her counterpart in the senate cooperated with the Democratic majority and was even included in Democratic leadership strategy sessions. His approach was to get as much for his colleagues and their policy preferences as he could through cooperation and compromise. Sauerbrey was quite the opposite. According to one of her colleagues, she "couldn't get a bill passed if she bought the votes." But she, and her successor as minority leader, with their confrontational, no-compromise approach, certainly made headway, picking up seats and gaining recognition. Now, the speaker has to think about where the Republicans are and what they will do before he acts.

Partisanship has not only had an impact in states where party previously meant relatively little, it has intensified in states that were partisan to begin with. California is an example. Willie Brown originally acquired the assembly speakership with Republican support, but after he consolidated his position within the Democratic caucus, he no longer needed that support. Thereupon, his treatment of the Republican minority became less beneficent, exacerbating partisan feelings. The sides hardened further in response to the ideology and practice of Republican governor George Deukmajian. By the 1990s the assembly had become highly partisan, confrontational, and given to procedural gamesmanship of almost every sort. Although the Republicans eked out a bare majority in the elections of 1994, Brown managed in the next session through skillful maneuvering to hang on to the speakership. And when the game appeared to be up, he succeeded, with the votes of a unanimous Democratic caucus and one Republican defector, in denying the GOP its own choice for speaker. Instead, Brown and his Democratic colleagues named the Republican speaker, producing an even more contentious atmosphere.

When a party has been out of power for some time, militant partisanship is not unusual once it finally retakes control. This occurred in the Ohio house, which had been in Democratic hands for decades but recently saw a philosophically conservative Republican party win a majority. Even where control has shifted back and forth, partisan heat can be generated. For example, in the Minnesota house, "as each party assumed power, it used its organizational and procedural power to humiliate the minority, producing a thirst for revenge among the members who could hardly wait for their turn in power to get even."[46]

Legislative Deinstitutionalization

In a classic study of the U.S. House of Representatives, Nelson Polsby applied the concept of institutionalization to a legislative body. His analysis demonstrated that, in terms of being well bounded or differentiated from its environment, the U.S. House over time had become institutionalized.[47] More recently, Peverill Squire examined the institutionalization of the California assembly and showed that it, too, had developed well-defined boundaries.[48] Indeed, in the 1970s and 1980s, many legislatures were undergoing institutionalization. In addition to the California assembly, legislatures in Florida, Iowa, Minnesota, New Jersey, New York, Ohio, and Wisconsin moved in that direction. In the 1990s, however, the situation changed dramatically. Legislatures are now in the process of deinstitutionalization. They are becoming less separated from their environments, more permeable, and less able to keep outside influences from penetrating internal structures and processes. Indeed, the outside environment is fast becoming an integral part of life and business inside the legislature.

Personnel Continuity

Legislatures are differentiated from their outside environments by their personnel. On the basis of tenure and turnover data, it is possible to observe how legislatures became more institutionalized in the 1970s and 1980s.

Over the course of these two decades, turnover steadily declined. In some states, such as Michigan, New York, and Ohio, it dropped to 10 percent or less. One study spanning four decades found that, overall, turnover in lower houses fell from 45 percent in the 1950s to 32 percent in the 1970s to 28 percent by 1985. In thirteen of the eighteen houses examined turnover declined and retention increased. For example, retention rose from 65 to 80 percent in Ohio, 57 to 73 percent in Iowa, 39 to 77 percent in Kentucky, 45 to 60 percent in Utah, and 50 to 69 percent in Oregon. A high proportion of legislators were retained in Rhode Island, New York, Pennsylvania, Michigan, and California. These low turnover rates can be explained by the fact that a high percentage of incumbents were seeking reelection, seven or eight out of ten, and a large proportion of these were subsequently winning, roughly nine out of ten.[49] Until lately, continuity in state legislative personnel has been substantial, or at least increasing.

Currently, however, turnover is on the rise. The California assembly, which only a few years ago Peverill Squire characterized as an institutionalizing organization, is now a deinstitutionalizing one. As of 1995, over half of the members had been in the assembly less than three years; of its eighty members, twenty-seven were newly elected in 1992 and twenty-seven were newly elected in 1994. These were the highest numbers of first-term members since 1966. Florida, too, has experienced an increase in turnover. As of 1995, over half the members of the Florida house had been there less than three years; of the 120 members, 47 came into office in 1992 and 29 in 1994. Maine is similar. In 1992, 47 percent of the 35 senators and 33 percent of the 151 representatives turned over; in 1994, the percentages were 46 and 47, respectively. This increase in turnover has been felt elsewhere. One out of three senates and almost one out of two houses experienced a turnover of at least 33.3 percent in either 1992 or 1994, or in both years.

One powerful deinstitutionalizing force that has emerged in the 1990s is constitutional or statutory limits on the terms of legislators. Between 1990 and 1996, as listed in Table 6-2, the electorates of twenty-one states voted for initiative (or referendum) propositions that limited the terms of legislators. Among the twenty-four states that provide for a direct or indirect initiative, only Alaska, Illinois, Mississippi, and North Dakota have yet to pass term limits for legislators.

Term limits failed to gain a popular majority on Mississippi's 1995 ballot, which can be considered a remarkable event. The proposed amendment to the constitution was unclear and the public was concerned that it might apply to appointed officials, such as fire chiefs, school superintendents, and members of boards of county hospitals, as well as to legislators. It was opposed not only by public officials but by the powerful Mississippi Farm Bureau Federation. After the term limits defeat in 1995, its proponents began promoting a proposal for "legislature only" term limits, which can be expected on a future Mississippi ballot.

The chance that a majority of legislators in non-initiative states will choose to limit their own terms is very low. A survey of seven states (four of which adopted term limits by initiative) showed that legislators opposed the idea, although Republicans were more supportive than Democrats.[50] Yet, public pressure might force legislators to put term limits on the ballot, allowing voters to register their preferences in a referendum. It would be difficult for legislators to refute the argument that citizens should have the power to

Table 6-2   Term Limits in State Legislatures, 1990–1996

| State | Number of years in term | |
(year of enactment)	Senate	House
Arizona (1994)	8	8
Arkansas (1992)	8	6
California (1990)	8	6
Colorado (1990)	8	8
Florida (1992)	8	8
Idaho (1994)	8	8
Louisiana (1995)	12	12
Maine (1993)	8	8
Massachusetts (1994)	8	8
Michigan (1992)	8	6
Missouri (1992)	8	8
Montana (1992)	8	6
Nebraska (1994)	8	—
Nevada (1994)	12	12
Ohio (1992)	8	8
Oklahoma (1990)	12	12
Oregon (1992)	8	6
South Dakota (1992)	8	8
Utah (1994)	12	12
Washington (1992)	8	6
Wyoming (1992)	12	6

Source: Compiled by the author.

decide. Once given that power, there is little doubt as to what the voters' decision will be, in light of past experience.

The Louisiana legislature was the first to bow to popular will—before the threat of an initiative loomed. On its own, it proposed a term limit amendment to the constitution for popular referendum. With an election only months away, and a number of newer members pressing hard, majorities in the Louisiana house and senate felt they had no choice but to accept term limits. The attitude of many was, "I don't believe in it, but my people want it." By crafting the amendment themselves, Louisiana legislators at least got themselves a longer term—twelve years.

As can be seen in Table 6-2, seven houses limit members to six years, sixteen senates and nine houses limit members to eight years, and five senates and four houses limit members to twelve years. The effects of term limits are already being felt. In California's assembly and Maine's senate and house, their full impact will occur as early as 1996. At that time, all of the members who were in the California assembly in 1990 when term limits were adopted will have to step down. Many of the members who were in the Maine legislature in 1993, when term limits were adopted in that state, to be applied retroactively, will not be eligible to run.

Members do not necessarily wait for their terms to expire before departing the legislature. As discussed previously, many leave when the opportunity to obtain another office presents itself. A number of legislators in California, for example, left in mid-term to compete for other elective offices. Such actions lead to a marked increase in the number of special elections and a disruption of the legislative process.[51] It is difficult to keep track of members as they hop, skip, and jump over the political playing field to keep their careers alive. Republican Phil Wyman of California is an example of the peripatetic state politician. According to the *California Journal*, he served in the assembly for fourteen years before running unsuccessfully for Congress in 1992. He came back to the legislature in 1993 after a special election to the senate, but then lost his seat in the regular election in 1994. The next year he announced that in 1996 he would run for a seat held by a term-limited Republican who would be obliged to give up his senate office.

Adherence to Norms

Legislatures are also differentiated from their outside environments by a distinctive set of norms. These norms constitute an unwritten understanding as to what is proper and improper conduct. If legislators share beliefs on how they ought to behave, the institution in which they function will be stronger vis-à-vis its environment. The question is whether legislative norms exist and, if they do, what they are and how they have changed over time.

One useful study for answering these questions surveyed senators in eleven states about twenty years ago.[52] Senators were asked whether they agreed with nineteen different items; on seven of the items norms did exist and were evident in nearly all of the states.[53] Whether norms pertain to the same extent today is doubtful. A recent national survey of 304 legislators who had served fifteen years or longer asked whether they thought that "legislators today are less likely to spend time learning the 'norms' or 'folkways' of the chamber and 'paying their dues.'"[54] Of those responding, 68.5 percent agreed, while only 20.3 percent disagreed. The survey also asked whether legislators agreed with the statement, "Overall, legislators today are less likely to abide by the informal rules of the chamber." Here, the split was closer, with 49.0 percent agreeing and 40.0 percent disagreeing.[55] The idea that norms are weaker now than previously is echoed in a study of the Minnesota legislature. It found that over the past twenty-five years senate leadership has moved from a process of articulating a shared political culture to one of mediating among factional interests.[56]

Collegiality may once have constituted a norm in many places, but it is now on the wane. The eleven-state survey of senators asked how they regarded "being known among other senators as a 'loner' and not having much to do with them outside the chamber." A norm proscribing such behavior was evident in the senates of seven of the eleven states; two other state senates came very close to satisfying normative requirements. Today, everyone in the legislature is a loner—more or less. Socializing with one's colleagues after hours is the exception, where it once was the rule.

Many members commute daily to the capitol, rather than stay away from their families for three or four nights a week. Those members who live within a hundred miles of the capital city can, and do, go home nightly. In geographically smaller states, like Rhode Island, New Jersey, Delaware, and Maryland, practically everyone can commute. In geographically larger states, like Nebraska, Indiana, Minnesota, and New Mexico, a large proportion of members live in the capital city or vicinity. Even legislators who stay over, returning to their districts for long weekends, see relatively little of one another. They used to lodge in the same hotels; now, most of the hotels are gone, replaced by condominiums or rental apartments. Legislators are spread out. While capital cities still support watering holes, where some members and somewhat more lobbyists tend to congregate, they are fewer and farther between. Clyde's in Tallahassee gets a smaller crowd; Fran O'Brien's in Annapolis does not do the business it once did; and the Bull Ring in Santa Fe has closed down. Much of the after-hours time of legislators nowadays is spent at receptions hosted by statewide business, trade, and professional associations and often attended by a delegation of people from the district. For some members, attending receptions is a chore (often they send their legislative aides to attend in their stead); for some, however, it is one of the few occasions when they see colleagues removed from the maelstrom of legislative business.

The mood is very different. Participants and observers comment on the lack of social interaction and collegiality among contemporary members. One hears repeatedly that, "It just isn't fun anymore." A Florida staff director described how in earlier times legislators "liked each other" and "laughed their butts off." Not today. The camaraderie is gone, as is the ability to poke fun at one another. "They don't have a good time" was his assessment. When the 304 veteran legislators surveyed were asked whether "there is less socializing and personal interaction, and fewer friendships among members today," 58.0 percent agreed while only 29.5 percent disagreed.

Not only has the nature of the legislative arena changed, but the nature of those who people it has changed as well. An eloquent explanation of this transformation was offered by William R. Bryant, Jr., a member of the Michigan house. Said Bryant, "With more ambitious, hard-working, highly-educated, and political career-minded legislators, there is less camaraderie, less seeking after common wisdom. There are more attempts at personal attainment and more proprietary notions."[57]

Trust is a byproduct of collegiality, of friendship, and even of law makers communing with one another in the statehouse snack bar or at a local watering hole. Like Bryant, journalist Alan Ehrenhalt has observed the change away from a close-knit group to an array of individualist professionals focused on their own careers and goals.[58] With less socializing and fewer friendships, and with more members going their own ways, trust and integrity may be in jeopardy.

The eleven-state survey had one item related to trustworthiness. It asked for agreement or disagreement with the practice of "concealing the real purpose of a bill or purposely overlooking some portion of it in order to assure passage." Almost all of the respondents opposed such a practice. Years later, veteran legislators were asked whether that norm had changed. Did they agree or disagree with the statement, "Legislators are more likely today to hide their legislative motives and try to conceal the real purposes of legislative actions." Responses were divided: 31.7 percent agreed that such a change had occurred, 36.6 percent disagreed, and 31.7 percent took neither position.

Long-time legislators, however, comment on the diminution of trust. They point out that you can no longer count on a legislator's word. For example, Alaska's speaker of the house, Ramona Barnes, referred to the time sixteen years earlier when she first came to the legislature. "The old-timers, their word was their bond," she recalled. "You did business with a handshake. That's all passing by the wayside." That feeling was echoed in Ohio. Vern Riffe, who retired in 1994, mentioned that the biggest difference then and now was that "you don't see the trust of the members for each other that you used to see." The former house majority leader, William Mallory, agreed: "When you gave your word, you lived up to your word. I don't think somebody giving their word necessarily is a commitment today. It depends on what happens in the next moment."[59] In Florida, too, commitment has lost meaning. Time after time, the vote counts taken by party leaders and by lobbyists mean very little. Twenty years ago, 90 percent of the legislators could be relied on for their word. Now only a handful can be counted on, as far as a commitment is concerned. The trustworthiness of individuals and, thus, the trustworthiness of the process is in decline.

"A reasonable level of civility and mutual respect is necessary . . . if a legislature is to function at all, as is a degree of mutual trust among members," wrote Bryant.[60] But the norm of *civility* also seems to be in peril. The eleven-state survey found substantial agreement in every senate, with the exception of Texas, proscribing "dealing in personalities in debate or other remarks made on the floor of the chamber." This norm has been severely eroded today, even in a state such as Virginia, which has been noted for its long tradition of civil deliberation in the legislature. Heightened partisanship bears heavy responsibility for the toll taken here.

Other norms have undergone erosion as a consequence of recent events, particularly the imposition of term limits. There is a belief among practitioners that members are no longer willing to serve an *apprenticeship*. The survey of veteran legislators asked for an "agree" or "disagree" response to the following statement: "Legislators today are less likely to be seen and not heard; they are less likely to show respect for, and seek the counsel of older, more experienced members." The ratio of agreement to disagreement on this item was 65.9 percent to 20.0 percent. Even though legislative veterans believe that it takes about six years to learn the ropes and become effective, they also recognize that few new law makers are willing to take the time—or wait around.

Today's professional politician wants to hit the ground running and gives little deference to anyone who has been around for a while.[61]

Apprenticeship may be on the wane, but it is doubtful that it ever really operated as a norm, despite the "good-old-days" reflections of some members. The eleven-state survey asked respondents whether "serving an apprenticeship period when you first enter the legislature" was expected. In fact, even then apprenticeship did not exist as a norm in any of the senates under examination. Twenty years later, such an expectation is completely out of the question, particularly in states with term limits where members set out to accomplish their objectives in as little time as possible. There is no reason to invest in a learning process.

As far as boundaries are concerned, the norm that ought to weigh heaviest is that of *institutional loyalty*. Whether or not many legislators ever singled out their institution as one deserving of loyalty is disputable. Some legislators did develop such feelings, at least over time; with experience and investment came loyalty. Those with institutional devotion tended to be disproportionately leaders, many of whom had a decade or more of service under their belt.

If institutional loyalty failed to achieve normative status in earlier years, it comes nowhere near to achieving it now. The impression is that fewer leaders and fewer members think in such terms, although the survey of veteran legislators found opinion divided. Just about as many agreed as disagreed—39.5 to 40.8 percent—that "legislators today have less commitment to the legislature itself." Yet, these same respondents acknowledged the negative effects of the electoral campaign on such a norm. It is not uncommon today for incumbent legislators, as well as challengers, to run against the legislature, the system, and its practices. When asked if they agreed or disagreed with the statement, "Legislators today are more likely to campaign against the legislature during electoral periods," 63.0 percent agreed, while only 17.8 percent disagreed. This hardly demonstrates loyalty to the legislature as an institution.

Add to all of this the imposition of term limits, and the possibility of widespread agreement on loyalty to the institution is virtually nil. When members enter the legislature with the certain knowledge that they will be leaving within a period of six, eight, or twelve years, their commitment has to be much reduced. They possess little time to develop it and no future in the legislature to justify it. One of the criticisms of term limits is that it destroys institutional memory; another might be that it discourages any memory of the institution whatsoever.

Managerial Autonomy

An institutionalized organization manages its internal life without substantial control or intervention from outside. Periodically, changes are made in the way state legislatures are run. Different generations, different parties, and different leaders alter the institution's management, at least to some extent.

But if such changes are mainly dictated by outside intervention or pressure, then the legislature's autonomy is in question. Although the authority of legislatures to govern themselves has always been restricted to some extent, that authority is more severely restricted today. The outside environment intrudes into internal processes and sometimes even determines institutional outcomes that were once decided by legislators themselves.

Paralleling this development, and doubtless related to it, is the intervention of outsiders into policy making itself. This is not to say that policy making was ever a purely inside enterprise. On most issues, however, legislative policy making was insulated to some degree from external forces. Today, outside forces are numerous, influential, unrelenting, and effective. They employ techniques that impact mightily on the decision-making prerogatives of legislative bodies. No longer is it sufficient for interest groups to communicate with legislators through their lobbyists alone. Now, they utilize public relations and grass-root campaigns to communicate with the public as well, who in their turn pressure law makers.[62] Lobbying was once a "relationships game," heavily dependent on entertaining, socializing, and personal connections.[63] Now, lobbying is more of a "constituents game," with legislators concerned with the mobilizing effects of grass-root and media campaigns in their districts. And this concern, of course, is directly related to legislators' growing preoccupation with the next election.

Although issue participation has expanded well beyond an inner circle, legislators still make the final decisions on the general shape, as well as the details, of legislation. But they are more attentive to and intimidated by the voices and pressures from without. While the challenge to the legislature's managerial prerogatives is not unrelated to these new patterns of lawmaking, a distinction can still be made between management on the one hand and lawmaking on the other. The former is an internal responsibility of a legislature, and the way in which it is met reflects an organization's institutional nature; the latter is not and does not.

Much of the loss of managerial control has occurred in the states that provide for the direct or indirect initiative to amend the constitution or enact a statute. The use of the initiative has been on the rise since the 1950s and 1960s, when there was relatively little initiative activity. The 1980s saw a marked increase, which has continued into the 1990s. The Council of State Governments reported that from 1981 to 1992, 23 states had 346 initiatives on the ballot, of which 153 passed. This figure includes 30 adoptions in California, 17 in Oregon, 10 in Colorado, 10 in Maine, and 9 in Washington. The initiative process has had the most profound impact in California, where the editors of the *California Journal* noted that, in effect, initiative sponsors were becoming the state's political leaders, while the governor and the legislature were being thrust into supportive roles.[64] In fact, many of the major public policy decisions coming out of California since Proposition 13 in 1978 were made by interest groups and the people of the state, with the legislature becoming increasingly less relevant.

A number of the propositions that have been put on the ballot and approved by the voters limit the legislature's authority to levy taxes or expend monies. California's Proposition 98, for example, which was passed in 1988, required at least 40 percent of the state's general fund to go to the schools. Additional examples of what has been called "ballot box budgeting" can be found in several other places. In 1992, Colorado citizens passed a measure that required voter approval of any increase in taxes. Two years later the people of Florida adopted one amendment to limit government spending and another that made it easier to amend the constitution to further limit taxes and spending. Arizona and Nevada voters mandated that a two-thirds vote by the legislature be required to implement a tax increase. Oklahoma required the approval of three-fourths of its law makers. Washington's electorate provided for limits on expenditures and a referendum to approve tax hikes. Other initiatives bypassing or limiting the legislature have been approved in the area of campaign finance in Missouri, Montana, Nevada, Oregon, and Washington.

While these measures restrict legislative authority over statewide policy, they do not directly restrict the managerial prerogatives of legislatures. But other measures, in addition to term limit initiatives themselves, have further limited the legislature's control over its own affairs. In recent years, initiatives have been introduced to reduce the size of the legislature, shorten the legislative session, convert from bicameralism to unicameralism, and require that the institution remain part time. California, Colorado, Florida, Illinois, Michigan, Nevada, Ohio, Oklahoma, Oregon, South Dakota, and Washington have all witnessed one or several such drives.

Two of the most notable assaults on legislative prerogatives occurred in Colorado and California. Colorado voters in 1988 tried to change the legislative process by passing the GAVEL (Give a Vote to Every Legislator) amendment to the constitution. This amendment required that every bill referred to a legislative committee be voted on in committee, thus preventing a committee chair from allowing bills to die by default; that bills reported out of committee go to the floor, thus negating the power of the rules committee; and that legislators not be permitted to commit themselves through a vote in party caucus, thus ending binding votes, especially on the budget bill.[65] California voters went even further. In 1984 they adopted Proposition 24, which was intended to strip the speaker of the authority to appoint committees, requiring instead the proportional division of legislative resources between the parties. This initiative never went into effect. A state court invalidated it on the grounds that the California constitution gave the legislature sole authority over its organization. However, in 1990 Proposition 140, described by one observer as "one of the most vicious acts of political retribution in recent American history,"[66] did survive judicial review. It not only brought term limits to California, but also required a 38 percent cut in the legislative budget, necessitating a reduction of about 600 staff positions. In addition, Proposition 140 abolished the legislature's retirement system, which had been established over twenty years earlier.

Outside control over legislative structure is evidenced as well by the electorate's refusal in a number of states to endorse legislative determinations on the length of sessions. Alaska's constitution of 1956 had authorized annual sessions of unlimited length. In 1984, out of frustration at the amount of time law makers were taking to divvy up oil revenues, voters amended the constitution to limit annual sessions to 120 days.[67] Although Montana's 1972 constitution provided for annual sessions, a referendum in 1974 returned the legislature to biennial sessions of 90 days. In 1982 and 1988 the legislature made repeated efforts to get annual sessions, but Montana voters decided otherwise. In 1993 the legislature made another attempt, but could not get the two-thirds legislative vote necessary to put it on the ballot.[68]

State legislatures are also limited in their control of members' compensation—also a management prerogative. Compared to the one-half of the states that had constitutional limits on pay in the 1960s, only a few have such restrictions now. But in some states legislative pay still remains low. New Mexico is an example of a state with a constitutional restriction on pay. Currently, its constitution prohibits any compensation, perquisite, or allowance, save for a per diem of $75 while the legislature is in session and 25 cents per mile for one, round-trip journey to the capitol each session. (Only one state, New Hampshire, pays its legislators less than New Mexico.) Since 1951, the legislature has put compensation provisions on the ballot on eleven occasions, but has been overruled by the electorate eight times. The last compensation increase was adopted in 1982, thanks to support from the press, the business community, and Common Cause, as well as the misleading wording of the title of the amendment, which asked the electorate to vote on "limiting per diem to $75 a day." In 1994, legislators made an ambitious effort to expand per diem and reimburse legislators for interim expenses incurred in serving constituents or serving in leadership positions. They were defeated.

Even where legislatures have the statutory power to raise salaries, for political reasons they are hesitant to do so. Some have proceeded very cautiously, as in Montana. Here, legislators in 1993 were receiving a daily pay of $56.44. During the 1993 session they voted for a raise in salary, but by only one dollar per day.[69] Alaska legislators, thinking back to a 1976 referendum in which voters rolled back a pay raise, rescinded a pay increase they had given themselves three years earlier before the voters did it for them.

Other legislatures have been frightened away from exercising their responsibility to determine compensation. Currently, twenty states have independent compensation commissions. A number of others, in an effort to deflect public criticism, have tied legislator pay to that of state employees. Several legislatures have benefitted from the commission device. California's legislative leaders, for example, decided that it was politically advisable to place the salary issue into the hands of an independent citizens' compensation commission via Proposition 112. To ensure that it would be agreeable to the voters, the legislature added sweeteners to the proposition, such as ethics reforms including the banning of honorariums. The public approved the amendment, and within a short time the commission raised yearly salaries from $41,000 to $52,000.[70] But the commission device does not totally insulate legislatures. There is always some political risk in accepting commission recommendations, and sometimes legislators are not willing to run that risk. For example, in 1991 the Michigan legislature turned down a commission recommendation to increase salaries because of the symbolic and political implications of being fiscally rewarded during a period of budget cuts.

There is nothing closer to a legislator's heart than the nature, shape, and population of the district in which he or she runs. In the majority of states, legislative redistricting remains in the hands of the legislators. Legislative leaders and designated committees put together plans, while rank-and-file members have input along the way and a final vote. Yet, in numerous states courts have overruled legislative redistricting enactments, and on a number of occasions they have done the redistricting themselves.

In Arkansas, Colorado, Hawaii, Montana, Pennsylvania, Washington, Missouri, New Jersey, and Ohio, redistricting has been taken almost entirely out of legislative hands, with independent commissions entrusted with its formulation and enactment. In addition, Illinois resorts to a commission if the governor and the legislature fail to reach an agreement, and Iowa has assigned the authority for redistricting to the staff of the Legislative Service Bureau. Thus, in more than one-fifth of the states legislatures no longer have responsibility for, or direct power over, the drawing of district lines. Legislative leaders do get to appoint commission members in most places, and they undoubtedly have some influence, but the legislature as such has been removed from the redistricting process. Few activities have such a large bearing on the composition and control of the legislature, so the abandonment or loss of such authority undermines the strength of the institution.

Legislatures are also losing control over the life-styles and conduct of their own members. There was a time when breaches of ethics were handled within the legislature itself. Now, because of scandal, or the appearance of scandal disseminated by a sensationalizing media, legislatures have lost much of their autonomy to manage in this area. At a formal level, in almost one-third of the states independent commissions currently have jurisdiction over the ethics of legislators.

Kentucky provides an example of how such a commission arises and operates. After a scandal that resulted in the conviction of a number of its members, the Kentucky legislature—under great pressure from the press—passed an omnibus ethics law. Among other things, the law established an ethics commission as an agency of a new culture. This new culture is one in which the public not only decides who its representatives are, but also has a large say in how those representatives conduct themselves on a day-to-day basis. While adjudicating, in the words of its chairman, "according to the letter of the law," the early interpretations of the Kentucky ethics commission were as restrictive as the law allowed. Little weight was given to what the legislature's intent in passing the law might have been or to what legislators' needs might be. The commission conceived of itself as representing the public; it wanted to demonstrate its credibility to citizens of the state. In consequence, its relationship with the legislature was destined to be uneasy and adversarial.

On an informal level, legislators are responding to public pressures and altering their conduct in a number of respects. Increasing numbers of members are reluctant to travel at taxpayers' expense to out-of-state legislative meetings. They are fearful of how the media will portray the trip, how the opposition party and candidate will challenge it in the next campaign, and how their constituents will react. Many legislators now rely on their own campaign accounts for travel, even if on state business; some use personal funds; and quite a number have decided that travel out of the state is simply not worth the risk, so they stay put.

Even when it comes to internal operations, the media cannot be ignored. They are intrusive and influential. For example, in Minnesota in 1993, negative media coverage of a telephone scandal in the legislature, a skiing vacation taken by legislators, a legislative visit to Duluth, and the attendance of legislators at a national meeting in San Diego forced the speaker of the house to step down from her leadership position after sustained criticism. It also led to the enactment of ethics legislation, which among other things tightened up restrictions on gifts to legislators from lobbyists.[71] Throughout the nation legislative leaders are reluctant to take action on budgeting, staffing, travel allowances, and the like, lest their legislative party, and individual members, suffer at the hands of the "gotcha," muckraking journalism rampant in many state capitals today.

Institutions under Siege

If institutionalization is largely the result of the desires of those on the inside—the legislators themselves—deinstitutionalization is the result of the desires of those on the outside—principally, the media and the public. No longer can state legislative bodies be characterized as organizations that displace goals and focus resources on internal processes at the expense of external demands. Legislatures today are beset by external demands, to which they are extraordinarily responsive. *New York Times* correspondent Michael Wines wrote that "a somewhat slow and contemplative system" has been turned into "something more like a 500-channel democracy, with the clicker grasped tightly in the hands of the electorate."[72] Legislatures are criticized for not being responsive. But their problem is not that they listen too little, but they listen too much—to television, videos, faxes, computers, 800 numbers, grass roots, phone banks, and poll after poll.

The public's expectations of government have been stimulated in large measure by government itself. People want what government delivers, and in particular the services that address their specific needs. But most of them also feel that taxes can and should be lowered. Democrats and Republicans alike are faced with the dilemma of satisfying individual needs without losing sight of the larger, overriding public interest.

Today's popular wants are articulated and, to some degree, created by interest groups of every shape and variety. These groups add their often powerful, insistent voices to the pressuring legislatures to meet their demands. Those with large membership and broad appeal are unwilling to take no for an answer and are even resistant to compromise. Legislators, with fewer defenses than formerly, are being battered from all sides.

The media compound these problems. The legislature is far more open than it used to be, and both print and electronic media coverage of legislatures has increased since the early 1970s. The nature of this coverage is anything but favorable, however. The press tends to report the worst examples of legislative behavior, disregarding positive achievements. The media contend that it is these types of stories in which their audiences are most interested. And certainly there are cases of waste, partisan game-playing, stalemate, and illegal and unethical behavior. Indeed, legislators have been convicted of corrupt practices in the wake of FBI or local law enforcement stings in California, Arizona, South Carolina, and Kentucky. That people should generalize from what they view on television, hear over talk radio, or read in the newspaper, though, is unfortunate. Such generalizations are based on aberrant behavior and hardly represent usual legislative performance. The case against the legislature is grossly distorted, but is it any wonder that citizens have lost confidence in their legislatures, just as they have lost confidence in other institutions? Whatever their sins, they are by no means commensurate with the bad press state legislatures receive and the low esteem in which they are held.[73]

It is ironic that the public's regard for legislatures declined just as they modernized and developed the capacity to govern, and expanded their role. Legislatures certainly became larger targets for the aim of critics. And recent trends—notably professionalization and politicization—have something to do with the heightened public cynicism.

Today's legislators run their own campaigns, promote the interests of their districts, and pursue their political ambitions as individual entrepreneurs. The capital community of legislators, lobbyists, and others is more diffuse. Few values are shared, and legislative norms have weakened.

The legislative process has become less deliberative. Given the goals of members, the demands of interest groups, and the heavy workload, deliberation often gives way to expediency—not always an optimum trade-off. Members frequently are unwilling to say no to their colleagues, lest their colleagues say no to them. They are also adverse to saying no to constituents, lest their constituents say no to them at the ballot box. The entire process has become porous—much seeps in that probably should not.

Legislative leadership has weakened as well. Leaders will likely serve shorter tenures in the years ahead than they have in years past. More are being challenged by their own caucuses and by bipartisan coalitions; some are being overthrown. In states with term limits ranging from six to twelve years, it is improbable that rank-and-file members will permit house speakers, senate presidents, or presidents pro tem to hold top office for more than two or four years. The long leadership tenures of a Willie Brown of California, a Vern Riffe of Ohio, or a John Martin of Maine will not be repeated. Leadership authority to appoint members to committees, to name committee chairpersons, and to calendar bills is being whittled away in a number of places and is being challenged in others. Perhaps the most significant power left to leaders is that of raising and allocating campaign funds, but that too will probably decline in the current climate. Some time ago, most legislative leaders adopted as their principal legislative mode that of consensus building and facilitating, rather than pushing through their own policy agendas. However, even these modes will be more difficult to accomplish in the period ahead.

The effects of term limits are just beginning to be felt. Those states with more professionalized legislatures, such as California, Michigan, and Ohio, will feel its effects more severely than those with citizen legislatures, such as Montana, South Dakota, and Utah. But even the latter will be affected. Power is apt to shift, to some degree, from the legislature to other agencies—to the governor, to executive bureaucracies, to interest groups and lobbyists, or to the media and whatever public becomes mobilized. And institutional memory and institutional commitment will decline further.

If the legislature has among its responsibilities providing a process capable of resolving conflict and building consensus, then surely it has its hands full. Simply maintaining itself as a political institution will be a challenge. These prospects are not happy ones. In all likelihood the fabric of the legislative institution will continue to unravel. David S. Broder wrote not long ago: "It's all too easy in stressful times, for everyone to forget how valuable—and how fragile—these representative institutions are."[74] In fact, people may not have forgotten; they simply may never have really known.

Notes

1. For an account of the legislative reform movement, see Alan Rosenthal, "Reform in State Legislatures," *Encyclopedia of the American Legislative System*, II, ed. Joel H. Silbey (New York: Scribner's, 1994).
2. Alan Ehrenhalt, *The United States of Ambition: Politicians, Power and the Pursuit of Office* (New York: Random House, 1991).
3. In Minnesota, although almost one-third of the members surveyed admitted to being full time, 88 percent believed the legislature should not be full time, and 90 percent believed legislators should have another occupation. Charles H. Backstrom, "The Legislature as Place to Work: How Minnesota Legislators View Their Jobs" (Paper prepared for the Hubert H. Humphrey Institute of Public Affairs, University of Minnesota, December 1986), 5.
4. The percentages of full-time members reported here are estimates furnished by instate sources. Those who publicly identify their occupations as "legislator" for state blue books and directories tend to be somewhat fewer. See National Conference of State

Legislatures, *State Legislators' Occupations: A Decade of Change* (Denver, Colo.: National Conference of State Legislatures, March 25, 1987); Peverill Squire, "Career Opportunities and Membership Stability in Legislatures," *Legislative Studies Quarterly* 13 (February 1988): 75, 78.

5. An alternate categorization, based on session length, staffing, compensation, and membership turnover, groups states into three classes. In the first are eight states with the more professionalized legislatures; in the third are seventeen with less professionalized legislatures. In the second are twenty-five states somewhere in between. See Karl T. Kurtz, "The Changing State Legislatures," in *Leveraging State Government Relations*, ed. Wesley Pedersen (Washington, D.C.: Public Affairs Council, 1990), 23–32.

6. Malcolm E. Jewell and Penny M. Miller, *The Kentucky Legislature* (Lexington: University Press of Kentucky, 1988), 15.

7. Brian Weberg, "Changes in Legislative Staff," *Journal of State Government* 61 (November/December 1988): 190–197.

8. Kevin Sack, "The Great Incumbency Machine," *New York Times Magazine,* September 27, 1992, 48.

9. Quoted in the *New York Times,* January 17, 1988.

10. John Brandl, "Reflections on Leaving the Minnesota Legislature," *Humphrey Institute News* (June 1990): 14–15.

11. Ehrenhalt, *The United States of Ambition,* 17–18, 20, 203.

12. Morris P. Fiorina, *Divided Government* (New York: Macmillan, 1992), 48–51, and Fiorina, "Divided Government in the American States: A Byproduct of Legislative Professionalism?" *American Political Science Review* 88 (June 1994): 307.

13. Ehrenhalt, *The United States of Ambition,* 20.

14. The gains made by African-Americans and Hispanics may be reduced somewhat by the Supreme Court's 1995 redistricting decision declaring unconstitutional Georgia's 11th Congressional District.

15. Dianna Gordon, "Citizen Legislators—Alive and Well," *State Legislatures* (January 1994): 27.

16. Samuel C. Patterson, "Legislative Politics in Ohio," in *Ohio Politics,* ed. Alexander P. Lamis (Kent, Ohio: Kent State University Press), 240; Gerald A. McBeath and Thomas A. Morehouse, *Alaska Politics and Government* (Lincoln: University of Nebraska Press, 1994), 145.

17. John R. Hibbing, "Modern Legislative Careers," in *Encyclopedia of the American Legislative System,* I, ed. Joel H. Silbey (New York: Scribner's, 1994), 497.

18. Unless otherwise noted, here and below quotations are from interviews conducted by the author.

19. For a study of voluntary departure in Indiana and Missouri, see Wayne L. Francis and John R. Baker, "Why Do U.S. State Legislators Vacate Their Seats?" *Legislative Studies Quarterly* 11 (February 1986): 119–126.

20. Jerry W. Calvert, "Reform, Representation, and Accountability—Another Look at the Montana Legislative Assembly," in *Legislative Reform and Representative Government in Montana* (Burton K. Wheeler Center, Montana State University), 6–7.

21. Diane D. Blair, *Arkansas Politics and Government* (Lincoln: University of Nebraska Press, 1988), 165.

22. John A. Straayer, *The Colorado General Assembly* (Niwot, Colorado: University Press of Colorado, 1990), 65.

23. Patterson, "Legislative Politics in Ohio," 240.

24. Bruce Cain, John Ferejohn, and Morris Fiorina, *The Personal Vote* (Cambridge, Mass.: Harvard University Press, 1987), 7. See also Lawrence C. Dodd, "A Theory of Congressional Cycles: Solving the Puzzle of Change," in *Congress and Policy Change,* ed. Gerald C. Wright, Jr., Leroy N. Rieselbach, and Lawrence C. Dodd (New York: Apathon Press, 1986), 3–44.

25. Joel A. Thompson and Gary Moncrief, "The Evolution of the State Legislature: Institutional Change and Legislative Careers," in *Changing Patterns in State Legislative Careers*, ed. Gary Moncrief and Joel A. Thompson (Ann Arbor: University of Michigan Press, 1992), 203.

26. William R. Bryant, Jr., *Quantum Politics: Greening State Legislatures for the New Millennium* (Kalamazoo: New Issues Press, Western Michigan University, 1993), 126.

27. Karl T. Kurtz, "The Old Statehouse: She Ain't What She Used to Be," National Conference of State Legislators, July 26, 1993.

28. A study comparing the period 1968–1976 with 1978–1986 indicated that no significant change occurred from the earlier to the late period in the percentages of incumbents winning reelection. David Breaux and Malcolm Jewell, "Winning Big: The Incumbency Advantages in State Legislative Races," in *Changing Patterns in State Legislative Careers*, 87–105.

29. Harvey J. Tucker and Ronald E. Weber, "Electoral Change in the U.S. States: System Versus Constituency Competition," in *Changing Patterns in State Legislative Careers*, 81.

30. Anthony Gierzynski and David Breaux, "Money and Votes in State Legislative Elections," *Legislative Studies Quarterly* 16 (May 1991): 207.

31. Kenneth T. Palmer, G. Thomas Taylor, and Marcus A. Librizzi, *Maine Politics and Government* (Lincoln: University of Nebraska Press, 1992), 42–43.

32. Tom Dunkel, "In Vermont, Common Folk Make the Laws," *Insight*, May 18, 1992, 12.

33. Kurtz, "The Old Statehouse: She Ain't What She Used to Be," 3.

34. See Richard A. Clucas, *The Speaker's Electoral Connection: Willie Brown and the California Assembly* (Berkeley: University of California, Institute of Governmental Studies Press, 1995).

35. Malcolm E. Jewell and Marcia Lynn Whicker, *Legislative Leadership in the American States* (Ann Arbor: University of Michigan Press, 1994), 114–115; also, Gierzynski, *Legislative Party Campaign Committees in the American States* (Lexington: University Press of Kentucky, 1992), 56–57.

36. Jeffrey M. Stonecash, "Campaign Finance in New York Senate Elections," *Legislative Studies Quarterly* 15 (May 1990): 254.

37. Chao-Chi Shan and Jeffrey M. Stonecash, "Legislative Resources and Electoral Margins: New York State Senate, 1950–1990," *Legislative Studies Quarterly* 19 (February 1994): 79–93.

38. Quoted in Rob Gurwitt, "Legislatures: The Face of Change," *Governing* (February 1993): 32.

39. Keith E. Hamm, Ronald D. Hedlund, and R. Bruce Anderson, "Political Parties in State Legislatures," in *Encyclopedia of the American Legislative System* II, ed. Joel H. Silbey (New York: Scribner's, 1994): 947–981; Patterson, "Legislative Politics in Ohio," 250.

40. Gary Moncrief, Joel A. Thompson, and Karl T. Kurtz, "The Old Statehouse Ain't What She Used to Be: Veteran State Legislators' Perceptions of Institutional Change" (paper prepared for delivery at the 1993 Annual Meeting of the American Political Science Association, Washington, D.C., September 2–5, 1993).

41. Burdett A. Loomis, *Time, Politics and Policies: A Legislative Year* (Lawrence: University of Kansas Press, 1994), 54–55.

42. Royce Hanson, *Tribune of the People* (Minneapolis: University of Minnesota Press, 1989), 96.

43. Sherry Bebitch Jeffe, "For Legislative Staff, Policy Takes a Back Seat to Politics," *California Journal* (January 1987): 42.

44. *Washington Post*, February 27, 1995.

45. Quoted in Sharon Randall, "Out of Power: Struggling for Influence," *State Legislatures* (February 1990): 22.

46. Hanson, *Tribune of the People*, 66.

47. Nelson W. Polsby, "The Institutionalization of the U.S. House of Representatives," *American Political Science Review* 62 (March 1968): 144–168.

48. Peverill Squire, "The Theory of Legislative Institutionalization and the California Assembly," *Journal of Politics* 54 (November 1992): 1026–1054.

49. Breaux and Jewell, "Winning Big," 94–95; Malcolm E. Jewell and David Breaux, "The Effect of Incumbency on State Legislative Elections," *Legislative Studies Quarterly* 13 (November 1988): 499–501.

50. Glenn Sussman, Nicholas P. Lovrich, Byran W. Daynes, and Jonathan P. West, "Term Limits and State Legislatures," in *Extension of Remarks*, ed. Lawrence C. Dodd (July 1994), 3.

51. Elizabeth Capell, "The Impact of Term Limits: Early Returns from California," in *Extension of Remarks*, 4, 7, 9.

52. E. Lee Bernick and Charles W. Wiggins, "Legislative Norms in Eleven States," *Legislative Studies Quarterly* 8 (May 1983): 191–200.

53. If at least 70 percent responded in the expected direction, and if the item received either a high or a low score in the expected direction on a five-point scale, a norm was said to exist.

54. Unfortunately, this question combines two separate concepts—that of attending to norms generally and that of apprenticeship.

55. Moncrief, Thompson, and Kurtz, "The Old Statehouse Ain't What She Used to Be."

56. Hanson, *Tribune of the People*, 120.

57. Bryant, *Quantum Politics*, 128.

58. Ehrenhalt, *The United States of Ambition*.

59. Lee Leonard, in Columbus *Dispatch*, December 12, 1994.

60. Bryant, *Quantum Politics*, 138.

61. Ehrenhalt, *The United States of Ambition*, 34–35.

62. Laureen Lazarovici, "The Rise of the Wind-makers," *California Journal* (June 1995): 16.

63. Alan Rosenthal, *The Third House: Lobbyists and Lobbying in the States* (Washington, D.C.: CQ Press, 1993), 112–128.

64. See John McFarland, "Protestant Reformers Who Thought Politics Was Sin," *California Journal* (October 1984): 388, Editors' Note.

65. Thomas E. Cronin and Robert D. Loevy, *Colorado Politics and Government* (Lincoln: University of Nebraska Press, 1993), 186–190.

66. William Schneider, " 'Off with Their Heads?'," *The American Enterprise* (July/August 1992): 32.

67. McBeath and Morehouse, *Alaska Politics and Government*, 121.

68. Calvert, "Reform, Representation, and Accountability," 2–3.

69. Ibid., 3.

70. Charles M. Price, "The Guillotine Comes to California: Term-Limits Politics in the Golden State," in *Limiting Legislative Terms*, ed. Gerald Benjamin and Michael J. Malbin (Washington, D.C.: CQ Press, 1992), 118–119.

71. Alan Rosenthal, *Drawing the Line: Legislative Ethics in the States*, (Lincoln: University of Nebraska Press, forthcoming 1996), Ch. 7.

72. Michael Wines, *New York Times*, October 16, 1994.

73. Martin Linsky, "Legislatures and the Press: The Problem of Image and Attitudes," *Journal of State Government* 59 (Spring 1986): 41.

74. David S. Broder, "Legislatures under Siege," reprinted in *State Legislatures* (July 1991), 21.

7

Supreme Courts in the Policy Process

Lawrence Baum

S tate supreme courts are far less visible than governors and legislatures, but they rule on a wide range of important issues. Supreme courts[1] adjudicate disputes over the apportionment of legislatures and the veto powers of governors. They help to allocate power over the governance of corporations and public schools. Their decisions define the responsibilities of employers toward employees, drivers toward pedestrians.

Supreme courts address such issues within a broad context. Their interpretations of law are influenced by other institutions in government and politics. And their interpretations spur reactions by the same institutions: a supreme court decision is not necessarily the final word on a legal issue.

While the policies of supreme courts have always been a complex mix of competing trends, the most powerful theme in those policies during the 1970s and 1980s was a liberalism on civil liberties and economic issues. Inevitably, groups that favored more conservative policies reacted against those policies. These groups sought action in other forums to overturn unfavorable decisions as well as change in the policies of supreme courts themselves.

In the 1990s, those efforts have achieved considerable success. As conservative political forces have become more powerful in state and national politics, other institutions are more willing to attack liberal lines of policy in state supreme courts. And the center of ideological gravity in state supreme court policy has shifted to the right. This chapter focuses on these developments and their implications for an understanding of state politics.

State Supreme Courts in the Policy Process

Areas of Activity

In legal terms, state supreme courts take action of three general types. The first is interpretation of state statutes in such fields as criminal law, labor relations, and environmental protection. Through its interpretations, a supreme court shapes a statute's meaning and thus its practical impact. For example, in 1994 New York's highest court held that an employee could receive workers' compensation benefits for aggravation of asthma due to second-hand cigarette smoke in her workplace. In 1995 the Kansas supreme court ruled that the Boy Scouts of America was not a "public accommodation," so the organization was not covered by a Kansas law against discrimination. And in

1995 the Arkansas Supreme Court ruled that a Wal-Mart store's practice of selling some items below its own cost was not an attempt to destroy competition and thus did not violate state law.[2]

Second, state supreme courts are involved in the development and interpretation of the "common law." In certain areas of the law, basic legal rules have been established almost entirely through state court decisions rather than statutes. Even though legislatures hold the power to make the rules themselves, they largely defer to the courts. The most important common law areas are property law, which covers the rules governing ownership and transfer of property; contract law, which covers the rules for the enforcement of contracts; and tort law, which in most cases concerns liability for wrongful acts causing property damage, personal injuries, or death.

While legislatures today play a more active role in the common law fields, courts remain the primary decision makers. Indiana's chief justice noted in 1991 that the Indiana statutes had "grown to more than 12,000 pages," but "subjects like torts, contracts, landlord/tenant, and employment are still governed substantially by common law." [3]

Finally, state supreme courts interpret the federal and state constitutions. Their interpretations of the federal Constitution are subject to review by the U.S. Supreme Court. In contrast, state supreme courts are the ultimate interpreters of their own state constitutions. Federal courts must accept the meaning of state constitutional provisions and of state statutes, as determined by a state's highest court. This role allows supreme courts to address such issues as the division of legal power between governors and legislatures, the balance between free speech and other values, and the obligation of state taxpayers to fund public schools.

Variable Roles

As policy makers, state supreme courts change a good deal over time and differ considerably from one another. This variation falls primarily along two dimensions: the importance of the policies they make and the substance of those policies. The importance of court policies is often analyzed in terms of activism, a complex and multifaceted concept.[4] As used here, the term refers to the making of policies that have a potentially powerful impact, especially when the court departs from existing judicial doctrines or when it directly challenges the policies of other institutions. Departures from existing doctrines are clearest when a court overturns its own precedents. Challenges to other institutions are clearest when a court rules that a statute is unconstitutional. Such rulings also illustrate differences in activism: the frequency with which state supreme courts overturn state statutes has varied considerably among the states and over time.[5]

Activism aside, courts differ in the positions they take on legal issues. Most of these differences can be summarized in terms of the liberal-conservative spectrum. A liberal court generally favors the interests of "economic underdogs" and those who seek legal protection for their civil liberties, while a conservative court is less sympathetic to those interests. On this dimension, too, the state supreme courts have varied a good deal.

Relationships with Other Policy Makers

State supreme courts are part of a larger policy-making system, and they are connected to other policy makers in several ways. Like other state institutions, supreme courts operate in the context of federalism, both "vertical" (the federal-state relationship) and "horizontal" (relationships among states).[6]

Their primary vertical relationship is with the U.S. Supreme Court. If a state supreme court rules on an issue of federal law, the losing litigant can ask the U.S. Supreme Court to consider the case. Because the Supreme Court is the ultimate interpreter of the U.S. Constitution and federal statutes, state judges are obliged to follow those interpretations whenever they are relevant to a case in their own court. In this way, the Supreme Court influences the content of state supreme court decisions. At the same time, state supreme courts have some leeway in how they apply Supreme Court rulings to situations within their own states, and their use of this leeway shapes the ultimate impact of those rulings. The Supreme Court and state supreme courts also influence each other's agendas with their decisions and their policy choices.

Another vertical relationship is with Congress. State courts sometimes interpret federal statutes. More important, Congress can preempt state law where the Constitution gives it the power to act. To take one example, Congress can use its broad power to regulate interstate commerce as a means to overturn state supreme court rulings on issues related to commerce.

Horizontally, a state supreme court is parallel to supreme courts in other states, courts that often face similar legal and policy issues. Not surprisingly, state supreme courts provide policy cues to each other. While no court is obliged to adopt the rulings of courts in other states, judges often choose to follow specific initiatives of other supreme courts and broader trends in state courts across the nation.

Within its own state, a supreme court operates alongside the state legislative and executive branches. Along with its role as interpreter of statutes, a state supreme court also holds the power to invalidate statutes on constitutional grounds and to invalidate action by the executive branch on the ground that it is inconsistent with a statutory or constitutional provision. For their part, the other branches hold legal power over the state courts on matters ranging from jurisdiction to budgets, and this power gives them influence over the courts. They can also adopt statutes to modify or overturn state court decisions on statutory or common law decisions, and they can initiate constitutional amendments to overturn decisions interpreting the state constitution.

The electorate also affects the state supreme court. Voters hold the power to accept or reject proposed constitutional amendments, and in about half the states they can adopt amendments on their own through the initiative process.

Some amendments are directed at judicial policies. In most states voters select supreme court justices through partisan or nonpartisan elections, and in many others they vote on whether to retain supreme court justices who were initially selected by a nominating commission and the governor. Altogether, judges in about three-quarters of the states face the voters.[7]

Interest groups help to forge links between state supreme courts and other institutions. Disappointed by the outcome in one institution, a group often turns to another for redress. Some litigants who are unhappy with state supreme court decisions seek to have the U.S. Supreme Court consider their case. There are also a great many political "appeals." Groups go to court to challenge state statutes or actions by the executive branch. And groups whose interests are injured by supreme court decisions can go to the legislature, the voters, or the federal government to secure more favorable action.

The Liberal Trend

Change in State Supreme Court Policies

For most of the nation's history, the policies of state supreme courts were more conservative than liberal. On economic issues, conservatism meant support for business interests over the interests of competing groups such as employees and consumers. In civil liberties, conservatism meant narrow interpretation of legal protections for individual liberties. Of course, a great many decisions diverged from this conservative stance, but they were exceptions to the general pattern.[8]

In comparison with this historical pattern, between the 1950s and the 1980s state supreme courts as a whole took relatively liberal positions on legal issues. This ideological shift was most evident in two areas: tort law and civil liberties.

Tort Law. In tort law, most supreme courts in the nineteenth century adopted basic rules that limited legal liability for property damage, injuries, and death.[9] For example, the fellow servant rule relieved employers of responsibility for injuries caused by the conduct of fellow employees. Under the contributory negligence rule, an injured party who bore any share of the fault for the injury could not recover damages from someone who was primarily at fault.

Beginning in the first half of the twentieth century, and accelerating in the 1950s, this direction of tort policy was largely reversed.[10] On issue after issue, supreme courts eliminated traditional doctrines that limited tort liability, replacing them with doctrines that favored plaintiffs (those seeking compensation for losses) over defendants (those allegedly responsible for damage or injuries). Every state participated in this shift to some degree, and most changed their traditional doctrines in major ways.

The range of issues involved in the reversal of traditional doctrines is impressive. And in undertaking these changes, courts frequently had to overturn well-established legal principles. When the South Carolina Supreme Court in 1985 abolished the immunity of state and local governments from lawsuits, it overruled at least 118 of its past decisions, handed down from 1820 through 1984.[11]

Civil Liberties. During the 1950s and 1960s, the U.S. Supreme Court gave unprecedented support to civil liberties. It broadened the scope of legal protection for freedom of expression, expanded the civil rights of racial minority groups, and established a variety of new protections for criminal defendants. In this period, not all state supreme courts supported the positions of the U.S. Supreme Court. While state courts could not legally reject the Supreme Court's interpretations of the federal Constitution, some weakened the Court's impact through narrow interpretations of its decisions or even evaded the Court's rulings altogether. Such opposition was particularly strong on issues of racial equality, as some southern supreme courts worked to maintain the status quo of segregation.[12]

When the Burger and Rehnquist courts later began to interpret federal protections of civil liberties more narrowly, some state supreme courts responded by adopting expansive interpretations of their own constitutions—holding that state constitutions protect rights to a greater degree than the U.S. Constitution. State courts always were free to do so, provided that the rights they established did not conflict with federal rights. But such action first became common during the Burger Court. The number of decisions establishing independent state rights grew enormously from the early 1970s on.[13]

By no means have all supreme courts participated in this development. Most courts still rely primarily on the U.S. Constitution and Supreme Court decisions in their rulings on civil liberties.[14] Others have turned to their state constitutions, but usually to interpret them as providing only those protections guaranteed by the federal Constitution. Those supreme courts that make frequent use of their constitutions to protect liberties are relatively small in number and are concentrated in the West and Northeast.[15]

Overall, state supreme courts use state constitutions to expand civil liberties in only a distinct minority of the cases that allow them to do so.[16] But the number of such rulings is high enough to constitute a major development. Each year, there is a substantial list of cases in which state supreme courts establish protections for civil liberties on the basis of their own constitutions, on issues ranging from gender equality to free speech in private shopping malls.[17]

Sources of the Liberal Trend

What accounts for the liberal trend in state supreme courts, this departure from the historical pattern? Several interrelated conditions have played a part in creating and sustaining this trend.

One condition is change in social and political attitudes within the judiciary. In tort law, state supreme court policies reflect changes in societal views about accidents and injuries; during the twentieth century, people increasingly accepted the premise that those who suffer serious losses should be compensated. Reinforced by the increasing availability of insurance to pay court judgments against defendants, this feeling led to greater sympathy for individuals who seek compensation through the courts. One observer described the result as "a change in the ideology that courts bring to tort cases." [18]

In civil liberties, the Warren Court helped to reshape lawyers' thinking by showing that protection of civil liberties could be an appropriate role for the courts. As judges who received their legal training in the 1960s joined the state supreme courts, many brought with them an expectation that the courts should play such a role. As Justice Christine Durham of Utah said,

> most of us who sit on state supreme courts, and most of the lawyers who appear before us, were educated during a generation of expansivist, creative, and enormously "generative" thinking on the subject of the federal constitution and in the context of civil liberties. We saw in the Warren Court era an enormous and impressive reshaping of our attitudes and our assumptions about what the constitution meant for individual liberties in the U.S.[19]

The social composition of state supreme courts also changed,[20] and some of the changes helped to foster a different set of collective attitudes. The proportion of justices with law school training grew considerably in the twentieth century. The number of white Protestant men declined, as did the number of people from economically comfortable backgrounds. Each of these changes has had an impact on the collective thinking of state supreme courts. One specific change relevant to civil liberties is the declining presence of criminal prosecutors: in the 1960s, about half of all justices had served as prosecutors, while in 1980 only one-fifth had served in that capacity.[21]

A second condition is changes in legal services and interest group activity. People with civil liberties claims frequently had difficulty bringing those claims to and through the court system. But the increasing availability of lawyers to people with low incomes and the growth of interest groups concerned with civil liberties facilitated litigation in which people alleged violations of their individual rights.

Finally, policy developments within the judiciary had an impact. As state supreme courts take cues from each other, a certain momentum can develop: if a doctrine has been adopted in a number of states, judges may come to view it as the accepted approach to a particular issue, and its widespread acceptance influences additional courts to adopt it.

After World War II, liberal innovations in tort law benefited from this kind of momentum. Improvements in communication increased judges' awareness of developments in other supreme courts, and their opinions often revealed a desire to follow a trend in tort doctrines. Thus, the general movement of state courts toward support for tort plaintiffs exerted considerable influence on judges who did not want to be left behind.

In civil liberties, state supreme courts have been spurred by the growing conservatism at the federal level. This development has created an opportunity for state judges to assert their independence from the U.S. Supreme Court by establishing civil liberties protections based on state constitutions. For those judges who favored strong protections of liberties, the opportunity was quite attractive. And civil liberties groups such as the American Civil Liberties Union began to transfer their litigation activity to the state level, thereby giving state courts more opportunities to expand liberties.

Political scientist Richard P. Nathan has noted a cyclical pattern in American history, a tendency for state governments to play their most active and innovative roles during periods of conservatism in the national government.[22] More specifically, Nathan and Martha Derthick have argued that "the Burger Court was to the judicial system what the Reagan Administration has been to the Presidency: a conservatizing force that deflected liberal effort to the state level."[23] State supreme court justices who participated in the broadening of rights wrote with evident pride about their courts' filling the vacuum left by the U.S. Supreme Court and giving more life to state courts and state constitutions.[24]

Responses to the Liberal Trend

Like other developments in state supreme courts, the liberal trends in torts and civil liberties evoked responses in other state institutions and the federal government. As we would expect, interest groups have done much to spur those responses.

Because they can overturn common law decisions with new statutes, state legislatures are attractive targets for groups representing tort defendants. Legislatures did much to reinforce the pro-plaintiff trend in state courts, because the same changes in social thinking that influenced judges affected legislators. In recent years, however, defendant groups have built on the sympathy of most state legislators for business interests by raising fears about the social and economic costs of pro-plaintiff doctrines. They have won some important legislative victories, particularly in medical malpractice.

But the success of defendant groups has been limited by the strong lobbying of groups representing plaintiffs. As a result, defendant groups have worked in other forums as well. The most important are Congress, which can preempt state tort rules, and the electorate, which can override judicial doctrines directly and change a court's thinking by electing new judges. Defendant groups have had some success with voters. And after these groups made little headway in Congress for several years, in 1995 both houses passed bills limiting the amounts of money that could be awarded to plaintiffs under some circumstances.

Most judicial action to expand civil liberties is unpopular among state legislators, but the legislature is in a weaker legal position in civil liberties than in torts. Decisions that find new rights in state constitutions generally can be overturned only through the cumbersome process of amending constitutions. As a result, legislative action has been limited to a few proposals for constitutional amendments. But legislators do have powers over courts as institutions and over their judges. For example, the New Jersey legislature limited the state courts' jurisdiction in an area over which the two branches were in conflict. In another case, it confirmed the chief justice of its supreme court for a new term only after legislators had publicly criticized him for his court's activism.

As in tort law, those who oppose the liberal policies of some supreme courts on civil liberties have turned to the federal government and to the voters. The U.S. Supreme Court has created some procedural difficulties for state courts that attempt to establish independent rights under state constitutions, but it has not—and cannot—eliminate their power to do so. In a few instances, voters have overridden unpopular civil liberties decisions by adopting initiatives and referendums or defeating judges who are identified with those decisions.

Like supreme court decisions themselves, reactions to those decisions by other institutions may not settle the issues in question. In some areas, a long and complex interaction has taken place between supreme courts and other policy makers over matters on which there remains disagreement. Such interactions underline the interdependence of state supreme courts and other participants in the policy-making process.

Specific Areas in Civil Liberties and Torts

Because it is difficult to generalize about fields as broad as civil liberties and torts, it will be useful to look closely at some specific areas within those fields. The areas examined—product liability, criminal procedure, and school finance—illustrate some patterns in the work of state supreme courts and in their interactions with other policy makers.

Product Liability

Among the most important areas of tort law is product liability, which concerns liability for damage caused by defective products. As the twentieth century began, two doctrines severely limited the ability of consumers to sue manufacturers for allegedly defective products. The privity rule prohibited suits against any party except the business that had sold a product directly to the consumer; the negligence rule required consumers to prove negligence in the manufacture of a defective product.

From 1913 on, state supreme courts created exceptions to these rules for food and drink and for inherently dangerous products. After World War II, more courts adopted these exceptions. Then they began to overthrow the rules themselves. The first major steps were taken by the supreme courts of Michigan in 1958 and New Jersey in 1960.[25] In a 1963 decision, the California Supreme Court went even further in eliminating the privity and negligence requirements. The California court held that a manufacturer was strictly liable, whether or not proved negligent, for damages caused by defective products.[26]

The strict liability rule was a radical departure from traditional tort rules; in effect, it replaced one legal framework with another. Yet other states quickly jumped on the bandwagon. Within four years, courts in a dozen other states had followed California's lead, and by 1976 thirty-seven states had established strict liability by judicial decision. Today, all but a few states operate under the strict liability rule. The speedy and overwhelming acceptance of this rule underlines the strength of the liberal wave in tort law.

The pro-plaintiff trend in product liability did not end with the adoption of strict liability.[27] A variety of other doctrines favoring injured parties gained acceptance in state supreme courts. In the 1970s and early 1980s, for example, state courts greatly expanded the liability of manufacturers for defective product designs.

Inevitably, groups whose interests were injured by this trend sought to reverse it. Manufacturers are the primary defendants in product liability cases. In seeking more favorable policies they have worked with several other tort defendant groups, including other business interests, the medical community, and insurance companies.

The heart of this campaign has been an effort to convince judges, other policy makers, and the general public that pro-plaintiff trends in tort law have had damaging consequences. Through widespread advertising and other means, defendant groups seek to connect judicial doctrines favoring plaintiffs with what they depict as a burgeoning of lawsuits. They argue that such lawsuits have a variety of negative results, ranging from decisions by manufacturers not to produce desirable products to a general weakening of American economic competitiveness.

One purpose of this campaign is to influence the attitudes of citizens and thus potential jurors in product liability cases. Whether or not the campaign is valid, there is evidence that juries have lately become less favorable to plaintiffs in such cases. According to one analysis, the rate of success for defendants in New York cases rose from 51 percent in the period 1981–1987 to 62 percent in the period 1988–1994.[28]

Defendant groups have taken more direct action to change legal doctrines. One target is the supreme courts themselves. In addition to their arguments in court, business groups and their allies have sought to influence the membership of supreme courts by contributing money to judicial candidates. In response, groups that favor the interests of plaintiffs have entered the electoral process as well. The most important of these groups are the lawyers who represent tort plaintiffs, usually called "trial lawyers." Groups concerned with product liability and other tort law issues often limit themselves to funding of candidates whom they perceive as favorable to their interests. But in Texas, where the supreme court hears only civil cases, tort issues have become the centerpieces of public debate in supreme court elections as well as the source of massive funding for candidates.[29]

Groups on both sides of product liability and other tort issues were particularly prominent in judicial elections in 1994. They battled in several states, including Michigan, Mississippi, North Carolina, Texas, and Washington. The most heated battles were over the Alabama Supreme Court, perceived by business groups as hostile to their positions. In particular, those groups sought to defeat chief justice Sonny Hornsby; trial lawyers, however, worked for his reelection.[30] The result of that contest was so close that it was resolved with a narrow defeat for Hornsby almost a year after the 1994 election.

Business groups have achieved major successes as a result of their efforts. In 1986, financial contributions by defendant groups helped to defeat liberal justices in California and Ohio, and those supreme courts then adopted more conservative positions in tort law. Recent elections have made the Texas Supreme Court more conservative as well. But this shift in policy has not been limited to states where liberal justices were replaced by conservatives. Since the early 1980s, a broader change has taken place in state supreme court policies on product liability. This new trend is summarized well by legal scholars James A. Henderson, Jr., and Theodore Eisenberg:

> Courts once favorably inclined to break new ground and to discard doctrine blocking recoveries [of compensation for injuries] now are inclined to reflect more cautiously on the implications of their decisions. Courts continue to break new ground and discard doctrine in ways that favor plaintiffs. But they are increasingly apt to change the law to preclude liability rather than to promote it.[31]

Perhaps a slowing of the long pro-plaintiff trend was inevitable. But its occurrence in recent years seems to reflect the efforts of defendant groups to turn the tide. Some judges may have reassessed their positions in light of legislative actions and the activities of pro-defendant groups in judicial elections. More important, however, is the apparent effectiveness of the campaign to connect pro-plaintiff doctrines with a "liability crisis" and economic harm. Working in court systems with growing caseloads, judges may be receptive to arguments that litigation has become too common, that doctrines favoring injured parties have gone too far. In a new climate of opinion, many supreme courts seem to have adopted a new perspective on product liability.

Groups supporting the interests of defendants in product liability law have gone beyond the courts to legislatures, seeking to overturn unfavorable judicial doctrines through statutes. They have achieved considerable success in this effort. In the latter half of the 1980s, according to one count, legislatures in forty-one states adopted at least some of the product liability rules sought by manufacturers; legislatures continue to enact such legislation in the 1990s.[32] Many legislatures have established additional legal defenses in suits for product liability. One example is provisions holding that a manufacturer is not liable if the product in question adhered to the "state of the art" at the time it was made. Another common action is to establish direct or indirect limits on the amount of monetary damages that plaintiffs can win under certain circumstances.

The level of legislative success for defendant interests would have been even greater except for increasingly strong counterpressure from trial lawyers, often working alongside consumer groups and labor unions. The battle has become a ferocious one. Because of the ideological tenor of tort issues, Republican gains in the 1994 state legislative elections across the country strengthened defendant interests and thus increased the pressure for legislation on product liability. In 1995 Illinois passed a statute with several provisions that manufacturers had sought, and several other legislatures adopted new rules favoring defendants.[33]

Not surprisingly, business groups also turned to national policy makers. They have gone to the Supreme Court on the issue of punitive damages, which can be awarded to a plaintiff to punish a defendant for egregious conduct that resulted in an injury. In a series of cases, individual businesses supported by broader business groups argued that high punitive damages awards violate provisions of the U.S. Constitution. The Court's decisions have been mixed but largely unfavorable to these arguments.[34]

For the past two decades business groups have sought more comprehensive relief from Congress in the form of federal rules that would limit liability for defective products in both federal and state cases. Their efforts were strengthened by support from the Reagan and Bush administrations, but the critical step was election of Republican majorities to both houses of Congress in 1994. The "Contract with America" supported by Republican candidates for the House of Representatives in 1994 included "reform of product liability laws" through national legislation.[35] The House quickly passed a bill that limited liability in several ways, including a prohibition of most lawsuits more than fifteen years after a product is sold and limits on the awarding of punitive damages. The Senate later passed a narrower bill, and late in 1995 the differences between the two remained to be worked out in a conference committee.

Product liability illustrates the workings of a governmental system in which policy is made by multiple institutions at multiple levels. While contention over legal rules traditionally focused on state courts, today that contention occurs in state legislatures and Congress as well. Expansion of the battle over product liability has been facilitated by the economic resources of defendant groups, resources that have enabled them to fight in several arenas at once.

Criminal Procedure

State supreme courts have been most active in protecting civil liberties on issues of criminal procedure. One reason is that the Burger Court narrowed rights most quickly and most decisively in this area, providing state courts with a large void to fill if they wished. And the steady flow of criminal cases to state supreme courts provides frequent opportunities for those courts to act, while they see fewer cases in other areas of civil liberties.

During the Warren Court era, many state supreme court justices expressed a clear distaste for defendants' rights.[36] That distaste did not disappear when the Burger Court began to narrow those rights, and today most supreme courts seem to share the Rehnquist Court's conservatism on criminal procedure. But a number of supreme courts have more liberal collective views on these issues, and they have used their constitutions to resist the conservative trend at the national level.

A study by Barry Latzer charted the movement to broaden defendants' rights under state constitutions.[37] Latzer identified 232 decisions between the late 1960s and 1989 in which a state supreme court had rejected U.S. Supreme Court doctrines by finding broader protections of rights in their own constitutions. Those 232 decisions, made by forty-four state supreme courts, constitute a great deal of rights expansion. But twice as many decisions were handed down in which supreme courts interpreted their constitutions to provide no broader protections. And in most supreme courts, the usual practice was to adopt these narrow interpretations of their constitutions or not to look for rights in their constitutions at all.

Expansive interpretations of state constitutions have occurred most often in search and seizure, where the Supreme Court has narrowed rights to the greatest extent; state courts have overridden several of the Court's rulings through their state constitutions. The most important is the Court's 1984 decision establishing a "good faith" exception to the rule that excludes introduction of evidence seized on the basis of a faulty search warrant.[38] At least nine supreme courts have rejected the good faith exception in interpreting their own constitutions.[39] On other search and seizure issues, to take two examples, the Vermont Supreme Court in 1991 limited warrantless searches of cars, and the Minnesota Supreme Court in 1994 restricted police roadblocks to detect drunk driving.[40]

State courts have expanded rights in several other areas of criminal procedure. For instance, a 1992 Michigan decision struck down a mandatory life sentence for possession of large amounts of cocaine, and a 1994 Hawaii decision held that coercion by a private party could make a suspect's confession inadmissible as evidence.[41] And on the most contentious issue in criminal justice, the supreme courts of California, Colorado, Massachusetts, and Oregon all struck down the death penalty. But on the death penalty, as on most other issues, the courts expanding defendants' rights instead of adopting the Supreme Court's narrower position have been in the minority.

In an era of limited sympathy for criminal defendants, rulings that favor defendants often produce negative reactions. Legislators and governors criticize some liberal court decisions and initiate efforts to overturn them. But such overturnings generally require constitutional amendments, so that voters are the critical policy makers—deciding whether to ratify amendments proposed by the legislature or, in states that allow initiative measures, deciding whether to adopt amendments proposed by petition. Occasionally, voters have taken such action. Massachusetts voters reestablished the death penalty in 1982. Florida in 1982 and Pennsylvania in 1984 overturned state supreme court decisions to broaden the range of evidence that could be used against defendants.[42]

Voters also can remove judges who vote for expansions of defendants' rights. Rules of legal ethics nearly preclude discussion of policy issues by candidates. But in recent years the conservative views of most voters on criminal justice have encouraged many judicial candidates (or their supporters, who have more freedom to raise policy matters) to use such issues explicitly or implicitly in campaigns. They do so most often to criticize incumbents as unduly sympathetic to defendants.

Several such campaigns have occurred at the supreme court level, in states such as Louisiana, North Carolina, Oklahoma, and Wisconsin. Most often, these campaigns focus on capital punishment, with allegations that a justice has voted too often to overturn death sentences. Whether or not these attacks on incumbents are successful, they may influence the policy choices of other judges.[43] In a 1995 opinion, Justice John Paul Stevens of the U.S. Supreme Court wrote of "a political climate in which judges who covet higher office—or who merely wish to remain judges—must constantly profess their fealty to the death penalty."[44]

California voters have reacted strongly against expansions of defendants' rights. The California Supreme Court was the court that most frequently found independent protections for defendants in its state constitution, and this stance aroused considerable public wrath. The court's 1972 decision striking down the death penalty was overturned by a public vote later the same year, and in 1982 and 1990 the voters approved initiative measures that cut back on several defendants' rights under the state constitution.

After the California death penalty was restored, for many years the supreme court reversed the great majority of death sentences that it reviewed. The court's liberal justices faced growing criticism, and in 1986 capital punishment was the centerpiece of a heavily financed and well-publicized electoral campaign against Chief Justice Rose Bird and two of her colleagues. (In California, the public votes "yes" or "no" on retention of appellate judges in office.) Ultimately, all three justices were defeated—the first three appellate judges in California who failed to win the majority necessary to retain their positions.

In defeating the three justices, the majority of voters achieved the impact that they wanted. Appointments by a Republican governor made the court considerably more conservative, and it changed direction on criminal procedure issues.[45] Most notably, it affirmed the preponderance of death sentences that it reviewed. One newspaper editorial, citing what its writer regarded as highly questionable affirmances, accused the court of "pandering to public opinion."[46] Whether or not that accusation was justified, it underlines the potential influence of the public—and of the environment in general—on a supreme court's policies.

School Finance

Traditionally, public schools in the United States have been financed primarily by local property taxes.[47] As a result, the property values in a district strongly influence the level of funding for its schools. A district with limited wealth may tax its citizens at a high rate but produce considerably less funding per student than a wealthier district that has lower tax rates. State funding of public education grew over the years, and this funding typically reduced financial disparities among school districts. But major disparities remained, and state action to reduce them further was politically impossible.

In 1971 the California Supreme Court held that funding disparities in that state violated the equal protection guarantees in both the federal and state constitutions.[48] The decision helped spur the filing of similar lawsuits in most other states. But in 1973 the U.S. Supreme Court held that educational funding disparities in Texas did not violate the federal equal protection clause, thereby closing off challenges to state funding systems under the U.S. Constitution.[49] In response, litigants took their challenges to state courts under state constitutional provisions, primarily guarantees of equal protection. Several supreme courts struck down state funding systems, while about twice as many upheld them.

Since 1989 there has been a new wave of challenges to school funding systems, reaching the great majority of states. These challenges have come primarily under state constitutional provisions that make state governments responsible for providing education to their people. In the cases decided by supreme courts so far, the challenges have been successful more often than not. Altogether, since 1971 supreme courts in fourteen states have held their funding systems to be unconstitutional at least once (including three courts that switched positions on this issue over time), while fourteen other supreme courts have consistently upheld their states' systems. As the new wave of challenges continues, several other supreme courts are likely to address this issue in the next few years.

Decisions striking down systems of school funding require legislative implementation; state legislatures must adopt new systems to overcome inequalities among districts. Some state governments have acted readily to comply with the requirements of supreme court decisions. In Kentucky, for example, the legislature responded to a 1989 supreme court decision by providing major new funding for education. Kentucky legislators may have welcomed the decision as an impetus for improvement of the state's education system.[50]

Frequently, however, legislatures have balked at carrying out a supreme court's mandate. Perhaps the most striking example is New Jersey. The state's legislature provided funding to carry out a 1973 decision only after three years and a supreme court order that closed the state's schools until the legislature acted.[51] Advocates for low-income districts argued that the legislative action still left the state short of full compliance with the supreme court's mandate, and in 1990 the court required a massive transfer of funds to low-income districts.[52] The state legislature acted to carry out the decision, but in 1994 the supreme court held that the legislative action was inadequate,[53] and the implementation process is continuing.

As the examples of Kentucky and New Jersey suggest, education funding issues can create a variety of relationships between courts and the other branches. Supreme court decisions may serve as catalysts for major changes in education systems; indeed, some legislatures have acted to modify their systems even before a lawsuit has reached its supreme court. Yet legislators often are reluctant to create new funding systems that require substantial spending in difficult fiscal times or that hurt the interests of property-rich areas. For this reason, there is likely to be growth in the number of states with explicit or implicit conflicts between the supreme court and the legislature.

Conclusion

State supreme courts rule on legal issues within a larger world of politics and policy making. There is no area of policy and no significant issue on which they act alone and unnoticed.

This situation is inevitable. Most fundamentally, it results from the basic structure of American government, in which power to make policy is shared between levels of government and among the branches at each level. In turn, that sharing of power encourages interest groups to "appeal" from one institution to another in their efforts to obtain favorable policy.

This is a particularly good time to view the relationship between state supreme courts and the rest of government and politics. The activism of supreme courts on issues in civil liberties and tort law has aroused a good deal of opposition as well as support, and in tort law the opponents and supporters include many of the major economic groups in the United States. As a result, there has been contention over supreme court policy in other branches of the state government as well as the federal government, and groups on both sides have sought to influence supreme courts themselves.

Relationships between state supreme courts and other institutions feature different issues and ideological lines in different eras. The recent liberal trend in supreme courts was at least unusual in the history of state courts, and it produced counterreactions from groups that typically had approved of state court policy. But we can expect complex reactions and counterreactions to supreme court policies in any era. In our system of government, it is inevitable that state supreme courts are one participant in a continuing process of policy development that sprawls across levels and branches of government.

Notes

Author's Note: The author thanks Joel Blumberg for research assistance on this chapter.
1. Throughout this chapter, the term *supreme court* will be used to refer to the highest court of each state. Most of these courts are known formally as supreme courts, but exceptions exist. For instance, in New York, the court called the supreme court is a lower court and the highest court is the court of appeals. The supreme courts of Texas and Oklahoma hear only civil cases; each state has a court of criminal appeals that is in effect its supreme court for criminal cases. Where Supreme Court is capitalized, without any state designation, it refers to the Supreme Court of the United States.
2. The decisions were, respectively, *Matter of Johannesen v. Department of Housing Preservation and Development*, 638 N.E.2d (New York 1994); *Seabourn v. Council*, 891 P.2d

385 (Kansas 1995); and *Wal-Mart Stores v. American Drugs Inc.*, 891 S.W.2d 30 (Arkansas 1995).

3. Randall T. Shepard, "Indiana Law, the Supreme Court, and a New Decade," *Indiana Law Review* 24 (1991): 502.

4. Bradley C. Canon, "A Framework for the Analysis of Judicial Activism," in *Supreme Court Activism and Restraint*, ed. Stephen C. Halpern and Charles M. Lamb (Lexington, Mass.: Lexington Books, 1982), 385–419.

5. Oliver Peter Field, *Judicial Review of Legislation in Ten Selected States* (Bloomington: Bureau of Government Research, Indiana University, 1943); and Craig Emmert, "Judicial Review in State Supreme Courts: Opportunity and Activism" (Paper delivered at the annual meeting of the Midwest Political Science Association, Chicago, April 8–10, 1988).

6. G. Alan Tarr and Mary Cornelia Aldis Porter, *State Supreme Courts in State and Nation* (New Haven: Yale University Press, 1988), 2.

7. Council of State Governments, *The Book of the States, 1994–1995* (Lexington, Ky.: Council of State Governments, 1994), 190–192.

8. See Stanton Wheeler, Bliss Cartwright, Robert A. Kagan, and Lawrence M. Friedman, "Do the 'Haves' Come Out Ahead? Winning and Losing in State Supreme Courts, 1870–1970," *Law and Society Review* 21 (1987): 403–445.

9. Lawrence M. Friedman, *Total Justice* (New York: Russell Sage, 1985), 53–60.

10. See Lawrence Baum and Bradley C. Canon, "State Supreme Courts as Activists: New Doctrines in the Law of Torts," in *State Supreme Courts: Policymakers in the Federal System*, ed. Mary Cornelia Porter and G. Alan Tarr (Westport, Conn.: Greenwood Press, 1982), 83–108.

11. *McCall v. Batson*, 329 S.E.2d 741 (South Carolina 1985).

12. Tarr and Porter, *State Supreme Courts in State and Nation*, 74–82.

13. Ronald K. L. Collins, Peter J. Galie, and John Kincaid, "State High Courts, State Constitutions, and Individual Rights Litigation since 1980: A Judicial Survey," *Publius* 16 (Summer 1986): 141–161.

14. On self-incrimination issues, one study found that fourteen states based all of their decisions on federal law; another seventeen based more than three-quarters of their decisions on federal law. Michael Esler, "State Supreme Court Commitment to State Law," *Judicature* 78 (July–August 1994): 25–32.

15. Collins, Galie, and Kincaid, "State High Courts, State Constitutions, and Individual Rights Litigation since 1980"; and G. Alan Tarr, "The Past and Future of the New Judicial Federalism," *Publius* 24 (Spring 1994): 75.

16. Tarr, "The Past and Future of the New Judicial Federalism," 73–79. In the field of privacy, to take one example, most cases in state supreme courts have been decided on the basis of the U.S. Constitution, and most rulings have rejected right-to-privacy claims. Gregory N. Flemming, David B. Holian, and Susan Gluck Mezey, "State Supreme Courts and the New Judicial Federalism: Privacy Decision Making, 1965–1992" (Paper delivered at the annual meeting of the Midwest Political Science Association, Chicago, April 15–17, 1993).

17. See the annual summaries of decisions interpreting state constitutions in the *Rutgers Law Journal*—e.g., "Developments in State Constitutional Law: 1993," *Rutgers Law Journal* 25 (Summer 1994): 999–1270; and "Developments in State Constitutional Law: 1992," *Rutgers Law Journal* 24 (Summer 1993): 1101–1456. The shopping mall cases illustrate the generalizations discussed in this paragraph. The development of state constitutional rights in this area is summarized in *New Jersey Coalition v. J.M.B. Realty Corp.*, 650 A.2d 757 (New Jersey 1994).

18. Peter H. Schuck, "The New Judicial Ideology of Tort Law," in *New Directions in Liability Law*, ed. Walter Olson (New York: Academy of Political Science, 1988), 6.

19. Lawrence Baum and David Frohnmayer, eds., *The Courts: Sharing and Separating Powers* (New Brunswick, N.J.: Eagleton Institute of Politics, Rutgers University, 1989), 17.

20. See Robert A. Kagan, Bobby D. Infelise, and Robert R. Detlefsen, "American State Supreme Court Justices, 1900–1970," *American Bar Foundation Research Journal*

(Spring 1984): 371–408; and Henry R. Glick and Craig F. Emmert, "Stability and Change: Characteristics of State Supreme Court Judges," *Judicature* 70 (August/September 1986): 107–112.

21. Glick and Emmert, "Stability and Change," 108.

22. Richard P. Nathan, "Federalism—The Great 'Composition,'" in *The New American Political System*, 2d ed., ed. Anthony King (Washington, D.C.: American Enterprise Institute for Public Policy Research, 1990), 231–261.

23. Richard P. Nathan and Martha Derthick, "Reagan's Legacy: A New Liberalism among the States," *New York Times*, December 18, 1987, A39.

24. See, for example, Robert F. Utter, "Freedom and Diversity in a Federal System: Perspectives on State Constitutions and the Washington Declaration of Rights," *University of Puget Sound Law Review* 7 (1984): 491–525.

25. *Spence v. Three Rivers Building and Masonry Supply Inc.*, 90 N.W.2d 873 (Michigan 1958); and *Henningsen v. Bloomfield Motors*, 161 A.2d 69 (New Jersey 1960). These decisions held that manufacturers make an implied warranty of their products' safety to the ultimate consumers of the products.

26. *Greenman v. Yuba Power Products*, 377 P.2d 897 (California 1963).

27. James A. Henderson, Jr., and Theodore Eisenberg, "The Quiet Revolution in Products Liability: An Empirical Study of Legal Change," *UCLA Law Review* 37 (February 1990): 483–488.

28. Russell F. Moran, "Juries Are Just Saying No," *New York Times*, January 16, 1995, A11.

29. See Anthony Champagne, "Judicial Reform in Texas," *Judicature* 72 (October/November 1988): 148–149; and Donald W. Jackson and James W. Riddlesperger, Jr., "Money and Politics in Judicial Elections: The 1988 Election of the Chief Justice of the Texas Supreme Court," *Judicature* 74 (December/January 1991): 184–189.

30. "Tort Reformers Focus on Judicial Elections in Six States," *Liability Week*, November 7, 1994.

31. Henderson and Eisenberg, "The Quiet Revolution in Products Liability," 498.

32. Linda Lipsen, "The Evolution of Products Liability as a Federal Policy Issue," in *Tort Law and the Public Interest*, ed. Peter H. Schuck (New York: W. W. Norton, 1991), 248; "Tort Revision," *National Law Journal*, December 26, 1994/January 2, 1995, C12.

33. Rick Pearson, "Legislation Limiting Damage Awards Clears the Senate and Heads to Edgar's Desk," *Chicago Tribune*, March 5, 1995, 2:3; and Carol McHugh Sanders, "Illinois Leaving Its Wake in Swift Current of Tort Law Changes," *Chicago Daily Law Bulletin*, April 22, 1995, 1, 10.

34. The most recent decisions are *TXO Production Corp. v. Alliance Resources Corp.*, 113 S. Ct. 2711 (1993), which held that punitive damages awards must be subject to appellate review; and *Honda Motor Co. v. Oberg*, 114 S. Ct. 2331 (1994), a complex decision that upheld a $10 million punitive damages award.

35. Joan Biskupic, "To Discourage Lawsuits, House GOP Would Preempt State Laws," *Washington Post*, December 15, 1994, A25.

36. Bradley C. Canon, "Organizational Contumacy in the Transmission of Judicial Policies: The Mapp, Escobedo, Miranda, and Gault Cases," *Villanova Law Review* 20 (November 1974): 50–79.

37. Barry Latzer, "The Hidden Conservatism of the State Court 'Revolution,'" *Judicature* 74 (December/January 1991): 190–197. See also Latzer, *State Constitutions and Criminal Justice* (Westport, Conn.: Greenwood Press, 1991).

38. *United States v. Leon*, 468 U.S. 897 (1984). The Court held that, if an officer who seizes evidence on the basis of a faulty search warrant reasonably believed that the warrant was valid, the evidence could be admitted in court.

39. See Leigh A. Morrissey, "State Courts Reject *Leon* on State Constitutional Grounds: A Defense of Reactive Rulings," *Vanderbilt Law Review* 47 (April 1994): 917–941; and *State v. Canelo*, 653 A.2d 1097 (New Hampshire 1995).

40. The decisions were, respectively, *State v. Savva*, 616 A.2d 774 (Vermont 1991); and *Ascher v. Commissioner of Public Safety*, 519 N.W.2d 183 (Minnesota 1994).

41. The Michigan decision was *People v. Bullock*, 485 N.W.2d 866 (Michigan 1992), which was in contrast with the Supreme Court's decision involving the same statute in *Harmelin v. Michigan*, 501 U.S. 957 (1991). The Hawaii decision was *State v. Bowe*, 881 P.2d 538 (Hawaii 1994), which was in contrast with the Supreme Court's decision in *Colorado v. Connelly*, 479 U.S. 157 (1986).

42. Janice C. May, "Constitutional Amendment and Revision Revisited," *Publius* 17 (Winter 1987): 175–176.

43. See Melinda Gann Hall, "Electoral Politics and Strategic Voting in State Supreme Courts," *Journal of Politics* 54 (May 1992): 427–446.

44. *Harris v. Alabama*, 115 S. Ct. 1031, 1039 (1995).

45. See Claire Cooper, "Making a Federal Case Out of It," *California Lawyer*, April 1993, 27–28; and John H. Culver, "The Transformation of the California Supreme Court" (Paper delivered at the annual meeting of the Western Political Science Association, Portland, Oregon, March 16–18, 1995).

46. "Death without Deliberation," *San Francisco Examiner*, February 17, 1991, A16. The trend in California is described and analyzed in Craig F. Emmert and Carol Ann Traut, "The California Supreme Court and the Death Penalty," *American Politics Quarterly* 22 (January 1994): 41–61.

47. This discussion of state school funding draws from Bill Swinford, "A Predictive Model of Decision Making in State Supreme Courts: The School Financing Cases," *American Politics Quarterly* 19 (July 1991): 336–352; Swinford, "Shedding the Doctrinal Security Blanket: How State Supreme Courts Interpret Their State Constitutions in the Shadow of *Rodriguez*," *Temple Law Review* 67 (1994): 981–1001; and William H. Thro, "Judicial Analysis During the Third Wave of School Finance Litigation: The Massachusetts Decision as a Model," *Boston College Law Review* 35 (May 1994): 597–617. For a discussion of other aspects of school funding, see chapter 9 in this book, by Margaret Goertz.

48. *Serrano v. Priest*, 487 P.2d 1241 (California 1971).

49. *San Antonio Independent School District v. Rodriguez*, 411 U.S. 1 (1973).

50. William Celis III, "Kentucky Begins Drive to Revitalize Its Schools," *New York Times*, September 26, 1990, B6.

51. Richard Lehne, *The Quest for Justice: The Politics of School Finance Reform* (New York: Longman, 1978). The decision was *Robinson v. Cahill*, 303 A.2d 273 (New Jersey 1973).

52. *Abbott v. Burke*, 575 A.2d 359 (New Jersey 1990).

53. *Abbott v. Burke*, 643 A.2d 575 (New Jersey 1994). See Jerry Gray, "New Jersey School Financing Ruling Is Seen as Push Toward More State Control," *New York Times*, July 14, 1994, A12.

8

Accountability Battles in State Administration
William T. Gormley, Jr.

S tate bureaucracies have paid a price for their growing importance, and that price is a loss of discretion. In recent years, state bureaucracies have become more permeable, more vulnerable, and more manipulable. They are subject to a growing number of controls, as governors, state legislators, state judges, presidents, members of Congress, federal bureaucrats, interest groups, and citizens all attempt to shape administrative rule making, rate making, and adjudication at the state level. Of equal significance, they are subject to tougher, more restrictive, and more coercive controls.

In other words, state bureaucracies have become more accountable for their actions. In a sense, this is both understandable and desirable. Even state bureaucrats concede the virtues of accountability, at least in theory. Yet accountability is a multidimensional concept. Increasingly, the question is not whether state bureaucracies shall be accountable but to whom. A related question is how accountability can best be structured to avoid damage to other important values, such as creativity and flexibility.

A variety of controls that limit the discretion of state bureaucracies recently has proliferated, primarily in the areas of legislative oversight, executive management, due process, and regulatory federalism. For example, "coercive controls" rely on coercion for bureaucratic performance, while "catalytic controls" may yield comparable progress with fewer adverse side-effects. The emergence of accountability battles pit competing claimants against one another, in bitter struggles over authority, with state bureaucracies as the ultimate prize. A key development in 1995 was strong pressure to shift control over shaping state programs and agencies from the federal government to the states' governors. As categorical grants and entitlements give way to block grants and discretionary spending, governors will acquire greater authority while the federal government cedes authority to the states.

The Proliferation of Controls

During the 1970s, 1980s, and into the 1990s, as state bureaucracies grew larger and more important, politicians, judges, and citizens strengthened their leverage over state bureaucracies by institutionalizing a wide variety of control techniques. Some of these techniques, such as sunset laws and ombudsmen, were new. Others, such as executive orders and conditions of aid, were old but not much utilized. Control techniques also differed in their directness, formality, durability, and coerciveness. However, they all shared a common purpose—to make state bureaucracies more accountable to other public officials or to the people.

Legislative Oversight

During the 1970s, state legislatures discovered oversight as a form of bureaucratic control. Legislative committees took an active interest in bureaucratic implementation or nonimplementation of state statutes and conducted hearings aimed at identifying and resolving problems. This became easier as the legislator's job became a full-time profession in most states and as legislative staffs became larger and more professional. More than their congressional counterparts, state legislators decided not to leave oversight to chance. Perhaps oversight needed an extra push at the state level. In any event, state legislatures established regular mechanisms for legislative review.

Following the lead of Colorado, approximately two-thirds of the state legislatures adopted sunset laws, which provide for the automatic expiration of agencies unless the state legislature acts affirmatively to renew them. Although the threat of extinction is far-fetched in the case of large agencies, the threat of review must be taken seriously by all agencies. The sunset review process is especially important for obscure agencies that might otherwise escape scrutiny by legislative committees.

In addition to sunset laws, many state legislatures substantially upgraded the quality of their legislative audit bureaus. Gradually, these organizations came to place greater emphasis on program evaluation and policy analysis, less emphasis on auditing and accounting. To ensure careful, well-crafted evaluations, state legislatures augmented the staffs assigned to these organizations.

Finally, the overwhelming majority of state legislatures provided for legislative review of administrative rules and regulations. In sixteen states, legislative vetoes enable the legislature to invalidate an administrative rule or regulation. Through the legislative veto process, state legislatures have exercised closer scrutiny of administrative rule making. The U.S. Supreme Court declared the legislative veto unconstitutional at the federal level,[1] and state courts have invalidated legislative vetoes in eight states.[2] Nevertheless, the legislative veto continues to be an important mechanism for legislative control in one-third of the states.

In thinking about legislative controls, a useful distinction can be made between inward-looking and outward-looking legislative changes. As political scientist Alan Rosenthal has observed, state legislatures have become more fragmented, more decentralized, and less cohesive in recent years. In some sense, this might be characterized as legislative decline. However, a fragmented legislature is not necessarily weaker in its dealings with other units of government, such as state bureaucracies. A highly fragmented legislature may provide more occasions for legislative oversight and more incentives for individual legislators to engage in oversight. Thus, as legislatures become weaker internally, they may become stronger externally. This is especially true of those forms of legislative control that do not require a legislative majority.

Executive Management

For years, governors have complained about the fragmented character of the executive branch. Many executive branch officials are elected or appointed to office for fixed terms that do not coincide with the governor's term. The number of state agencies, boards, and commissions can be overwhelming and disconcerting. Also, agencies have their own traditions and habits and may be reluctant to follow the priorities of a new governor. All of these factors have inhibited executive integration, coordination, and leadership.

During the 1970s, 1980s, and into the 1990s, many governors took steps to deal with these problems. Most governors spearheaded major reorganizations of the executive branch, striving for greater rationality and for a reduction in the number of boards and commissions. Minor reorganizations also were commonplace. In Minnesota, for example, five governors issued a total of 155 reorganization orders between 1970 and 1988.[3]

Governors also institutionalized cabinet meetings, subcabinet meetings, or both to secure greater coordination and integration. During the 1970s, approximately fourteen governors established a cabinet for the first time and approximately twenty-five governors established subcabinets to advise and coordinate in broad policy domains.[4] The hope was that these meetings would ensure that key executive branch officials marched to the same drumbeat.

In addition, governors relied on new budget techniques, such as zero-based budgeting, to increase their control over agency budget submissions and, ultimately, agency budgets themselves. Under zero-based budgeting, the previous year's budget base is not taken for granted, although it may be incorporated into alternative budget submissions. During the 1970s, approximately twenty-five states adopted a modified form of zero-based budgeting.[5]

At the same time, governors fought successfully for shorter ballots to bring more top state officials under gubernatorial control. Between 1962 and 1978, the number of elected state executives declined by 10 percent.[6] As a result of these reforms, governors today are more likely to deal with state agencies headed more often by gubernatorial appointees in whom they can have confidence.

Finally, executive orders have become more popular in recent years. Many executive orders are aimed at controlling state bureaucracies, and some of them are both significant and controversial. For example, California governor Pete Wilson issued an executive order in June 1995 eliminating affirmative action preferences for state employees.[7] State hiring and promotion practices will change sharply as a result.

These gubernatorial control techniques have become even more important as a result of limitations on political patronage imposed by the U.S. Supreme Court in 1990. In *Rutan v. Illinois Republican Party*, the Court ruled that party affiliation could not be a factor in most state personnel decisions in Illinois.[8] That ruling, which has reverberated throughout the nation, has encouraged governors to control state agencies through other means.

Interest Representation

Unable or unwilling to control state agencies directly in every instance, politicians relied on surrogates to ensure better representation for favored points of view, such as consumers, environmentalists, and the elderly. Political scientists Matthew McCubbins and Thomas Schwartz referred to this phenomenon as "fire-alarm oversight" because politicians in effect depend on citizens or other public officials to spot fires in the bureaucracy and help extinguish them.[9] During the 1970s, 1980s, and into the 1990s, states took a number of steps to improve representation for broad, diffuse interests or other underrepresented interests, especially before state regulatory agencies—a "representation revolution" occurred.[10]

For example, many states established "proxy advocacy" offices to represent consumer interests in state public utility commission proceedings, such as rate cases. In some instances, attorneys general served this function; in other instances, separate consumer advocacy offices were established. Wisconsin, meanwhile, established a Citizens Utilities Board, funded by citizens through voluntary contributions but authorized by the state legislature to include membership solicitations in utility bills.[11] State legislatures in Illinois, Oregon, and New York subsequently established similar organizations, though without provisions for inserts.[12]

Disappointed in the performance of occupational licensing boards, state legislatures mandated lay representation on the boards in the hope that fewer anti-competitive practices would result. Wisconsin law specifies that at least one public member shall serve on each of the state's occupational licensing boards. California goes even further. Since 1976, California has required that all occupational licensing boards have a majority of public members, except for ten "healing arts" boards and the Board of Accountancy.[13]

Many state legislatures require public hearings in various environmental policy decisions. Pursuant to the California Coastal Act of 1972, a coastal zoning commission must call for a public hearing whenever a developer submits a construction permit request for a project that might have an "adverse environmental impact" on coastal resources.

Some interest representation reforms that occurred on the state level were mandated by or encouraged by the federal government. For example, Congress required states to cooperate with the Environmental Protection Agency (EPA) in providing for public participation under the Federal Water Pollution Control Act; the Resource Conservation and Recovery Act; the Comprehensive Environmental Response, Compensation, and Liability Act; and other statutes. Through the Older Americans Act, Congress required states to establish long-term care ombudsman programs to investigate complaints by nursing home residents and to monitor the development and implementation of pertinent laws and regulations.

Regulatory Federalism

The dynamics of regulatory federalism differ significantly from those of interest representation reforms. In both cases, politicians exercise indirect control over state bureaucracies, relying on surrogates to articulate their concerns. However, regulatory federalism is much more intrusive. If a consumer advocacy group recommends a new rule or regulation, a state agency may consider and reject it. If a federal agency instructs a state agency to adopt a rule or face a sharp cutback in federal funds, the state agency does not have much of a choice.

Regulatory federalism is a process whereby the federal government imposes conditions on state governments that accept federal funding.[14] Regulatory federalism arose as an adjunct to the new social regulations of the 1970s and as an antidote to the laissez-faire of general revenue sharing. Regulatory federalism includes a variety of techniques, such as direct orders (unequivocal mandates), crossover sanctions (threats in one program area if actions are not taken in another program), crosscutting requirements (obligations applicable to a wide range of programs), and partial preemptions (the establishment of minimal federal standards if states wish to run their own programs).[15] Some of these techniques apply to state legislatures; some apply to state agencies; many apply to both.

The number of federal statutes imposing significant new regulatory requirements increased dramatically during the 1970s. Given the Reagan administration's public support for federalism and deregulation, many observers expected regulatory federalism to decline during the 1980s. However, as political scientist Timothy Conlan has shown, the number of federal statutes with significant intergovernmental controls directed at the states increased even further.[16] Moreover, a disproportionate increase came about in the most coercive regulatory control techniques—namely, direct orders and crossover sanctions. In Conlan's words, "the 1980s rivaled the previous decade as a period of unparalleled intergovernmental regulatory activity."[17]

In 1995 regulatory federalism finally gave way to a concerted effort to devolve power to the states. Led by Republican governors and members of Congress, advocates of state discretion pushed for program consolidation, block grants, and the elimination of unfunded federal mandates. In some instances, these developments will allow state administrators to enjoy greater discretion than before. Certainly, they will have fewer federal auditing and paperwork requirements to meet. On the other hand, as the flow of federal dollars to the states diminishes, state administrators will find it difficult to extend funding and protection to previously uncovered target populations. For example, new federal child care legislation would allow state agencies to offer child care assistance to families who earn as much as 100 percent of their state's median family income, up from 75 percent in previous legislation.[18] Yet, an additional feature of the new legislation will eliminate a special child care program aimed at children at risk. Consequently, the states will probably be forced to ignore potential new beneficiaries to focus on these needier children whose program has been eliminated.

Due Process

In addition to serving as arbiters in intergovernmental disputes, federal judges have been active participants in efforts to control state bureaucracies. They have intervened vigorously in pursuit of such constitutional rights as "due process of law" and freedom from "cruel and unusual punishment." Dissatisfied with progress at the state level, they have gone so far as to seize, for example, state prisons and homes for the mentally ill or the mentally retarded, substituting their managerial judgment for that of state public administrators.

The 1971 case *Wyatt v. Stickney*[19] was the first in a long line of institutional reform cases in which federal judges decided to play a strong managerial role. Alabama's homes for the mentally ill and the mentally retarded were overcrowded, understaffed, dangerous, and unsanitary. In response to a class action suit, Judge Frank Johnson held that mentally disabled patients have a right to adequate and effective treatment in the least restrictive environment practicable. To secure that right, he issued extremely specific treatment standards and ordered rapid deinstitutionalization.

Shortly after the *Wyatt* decision, Judge Johnson found himself embroiled in an equally bitter controversy over Alabama's prisons. By most accounts, conditions in the state's prisons were deplorable. Rapes and stabbings were widespread, food was unwholesome, and physical facilities were dilapidated. In response to inmate complaints, Judge Johnson issued a decree calling for adequate medical care, regular fire inspections, and regular physical examinations.[20] When conditions barely improved, he issued detailed standards, including cell-space requirements, hiring requirements, and a mandatory classification system.[21]

The Alabama cases set the stage for a large number of similar cases throughout the country. In state after state, federal judges mandated massive changes in physical facilities, staffing ratios, health services, and amenities. They specified the size of prison cells, the credentials of new employees, and plumbing and hygiene standards. They shut down facilities and prohibited new admissions, even where alternative facilities were not available.

The U.S. Supreme Court in 1982 finally applied the brakes on mental health orders in *Youngberg v. Romeo.*[22] In that decision, the Court ruled that mentally retarded clients are constitutionally entitled to minimally adequate treatment and habilitation but that professionals, including state administrators, should be free to decide what constitutes minimally adequate training for staff. Thus, the decision was viewed as a partial victory for state administrators.

More recently, the Court restricted other federal courts from correcting prison conditions in the absence of "deliberate indifference." In *Wilson v. Seiter*, the Court ruled that federal judges may address "cruel and unusual punishment" by state prison officials only if the plaintiff has demonstrated that prison officials exhibited a "culpable state of mind."[23] This imposes a higher hurdle for prison reform interventions than was previously the case.

Types of Controls

It is useful when thinking about recent efforts to control state bureaucracies to imagine a spectrum ranging from catalytic controls at one end to coercive controls at the other end, with hortatory controls falling in between. Catalytic controls stimulate change but preserve a great deal of bureaucratic discretion. Coercive controls require change and severely limit bureaucratic discretion. Hortatory controls involve more pressure than catalytic controls but more restraint than coercive controls.[24]

Moreover, different types of controls have different types of effects. In their public policy implications, catalytic controls have been surprisingly effective and coercive controls have been notably counterproductive.

Catalytic Controls

Catalytic controls require state bureaucracies to respond to a petition or plea but do not predetermine the nature of their response. As a result, such controls are action-forcing but not solution-forcing. While they alter bureaucratic behavior, they nevertheless permit a good deal of discretion and flexibility. Examples of catalytic controls include public hearings, ombudsmen, proxy advocacy, and lay representation.

Public hearings have enabled environmentalists to win important victories in their dealings with state bureaucracies. For example, citizens have used public hearings on state water quality planning in North Carolina to secure important modifications of state plans concerning waste water disposal, construction, and mining.[25] Similarly, citizens used public hearings before the California Coastal Commission to block permits for development projects that would have an "adverse environmental impact" on coastal resources.[26]

Ombudsmen have been active in several areas but especially on nursing home issues. According to one report,[27] nursing home ombudsmen have been effective in resolving complaints on a wide variety of subjects, including Medicaid problems, guardianship, the power of attorney, inadequate hygiene, family problems, and the theft of personal possessions. Another study[28] found that nursing home ombudsmen provide useful information to legislators and planners.

Proxy advocates have effectively represented consumers in rate cases and other proceedings held by state public utility commissions. As a result of the interventions, utility companies have received rate hikes substantially lower than those originally requested. Proxy advocates also have been instrumental in securing policies on utility disconnections and payment penalties that help consumers who are struggling to pay their bills.[29] Even in complex telecommunications cases, proxy advocates have successfully promoted competition on behalf of consumers.[30]

Catalytic controls may be too weak in some instances. In several southern states, for example, public hearing requirements in utility regulatory proceedings have been pointless because consumer groups and environmental groups have not materialized to take advantage of such hearings.[31] Lay representation on occupational licensing boards also has been a disappointment. Lacking expertise, lay representatives typically have deferred to professionals on these boards.[32]

Overall, though, catalytic controls have been remarkably successful in making state bureaucracies more responsive to a vast array of formerly underrepresented interests. In effect, they have institutionalized what political scientist James Q. Wilson refers to as "entrepreneurial politics"[33] or the pursuit of policies that offer widely distributed benefits through widely distributed costs. Moreover, catalytic controls have achieved results without engendering bureaucratic hostility and resentment. Studies show that state administrators welcome citizen participation[34] and interest group interventions.[35] At their best, catalytic controls provide state bureaucrats with ammunition to justify policies that promote the public interest.

Hortatory Controls

Hortatory controls involve political pressure or "jawboning," usually by someone in a position of authority. They strike a balance between bureaucratic discretion and bureaucratic accountability. Some, such as sunset laws and administrative reorganizations, are relatively mild; others, such as partial preemptions and crossover sanctions, are relatively strong.

The strength of hortatory controls depends primarily on two factors: their specificity (are the goals of the controllers clear?) and the credibility of the threat (how likely is it that penalties will be invoked?). Thus, sunset laws are relatively weak because the threat of termination is remote, except in the case of extremely small agencies.

To argue that some hortatory controls are mild is not to say that they are ineffective. A study of legislative audit bureau reports reveals that they do lead to changes in legislation, administrative practice, or both. Research by legislative audit bureaus is more likely to be utilized by state legislators than other types of research.[36] The literature on administrative reorganizations reveals that they do not reduce government spending but that they can promote coordination and integration if they are well-crafted and well-executed.[37] The key seems to be to put agencies with interrelated missions under the same roof.

Research on sunset laws roughly parallels the findings on administrative reorganizations. As a cost-containment device, sunset legislation has been a failure. However, as a mechanism for focusing legislative attention on agencies and issues low in visibility, sunset legislation has been a success. In a number of states, such as Connecticut and Florida, sunset laws have resulted in significant changes in statutes and agency rules.[38]

Stronger hortatory controls have been even more effective, though they also have been dysfunctional in some respects. In response to quality control systems in welfare, "errors of liberality" have declined, but "errors of stringency" have increased.[39] In effect, states have sacrificed accuracy for cost-containment. States also have enforced federal regulations that they know to be unreasonable, in response to partial preemptions in environmental policy. For example, the Minnesota Pollution Control Agency enforced a rigid EPA definition of hazardous waste, even though it meant that a lime sludge pile could not be removed from a highway site, could not be used for waste-water treatment, and could not be used to clean an electric utility company's smokestack emissions.[40]

Strong hortatory controls place a premium on uniform standards and universal compliance with such standards. In some instances, such as civil rights, no practical alternative exists to strong controls, because local prejudices are too deeply ingrained to permit cooperation. In others, however, strong hortatory controls may impose premature closure, discouraging the innovation and experimentation that are necessary for the states to serve as "laboratories" for the nation and for other states.

Strong hortatory controls have been particularly prominent in intergovernmental relations. Indeed, conditions attached to federal grants-in-aid epitomize hortatory controls. Such conditions have remained formidable, despite periodic rhetoric in support of a new federalism. In 1995, however, Congress took steps to soften or eliminate certain restrictions that states found offensive. For example, Congress voted to eliminate federal speed limit requirements for automobiles on federally financed highways except for some rural freeways.[41]

Coercive Controls

Coercive controls rob state bureaucracies of their discretion. They compel a specific response, often within a specific time frame. Neither the solution nor the deadline may be reasonable, but the state bureaucracy does not have the luxury of responding reasonably. Immediate compliance becomes more important than rationality, and short-term "outputs" become more important than long-term "outcomes."

Coercive controls often trigger bureaucratic circumvention or resistance. In the former case, bureaucrats comply with the letter, but not the spirit, of a tough requirement. In the latter case, the bureaucracy goes to court. In both cases, an adversarial relationship develops that precludes cooperation, bargaining, and persuasion.

As a response to legislative vetoes, some state agencies have issued emergency rules, which are not subject to the usual legislative review process. In Wisconsin, for example, state agencies issued a total of fifty-four emergency rules during the 1985–1986 legislative session—a sharp increase over earlier years.[42] Reliance on emergency rules is especially unfortunate, because they do not involve public hearings. Thus, in escaping highly threatening legislative vetoes, agencies avoid less threatening public hearings as well.

Court orders have triggered some of the more dysfunctional bureaucratic responses. When Judge Frank Johnson required state prisons to reduce their overcrowding, Alabama prison officials simply released large numbers of prisoners, forcing county jails to take up the slack. Unfortunately, county jails were poorly equipped for the task; they lacked adequate space and personnel. Consequently, many prisoners, shipped to county jails, were forced to endure conditions even worse than those they had experienced in the state prisons.[43] Yet the state agency was technically in compliance with the court decree.

A key problem with coercive controls is that they place far too much emphasis on formal authority. Many state agencies depend considerably on a series of informal understandings. This is especially true of prisons, where quick-thinking guards and cooperative inmates help to maintain a delicate balance between order and chaos. When that balance is disrupted, tragedy may result. This is precisely what happened in Texas, when Judge William Justice restricted the use of force by prison guards and ordered an end to the state's "building tender" system, in which inmates in effect guarded other inmates. The court's order dissolved the informal networks that enabled the prisons to function on a daily basis. As guards became more timid, direct challenges to authority rose sharply. Disciplinary reports reveal abrupt and dramatic increases in incidents where a guard was threatened or assaulted.[44] Inmates also turned on each other, with their fists or with makeshift weapons. By generating rising expectations and undermining bureaucratic morale, Judge Justice created a temporary power vacuum that prison gangs quickly filled. The tragic result was a series of riots and violent episodes that left fifty-two inmates dead within two years.[45]

Accountability Battles

Accountability battles have become more prominent in state politics for three principal reasons: (1) the proliferation of controls; (2) the intensification of controls; and (3) the judicialization of controls. As controls multiply, some are likely to be contradictory. Competing claimants emerge. As controls intensify, contradictory controls generate more friction. Competing claimants press their claims. As controls spill over into the courts, disputes are resolved according to legal criteria. Moreover, the courts themselves become active participants in these battles. Frustrated with both state politicians and state bureaucrats, judges have decided that they can do a better job and that they are entitled to do so under the U.S. Constitution, the state constitution, or both.

State Legislatures versus Governors

Accountability battles between state legislatures and governors have erupted in recent years. Although such disputes are not new, they seem to focus increasingly on directives to administrative agencies and on questions of legal authority instead of political preference. As a result, state judges have found themselves playing a key role in arbitrating disputes between governors and state legislatures.

Legislative vetoes have aroused considerable conflict between state legislatures and governors, even when the same party controls both branches of government. In New Jersey, for example, the Democratic state legislature and Democratic governor Brendan T. Byrne clashed in court over a generic legislative veto and a more specific veto, whereby certain building authority proposals must be approved by both houses or the presiding offices of the legislature, depending on the nature of the proposal.[46] The New Jersey state supreme court upheld the specific legislative veto[47] but ruled the generic veto unconstitutional, citing violations of separation of powers and the presentment clauses of the state constitution.[48]

Executive orders also have triggered conflict between state legislatures and governors. In Pennsylvania, for example, Republican governor Dick Thornburgh issued an executive order "privatizing" the state's liquor control store system. The Democratic state legislature, which had just rejected such a plan, promptly took the governor to court. A Commonwealth Court judge ruled in favor of the legislature, noting that the governor's privatization plan was "without authority and contravenes the Sunset Act." He also accused both sides of playing an unseemly game of political football at the public's expense.[49]

Money, too, has fueled many disputes between state legislatures and governors. In Wisconsin, Republican governor Tommy Thompson refused to accept a decision by the Democratic state legislature to maintain welfare benefits at existing levels. Stretching the outer limits of his line-item veto authority, Thompson vetoed two digits and a decimal point from the state legislature's benefit formula, thereby effecting a 6 percent reduction in welfare benefits. The legislature promptly took the governor to court, but the Wisconsin supreme court upheld a generous interpretation of the governor's line-item power.[50] In 1990, the voters approved a constitutional amendment prohibiting "Vanna White" vetoes that build new words out of stray letters but allowed deletions of whole words, thus sustaining creative veto powers.[51]

Tensions between state legislatures and governors can be very stressful for administrative agencies, especially when the two branches of government are controlled by different political parties. During a bitter budget battle between Republican governor John Engler and Democrats in the Michigan State legislature in 1991, the child care licensing division was threatened with extinction and licensors received pink slips. A strong grass-roots lobbying campaign managed to save the division, but the experience was extremely unpleasant for state agency officials.[52]

Federal Politicians versus State Politicians

State bureaucracies routinely are asked to implement federal statutes, such as environmental protection statutes. Often these federal statutes contradict state statutes or the policy preferences of the state's governor. Under such circumstances, a showdown is likely, with the federal government citing the "commerce clause" or the "take care clause" of the U.S. Constitution, while the state government cites the Tenth Amendment.

The U.S. Supreme Court and other federal courts have usually sided with the federal government in accountability battles where the allocation of federal funds is at issue. If states accept federal funding, they also must accept the conditions the federal government attaches to those funds. However, many intergovernmental disputes do not involve federal funding but a federal effort to preempt state activity in a particular policy domain. Here, also, the U.S. Supreme Court has sided with the federal government, though with occasional exceptions.

In *National League of Cities v. Usery*,[53] the Supreme Court surprised many observers by rejecting the federal government's attempt to extend minimum wage and maximum hour provisions to municipal employees. In doing so, the Court said that the Tenth Amendment prohibited any federal action that impaired "the State's freedom to structure integral operations in areas of traditional governmental functions." Thus, a key provision of the 1974 Fair Labor Standards Act Amendments was ruled unconstitutional. The decision was an important victory for both state and local governments.

In subsequent cases, the Supreme Court wrestled gamely with the "traditional governmental functions" criterion and offered further clarification. For example, in *Hodel v. Virginia Surface Mining and Reclamation Association*,[54] the Court articulated a three-fold test for determining when Tenth Amendment claims shall prevail. Specifically, the Court extended protection to the states if federal regulations: (1) regulate the states as states; (2) address matters that are indisputably attributes of state sovereignty; and (3) impair the states' ability to structure integral operations in areas of traditional function. In *Hodel*—a strip mining case involving a partial preemption statute—the Court concluded that Congress had acted properly and with restraint. Similarly, in *FERC v. Mississippi*,[55] the Court applauded Congress for imposing modest constraints on state public utility commissions, when it could have preempted the field entirely.

Finally, after years of painful efforts to distinguish between "traditional government functions" and other functions, the Supreme Court abandoned that doctrine outright in *Garcia v. San Antonio Metropolitan Transit Authority*.[56] Writing for the majority, Justice Harry A. Blackmun concluded that "State sovereign interests . . . are more properly protected by procedural safeguards inherent in the structure of the federal system than by judicially created limitations on federal power."[57] In effect, the states would have to protect themselves through vigorous lobbying on Capitol Hill. The Supreme Court no longer would invoke a rule that was "unsound in principle and unworkable in practice."[58]

If the *Garcia* decision left state and local governments discouraged about the future of intergovernmental relations, a more recent decision has left them jubilant. In *U.S. v. Lopez* (1995), the Supreme Court ruled that Congress had exceeded its constitutional authority in prohibiting the possession of a gun within 1,000 feet of a school.[59] In effect, the Court ruled that the commerce clause, which has justified numerous federal mandates in the past, cannot be equated with national supremacy. In writing an opinion for the majority, Chief Justice William Rehnquist said that in the future the Court will have to determine whether a regulated activity "substantially affects" interstate commerce.[60] This could make it difficult, though not impossible, for Congress to restrict activities, such as the possession of weapons or drugs, that do not necessarily involve interstate sales or transportation.

Federal Judges versus State Politicians

In accountability battles between federal politicians and state politicians, federal judges have served as arbiters. In other disputes, however, federal judges have served as both arbiters and combatants. In numerous institutional reform cases, federal district court judges have ordered sweeping changes that are attainable only if state legislatures allocate more money than they wish to spend in a particular policy domain. These decisions have had tangible effects on state budgets.[61] The decisions also have raised important questions concerning both federalism and the power of the purse.

A number of federal judges have acted with vigor, for example, Judge Johnson's efforts to overhaul the Alabama prison system and Judge Justice's response to Texas' prison program. In other institutional reform cases, federal judges have ordered sweeping changes in state treatment of the mentally ill and the mentally retarded. In New York, Judges Orrin Judd and John Bartels demanded more ward attendants, eighty-five more nurses, thirty physical therapists, and fifteen more physicians at the Willowbrook Developmental Center on Staten Island. They prohibited seclusion of patients and called for the immediate repair of broken toilets. They also ordered a sharp decrease in the Willowbrook population, stressing the advantages of deinstitutionalization. To implement these reforms, they appointed and preserved a Willowbrook Review Panel, which developed into a powerful agent of change.

In Pennsylvania, Judge Raymond Broderick went even further, after learning of unsanitary, inhumane, and dangerous conditions at the Pennhurst State School and Hospital for the mentally retarded. In a strongly worded opinion, Broderick ordered the eventual closing of the Pennhurst facilities, with residents being relocated in community facilities. In the meantime, he insisted on clean, odorless, and insect-free buildings, no new admissions, and less reliance on forcible restraint and unnecessary medication. To achieve these results, he appointed a special master and set deadlines for compliance.

More often than not, accountability battles between federal judges and state politicians have been won by federal judges. In reviewing lower court decisions, appeals court judges and the U.S. Supreme Court have agreed that "cruel and unusual punishment" is intolerable in state prisons and that the mentally ill have a constitutional right to "treatment" if admitted to a state facility. However, appeals courts also have raised questions about the extraordinarily detailed and specific remedies mandated by federal district court judges.

In *Newman v. Alabama*,[62] the U.S. Court of Appeals for the Fifth Circuit ruled that Judge Johnson went too far in specifying the size of new prison cells, in appointing human rights committees, and in insisting on rehabilitation opportunities for all prisoners. In the words of the court: "The Constitution does not require that prisoners, as individuals or as a group, be provided with any and every amenity which some person may think is needed to avoid mental, physical and emotional deterioration." In *Ruiz v. Estelle*,[63] the U.S. Court of Appeals for the Fifth Circuit ruled that Judge Justice went too far in outlawing double cells in Texas prisons (but supported his ban on triple and quadruple cells). In *New York State Association for Retarded Children v. Carey*,[64] the U.S. Court of Appeals for the Second Circuit concluded that Gov. Hugh Carey could not be held in contempt of court for failing to provide funding for the Willowbrook Review Panel. In *Pennhurst State School and Hospital v. Halderman*,[65] the U.S. Supreme Court ruled that a right to treatment exists only if a state accepts federal funds and if federal conditions of aid are clearly and unambiguously stated. In *Youngberg v. Romeo*,[66] the U.S. Supreme Court ruled that even when a right to treatment exists, it should be operationalized by qualified professionals, not judges.

Thus, accountability battles between federal district court judges and state politicians have given way to battles between federal district court judges and federal appeals court judges. On questions of constitutional rights, the appeals court judges generally have deferred to federal district courts, to the chagrin of the states. On questions of remedies, however, the appeals courts have cautioned lower courts against excessive specificity that stretches the limits of judicial expertise.

Conclusion

State administrative agencies once enjoyed considerable autonomy. Ignored by virtually everyone but clientele groups, they were "semi-sovereign" entities. In the early 1970s, that began to change. As state budgets grew and state bureaucracies increased in importance, this era came to a close. To make state agencies more accountable, politicians and judges institutionalized a wide variety of reforms. Through direct and indirect means, they attempted to bring state bureaucracies under control.

Ironically, this occurred at precisely the same time as the growing professionalization of state agencies. Thanks to civil service reforms, budget increases, rising education levels, and growing pressure for specialization, state bureaucracies acquired greater experience and expertise. Today, they are more adept at problem solving than ever before and arguably more deserving of discretion. Thus, they chafe at external pressure, particularly when it is highly coercive.

General agreement exists that state agencies ought to be accountable. Even state bureaucrats cheerfully concede that point. However, consensus on the need for bureaucratic accountability has given way to "dissensus" on lines of authority. If governors and state legislators both claim an electoral mandate, who is right? If federal and state politicians both cite constitutional prerogatives, who is correct? If judges and politicians disagree on spending priorities, who deserves the power of the purse?

In the 1990s, state agencies are more accountable to their sovereigns than they used to be. Yet accountability has become a murky concept. Principal-agent theories of politics[67] work only when the principal's identity is clear to the agent. In numerous policy areas, state bureaucratic agents face dual principals or even multiple principals.

Thus, accountability battles rage, as competing sovereigns press their claims. As one might expect in a federal system, different actors have won accountability battles in different settings and at different times. The 1994 congressional elections saw power shift from federal policy makers (both politicians and bureaucrats) to state policy makers (especially governors). If this trend continues, state administrative agencies will be more accountable to state politicians, less accountable to federal overseers. However, the history of intergovernmental relations suggests that periodic grants of discretion to the states are usually followed by negative feedback and additional restrictions. If this cycle repeats itself, state administrative agencies will once again find themselves subject to diverse, intense, and sometimes irreconcilable political pressures.

Notes

1. *Immigration and Naturalization Service v. Chadha*, 462 U.S. 919 (1983).
2. L. Harold Levinson, "The Decline of the Legislative Veto: Federal/State Comparisons and Interactions," *Publius* 17:1 (Winter 1987): 115–132.
3. Thad L. Beyle, "The Executive Branch: Organization and Issues, 1988–1989," in *The Book of the States, 1990–1991* (Lexington, Ky.: Council of State Governments, 1990), 76.
4. Lydia Bodman and Daniel Garry, "Innovations in State Cabinet Systems," *State Government* 55:3 (Summer 1982): 93–97.
5. Thomas Lauth, "Zero-Base Budgeting in Georgia State Government: Myth and Reality," in *Perspectives on Budgeting*, ed. Allen Schick (Washington, D.C.: American Society for Public Administration, 1980), 114–132.
6. Larry J. Sabato, *Goodbye to Good-time Charlie: The American Govenorship Transformed* (Washington, D.C.: CQ Press, 1983).
7. John Miller and Abigail Thernstrom, "Losing Race," *The New Republic*, June 26, 1995, 17–20.
8. *Rutan v. Republican Party of Illinois*, 497 U.S. 62 (1990).
9. Matthew McCubbins and Thomas Schwartz, "Congressional Oversight Overlooked: Police Patrols versus Fire Alarms," *American Journal of Political Science* 28:1 (February 1984): 180–202.

10. William Gormley, Jr., "The Representation Revolution: Reforming State Regulation through Public Representation," *Administration and Society* 18:2 (August 1986): 179–196.

11. Involuntary bill inserts later were ruled unconstitutional in a California case that effectively invalidated a key provision of the Wisconsin law. See *Pacific Gas and Electric v. Public Utilities Commission of California*, 106 S. Ct. 903 (1986).

12. Beth Givens, *Citizens' Utility Boards: Because Utilities Bear Watching* (San Diego, Calif.: Center for Public Interest Law, University of San Diego Law School, 1991).

13. Howard Schutz, "Effects of Increased Citizen Membership on Occupational Licensing Boards in California," *Policy Studies Journal* 2 (March 1983): 504–516.

14. Regulatory federalism also may be used to describe the relationship between state and local governments. For more on the growing burdens placed by state governments on local governments, see Catherine Lovell and Charles Tobin, "The Mandate Issue," *Public Administration Review* 41:3 (May/June 1981): 318–331. See also Joseph Zimmerman, "Developing State-Local Relations: 1987–1989," in *The Book of the States, 1990–1991*, 533–548.

15. Advisory Commission on Intergovernmental Relations, *Regulatory Federalism: Policy, Process, Impact and Reform* (Washington, D.C.: Advisory Commission on Intergovernmental Relations, 1983).

16. Timothy Conlan, "And the Beat Goes On: Intergovernmental Mandates and Preemption in an Era of Deregulation," *Publius* 21:3 (Summer 1991): 43–57.

17. Ibid., 50.

18. For the details of this legislation, see S.850, a bill to amend the Child Care and Development Block Grant of 1990.

19. *Wyatt v. Stickney*, 324 F. Supp. 781 (M.D. Ala. 1971).

20. *Newman v. Alabama*, 349 F. Supp. 278 (M.D. Ala. 1972).

21. *James v. Wallace*, 406 F. Supp. 318 (M.D. Ala. 1976); and *Pugh v. Locke*, 406 F. Supp. 318 (M.D. Ala. 1976).

22. *Youngberg v. Romeo*, 102 S. Ct. 2452 (1982).

23. 111 S. Ct. 2321 (1991).

24. William Gormley, Jr., *Taming the Bureaucracy: Muscles, Prayers, and Other Strategies* (Princeton: Princeton University Press, 1989).

25. David Godschalk and Bruce Stiftel, "Making Waves: Public Participation in State Water Planning," *Journal of Applied Behavioral Science* 17:4 (October-December 1981): 597–614.

26. Judy Rosener, "Making Bureaucrats Responsive: A Study of the Impact of Citizen Participation and Staff Recommendations on Regulatory Decision Making," *Public Administration Review* 42:4 (July/August 1982): 339–345.

27. Administration on Aging, U.S. Department of Health and Human Services, *National Summary of State Ombudsman Reports for U.S. Fiscal Year 1982* (Washington, D.C.: U.S. Government Printing Office, 1983).

28. Abraham Monk et al., *National Comparative Analysis of Long Term Care Programs for the Aged* (New York: Brookdale Institute on Aging and Adult Human Development and the Columbia University School of Social Work, 1982).

29. William Gormley, Jr., *The Politics of Public Utility Regulation* (Pittsburgh: University of Pittsburgh Press, 1983).

30. Paul Teske, *After Divestiture: The Political Economy of State Telecommunications Regulation* (Albany: SUNY Press, 1990), 63–85.

31. Ibid.

32. Gerald Thain and Kenneth Haydock, *A Working Paper: How Public and Other Members of Regulation and Licensing Boards Differ: The Results of a Wisconsin Survey* (Madison: Center for Public Representation, 1983).

33. James Q. Wilson, ed., *The Politics of Regulation* (New York: Basic Books, 1980).

34. Cheryl Miller, "State Administrator Perceptions of the Policy Influence of Other Actors: Is Less Better?" *Public Administration Review* 47:3 (May/June 1987): 239–245.
35. Glenn Abney and Thomas Lauth, *The Politics of State and City Administration* (Albany: SUNY Press, 1986).
36. David Rafter, "Policy-Focused Evaluation: A Study of the Utilization of Evaluation Research by the Wisconsin Legislature," Ph.D. dissertation, University of Wisconsin, Madison, 1982.
37. Kenneth Meier, "Executive Reorganization of Government: Impact on Employment and Expenditures," *American Journal of Political Science* 24:3 (August 1980): 396–412; and Karen Hult, *Agency Merger and Bureaucratic Redesign* (Pittsburgh: University of Pittsburgh Press, 1987).
38. Doug Roederer and Patsy Palmer, *Sunset: Expectation and Experience* (Lexington, Ky.: Council of State Governments, June 1981).
39. Evelyn Brodkin and Michael Lipsky, "Quality Control in AFDC as an Administrative Strategy," *Social Service Review* 57:1 (March 1983): 1–34.
40. Eric Black, "Why Regulators Need a Don't-Do-It-If-It's-Stupid Clause," *Washington Monthly* 16:12 (January 1985): 23–26.
41. Don Phillips, "Federal Speed Limit, Set in 1974, Repealed," *Washington Post*, November 29, 1995, 1.
42. Douglas Stencel, "Analysis of Joint Committee for Review of Administrative Rules Caseload 1985–1986," unpublished manuscript, Madison, Wis., April 1987.
43. Tinsley Yarbrough, *Judge Frank Johnson and Human Rights in Alabama* (Tuscaloosa: University of Alabama Press, 1981).
44. James Marquart and Ben Crouch, "Judicial Reform and Prisoner Control: The Impact of *Ruiz v. Estelle* on a Texas Penitentiary," *Law and Society Review* 19:4 (1985): 557–586.
45. Aric Press, "Inside America's Toughest Prison," *Newsweek*, October 6, 1986, 46–61.
46. Levinson, "The Decline of the Legislative Veto," 121.
47. *Enourato v. New Jersey Building Authority*, 448 A. 2d 449 (N.J. 1982).
48. *General Assembly v. Byrne*, 448 A. 2d 438 (N.J. 1982).
49. Gary Warner, "Despite Ruling, Future of Liquor Stores Up in Air," *Pittsburgh Press*, December 30, 1986, 1.
50. Charles Friederich, "Lawmakers to Sue Thompson over Budget Vetoes," *Milwaukee Journal*, September 2, 1987, B3; and Doug Mell, "Thompson Vetoes Win in Court," *Wisconsin State Journal*, June 15, 1988, 1.
51. Charles Mahtesian, "The Captains of Conservatism," *Governing* (February 1995): 30–31.
52. Personal interview with Ted DeWolf, Michigan Department of Social Services, July 13, 1993.
53. *National League of Cities v. Usery*, 426 U.S. 833 (1976).
54. *Hodel v. Virginia Surface Mining and Reclamation Association*, 452 U.S. 264 (1981).
55. *FERC v. Mississippi*, 456 U.S. 742 (1982).
56. *Garcia v. San Antonio Metropolitan Transit Authority* 105 S. Ct. 1005 (1985).
57. 105 S. Ct. 1018 (1985).
58. 105 S. Ct. 1016 (1985).
59. Ann Devroy and Al Kamen, "Clinton Says Gun Ruling is a Threat," *Washington Post*, April 30, 1995, 1.
60. Jeffrey Rosen, "Fed Up," *The New Republic*, May 22, 1995, 13.
61. Linda Harriman and Jeffrey Straussman, "Do Judges Determine Budget Decisions?" *Public Administration Review* 43:4 (July/August 1983): 343–351.
62. *Newman v. Alabama*, 559 F. 2d 283 (5th Cir. 1977).
63. *Ruiz v. Estelle*, 679 F. 2d 1115 (1982).

64. *New York State Association for Retarded Children v. Carey*, 631 F. 2d 162 (1980).
65. *Pennhurst State School and Hospital v. Halderman*, 101 S. Ct., 1531 (1981).
66. *Youngberg v. Romeo*, 102 S. Ct. 2452 (1982).
67. Jonathan Bendor and Terry Moe, "An Adaptive Model of Bureaucratic Politics," *American Political Science Review* 79:3 (September 1985): 755–774.

9

State Education Policy in the 1990s

Margaret E. Goertz

In the United States, the authority for public elementary and secondary education[1] resides in the states, a "reserved" power arising from the Tenth Amendment of the U.S. Constitution. All state constitutions contain provisions requiring states to create a system of free public schools, but until the mid-1960s, the state role in education was largely limited to creating local education agencies (LEAs), setting broad goals and general guidelines, and providing financial support to LEAs. Education was viewed as "a state authority locally administered." Over the last thirty years, several forces led to a major expansion in state responsibilities: an explosion in federal education programs and mandates in the mid-1960s and 1970s; federal funds to support state administration of these programs and to strengthen the general capacity of state education agencies (SEAs); increases in state spending on education to address fiscal and programmatic inequities among school districts; and a national call for a renewed emphasis on academic excellence.

Today, states play a major role in the funding and regulation of education, and education has come to dominate the state policy agenda. With states providing nearly half of all public school revenues, elementary and secondary education now commands the largest share of state budgets. About one-third of state expenditures are devoted to this function.[2] Legislators must grapple annually (or biennially) with the size of the state education aid budget, the allocation of these funds to local districts, and the consequences of these decisions for the level of local education spending, state and local taxes, and funds available for other public services. States have also assumed considerable authority in many nonfiscal areas of education, ranging from teacher certification to the establishment of student performance standards to sanctions for poorly performing schools and school districts, extending the power of the state in areas that were once the sole responsibility of local school boards.

States vary on the substance and scope of their education policies, but they all focus their attention on five policy domains: curriculum and instruction, accountability and assessment, teachers, governance, and finance. The substance of policy discussions and resolutions in the 1990s in these domains reflects the changing environment of American education, the national education agenda, and the competing reform values of equity, excellence, efficiency, and choice. Equity focuses on equalizing or distributing educational resources and opportunities to meet moral or societal goals. Excellence focuses on the use of these resources to support professional or publicly determined standards of quality or proficiency. Efficiency focuses on holding educators accountable for the performance of their schools and students and/or rendering schools more productive. As used in this chapter, choice refers broadly to policies that place the control of education in the hands of schools, parents, and/or private contractors.[3]

The Environment of State Education Policy

Education policy in the 1990s and beyond will be shaped by fundamental changes that have occurred in its social, economic, and political environment over the last twenty-five years. Declining test scores throughout the 1970s undermined public confidence in the country's public school system and led business leaders to question the quality of the nation's future work force. An eroding U.S. position in the international economy turned policy makers' attention and energies to issues of efficiency, excellence, and choice in education and away from earlier concerns with equity. Policy leadership thrust upon the federal government by the Russian *Sputnik* launching in the late 1950s, the Supreme Court's desegregation rulings in the 1950s, and the War on Poverty of the 1960s shifted back to the states where fragmented and diffuse interest groups compete for control of the education agenda. Today, states are struggling to define and support a more rigorous educational program that meets the postindustrial needs of American business at a time when the school-aged population is growing in numbers, in poverty, and in cultural diversity, and when taxpayers are questioning the cost, quality, and efficiency of public education.

The Social Environment of Education

The social environment of education encompasses the nature of the population to be educated and society's expectations for its schools. Both are changing dramatically. Children in school today are considerably more likely to be poor, from nontraditional families, and members of racial/ethnic minority groups. The percentage of children under age eighteen living in poverty decreased from 26.5 percent in 1960 to 14.9 percent in 1970, due largely to the War on Poverty programs of the late 1960s, but climbed again to 21.1 percent in 1992.[4] Some of the recent growth in poverty is related to changing family structures. In 1992, one quarter of all families with children under the age of eighteen were headed by a single parent (or caretaker), compared to only 11 percent of such families in 1970. Over three million of the nation's 64 million children are being raised by grandparents.[5] Single parent households, especially those headed by members of racial/ethnic minorities, are more likely to live in poverty. In 1992, one-fourth of Hispanic and half of African-American children lived in female-headed households; two-thirds of these households had incomes below the poverty line. However, minority children living in two-parent households also had poverty rates that were two to three times those of their white peers.[6] Poverty may continue to increase as the nation's schools enroll larger numbers of minority students. Between 1976 and 1992, the proportion of white, non-Hispanic students in American public schools declined from 76.0 to 66.7 percent of the student population, while the proportion of African-American students increased slightly (15.5 to 16.5 percent), and the proportion of Hispanic students nearly doubled (6.4 to 12.3 percent).[7] The nation's school-aged population is projected to become increasingly nonwhite into the twenty-first century. By the year 2010, only 64 percent of the nation's youth (age 0–17) will be non-Hispanic white, while the percentage of Hispanic youth will climb to about 15 percent.[8]

The educational problems of these children are confounded by their growing racial and economic isolation from mainstream society. By 1984, nearly one-third of African-American and Hispanic students attended "intensely segregated" schools, that is, 90 percent or more minority, and more than two-thirds of these students attended schools that were more than 50 percent minority.[9] States are impacted differentially by the concentration and growth of poor, minority, and limited English proficient students. Southern states have the highest school-age poverty rates in the country, but the number of poor children grew substantially in the West and Southwest during the 1980s.[10] Thirteen states were racially homogeneous—they had 12 percent or less minority youth in 1992—while four states, including the country's two largest, California and Texas, had "majority-minority" school-aged populations (see Table 9-1). California and Texas are also home to almost half of the nation's limited English proficient students, and California alone accounted for nearly 40 percent of the national school-age immigrant population in 1990.[11] Every year California acquires more school children than are enrolled in each of the six smallest states in the country.

These demographics have three major implications for education policy.[12] First, schools are faced with an "imperiled generation" of children, with between one-quarter and one-third of today's school children at risk of failure in school.[13] School curricula, programs, and structure need to be redesigned to meet the needs of children who come from multiple language and cultural backgrounds, are potential low achievers, change schools frequently, and have health and family problems. Second, the link between education and financial and career success in adulthood is growing stronger as the number of jobs in the middle of the economic range—primarily in manufacturing—continues to decline. If educational services for poor and minority students are not improved, these individuals will become increasingly concentrated in the nation's low-paying service economy. Third, there is a growing gap between those who benefit from public services and those who pay for them. Those population groups with the largest vested interest in education are those with limited political power—low income and minority citizens. As poor and minority students become increasingly concentrated in inner city and rural schools, white

Table 9-1 Economic and Racial/Ethnic Make-up of the States (percent)

State	Persons Aged 5 and under below the Poverty Line (1990)	Public School Students by Race or Ethnicity (1992)			
		White[a]	Black[a]	Hispanic	Other[b]
Alabama	26.1	62.7	35.6	0.3	1.4
Alaska	13.6	66.1	4.7	2.3	27.0
Arizona	24.9	60.4	4.1	26.9	8.6
Arkansas	28.5	74.4	23.9	0.7	1.0
California	19.0	43.4	8.6	36.1	11.8
Colorado	17.9	74.5	5.4	16.8	3.5
Connecticut	11.7	73.8	2.9	10.7	2.5
Delaware	13.3	66.8	28.1	3.2	1.9
District of Columbia	27.0	4.0	89.1	5.6	1.3
Florida	20.3	60.3	24.4	13.4	1.8
Georgia	22.1	60.7[c]	37.9[c]	0.6[c]	0.8[c]
Hawaii	12.6	23.8	2.7	5.2	68.3
Idaho	19.6	92.6[c]	0.3[c]	4.9[c]	2.1[c]
Illinois	18.9	65.1	21.2	10.7	2.7
Indiana	16.8	86.2	1.0	1.9	0.8
Iowa	17.5	93.8	2.9	1.5	1.8
Kansas	16.8	84.1	8.2	5.0	2.7
Kentucky	27.9	89.7	9.5	0.2	0.2
Louisiana	33.4	52.2	45.1	1.0	1.6
Maine	15.7	98.3[c]	0.5[c]	0.2[c]	1.0[c]
Maryland	11.9	59.8	33.6	2.7	4.0
Massachusetts	14.5	79.8	8.0	8.5	3.8
Michigan	22.1	77.8	7.4	2.4	2.3
Minnesota	14.8	89.8	3.7	1.5	5.0
Mississippi	35.8	48.3	50.6	0.2	0.9
Missouri	20.4	82.6	15.5	0.8	1.1
Montana	24.3	88.0	0.5	1.4	10.1
Nebraska	17.3	88.9	5.5	3.2	2.3
Nevada	15.1	72.0	9.1	13.1	5.8
New Hampshire	8.5	97.0	0.8	1.0	1.2
New Jersey	11.7	63.7	18.7	12.6	5.0
New Mexico	30.3	40.9	2.3	45.8	11.1
New York	20.6	58.9	20.0	16.1	4.9
North Carolina	19.2	66.1	30.2	1.1	2.6
North Dakota	19.6	90.8	0.7	0.7	7.8
Ohio	21.1	83.0	14.6	1.3	1.1
Oklahoma	25.3	72.6	10.2	3.1	14.2
Oregon	19.7	87.5	2.4	5.3	4.8
Pennsylvania	17.5	81.7	13.5	3.1	1.8
Rhode Island	16.3	82.0	6.6	8.0	3.5
South Carolina	22.8	57.3	41.4	0.5	0.8
South Dakota	23.6	86.3	0.7	0.5	11.9
Tennessee	23.9	75.8	22.9	0.4	0.9
Texas	25.6	48.4	14.3	34.9	2.4
Utah	15.8	91.7	0.6	4.3	3.4

Table 9-1   *(continued)*

State	Persons Aged 5 and under Below the Poverty Line (1990)	Public School Students by Race or Ethnicity (1992)			
		White[a]	Black[a]	Hispanic	Other[b]
Vermont	13.5	97.7	0.6	0.3	1.4
Virginia	14.5	68.5	25.5	2.5	3.5
Washington	17.0	80.7	4.4	6.4	8.5
West Virginia	31.7	95.4	4.0	0.2	0.5
Wisconsin	17.7	84.8	8.7	2.8	3.5
Wyoming	18.3	89.6	0.9	6.1	3.3
United States	20.1	66.7	16.5	12.3	4.5

Source: Digest of Education Statistics, 1994 (Washington, D.C.: U.S. Department of Education, National Center for Education Statistics, October 1994), Tables 20 and 45.

[a] Excludes persons of Hispanic origin.

[b] Includes Asian or Pacific Islander and American Native/Alaskan Native.

[c] Data for 1986. Data not available for 1992.

middle-aged, middle class suburban dwellers have become less willing to pay for these public schools, leading state legislators to balk at school finance reforms that raise taxes and/or redistribute education resources. In addition, as the nation's population ages, fewer individuals have a direct stake in the public education system. The number of households with school-aged children, now only 20 percent of all households, will decline as the baby boomers age.[14]

Social values about education have changed as well over the last twenty years. At a time when the number of disadvantaged students in our nation's schools is growing, society has retreated from its commitment to equal educational opportunity. In the 1960s, the civil rights movement heightened public awareness of inequities in society and passage of the Elementary and Secondary Education Act in 1965 focused attention on issues of equality of educational opportunity. Passage of the Bilingual Education Act of 1968 and enactment of the Education for All Handicapped Children Act of 1975 (now called the Individuals with Disabilities Education Act) expanded educational access to students not proficient in the English language and to those with disabilities. The education reform movement of the 1980s and 1990s, however, has redirected attention to efficiency and choice. The educational policies of these decades have emphasized higher educational standards for students and teachers, greater accountability for school and student performance, and increasing parental choice. Today, there are signs of renewed interest in issues of equity. Educators and policy makers now discuss educational standards for *all* students, and the need to develop educational programs for at-risk students. Equity issues are also reemerging as a result of an unprecedented number of school finance court cases. Even today's business leaders are joining in this re-emphasis on equity, though as much out of concern for the nation's economic development as for revitalization of the equity agenda of former years.

The Economic Environment of Education

The education reform movement of the 1980s and 1990s has been dominated by economic concerns: declining U.S. competitiveness in an international economy; low industrial productivity; and changes in the skill level, size, and composition of the nation's labor force. Worker productivity must continually increase for the United States to successfully compete in the global economy. Yet, employers in large and small businesses alike decry the lack of preparation for work among high school students. At a time when work force skills are growing increasingly complex and undergoing rapid change, too many students lack the necessary reading, writing, mathematical, and problem-solving skills to meet entry-level job requirements.[15] Performance on national assessments of mathematics and science improved slightly between the mid-1970s and 1992, especially for nine- and thirteen-year-old students, but improvement was concentrated in the lower levels of proficiency, or basic skills areas. Students showed little change on the reading assessment during this period. They had difficulty applying these skills and knowledge to complex problems, and fewer than 10 percent demonstrated the knowledge and skills to do first-year college-level work. In addition, while the performance gap between white and non-white students narrowed during the 1970s and 1980s, a substantial disparity remains. In reading, writing, and science, for example, the average score for a seventeen-year-old African-American student is at or below the average score for a thirteen-year-old white student.[16] As poor and minority individuals come to constitute a larger and larger portion of the labor force, "business leaders have come to understand that the emerging labor supply problem is essentially an educational problem."[17]

Another aspect of the economic environment that affects state education policy is the availability of fiscal resources to support public education. While real spending (adjusted for inflation) on elementary and secondary education grew 22 percent in the 1970s and 48 percent in the 1980s, it rose only 3 percent between 1989 and 1993.[18] The environment for increases in school revenue in the rest of the 1990s is projected to be unfavorable. State support for education will be limited by moderate economic growth, a need to offset cuts in federal aid for health and social welfare programs, conservative state tax policy (see Chapter 3), and continued strong competition for state tax dollars from corrections and health programs.[19]

The Political Environment of Education

Until the late 1960s, state education policy was the province of broad-based education interest groups (state education departments, schools of education, superintendents, administrators, and teachers) and a small number of legislators who specialized in education policy. Groups like the Educational Conference Board in New York and the Princeton Group in New Jersey sought to build consensus among these educational interests on the policy goals and legislative priorities in their states. This structure fit the limited state role in education at the time. Three factors have contributed to the growing complexity of education politics today: the changing roles of the federal and state governments in education policy, the growing political and programmatic fragmentation of education, and the emergence of noneducation interests into the education policy arena.

The involvement of the federal and state governments in public education expanded rapidly in the late 1960s and early 1970s. While the federal government has always played a modest role in public education, concern over national security and poverty led it to support the development of curricular innovations in mathematics and science and to design and fund equal educational opportunity programs. Although federal aid to education never exceeded 9 percent of all spending on elementary and secondary education, the impact of its financial contribution has been far-reaching. The federal government supported the expansion and professionalization of state departments of education throughout the country, and in times of state fiscal constraint it continues to fund the majority of SEA positions in many states.[20] A limited amount of federal dollars, coupled with comprehensive civil rights legislation, has driven the scope and content of special education programming across the country. While the federal contribution has dropped to less than 7 percent, the federal government remains the primary funder of educational programs for children in poverty.

Expansion of the state role in education policy was driven in part by its role in the implementation of these new federal programs, but also by the expanding fiscal role of states (caused by exploding school populations and the first round of school finance court cases) and a corresponding call for accountability in the use of these new state education dollars. As state courts called for greater equalization of education funding, both the state share of local education expenditures and the absolute level of state education spending rose substantially. This growth led many states to implement testing and other policies in the 1970s to hold educators accountable for the operation and performance of their schools. A national call for higher academic standards in the 1980s expanded the state role further in the setting of student, teacher, and school standards.

The broadened roles of state and federal government in education policy changed state education politics in two ways. First, the state education agenda expanded. With state education aid the major component of state budgets, legislators became preoccupied with the increasingly contentious job of raising and allocating state dollars to local school districts. Every year, policy makers had to balance a complex equity, political, and economic agenda, as school finance decisions became intertwined with the politics of redistribution and the politics of taxation. On the nonfiscal side, the push for higher education standards and increased accountability thrust governors and legislators in the role of defining and measuring the goals and elements of a quality education, areas that had been the province of education professionals and local school boards. In recent years these issues have become controversial, as the conservative right challenges both the substance and the value-orientation of state standards and related policies.

Second, the number of actors interested and involved in shaping education policy decisions grew, transforming the political structure from a state-wide monolith to a fragmented system of education politics.[21] The growth of collective bargaining for teachers and the creation of interest groups organized around new categorical education programs shattered the old consensus-building structures, replacing them with competing centers of power—teacher unions, administrator groups, and bilingual, Title I, and special education advocates. In the early 1980s, business groups emerged as powerful new voices in shaping education policy. The absence of a broad consensus about the purpose of education led to a patchwork of state education programs to meet the demands of different and often competing interests. What was unique about the politics of state education reform in the 1980s was the relatively unimportant role of education interest groups in the formulation of new state policies. While opposed to specific aspects of the new reforms, education groups were stymied. Strong public and business support assured backing from governors and state legislators.[22] Traditional education groups have found it difficult to regain their previous influence in state education policy in the 1990s, as Republican governors and legislatures have found continued public and business support for a more conservative agenda of deregulation and choice. The business community has turned its attention to programs that facilitate the preparation of students for, and transition into, the world of work, such as job apprenticeships, "tech-prep," and school-to-work initiatives.

The politics of education also grew more complicated as governors emerged as major players in education policy, sometimes leading, sometimes challenging, traditional legislative prerogatives. Governors began to play a visible role in educational policy in the 1970s when many became leaders in school finance reform in their states, crafting proposals to respond to real or anticipated court orders to reform state funding systems and proposing new or increased state taxes to fund these reforms.[23] Their role increased dramatically in the 1980s, when a group of reform-minded governors undertook an education reform movement that sought to respond to calls by the public, the business community, and the president for improved education. Reform activities by individual governors coalesced in 1989 when President George Bush and the nation's governors embraced the concept of national education goals at a historic education summit.[24] Many states have since adopted these goals as part of their education reform agendas, and a few state courts have used them as standards for the reform of their school finance systems. Governors remain active leaders in education in the 1990s, although many have a revised education agenda—one focused on the devolution of power from the state to local school districts and even to individual schools, on increased parental choice in education, and on limiting growth in education spending.

The fragmentation of the education political environment creates a major barrier for policy makers who are committed to taking a more systemic approach to education reform. Reforms designed to dramatically improve teaching and learning in our nation's classrooms require the development of a largely unprecedented consensus around learning outcomes, purposeful coordination by independent agencies and policies bodies within and across levels of the system, the implementation of multiple, aligned policy interventions, and a rethinking of traditional governance patterns. In addition to multiple actors with diverse and conflicting interests, three other characteristics of the state political system pose barriers to more coherent policy making: the focus on elections, policy overload, and specialization. The emphasis placed on campaigning and elections over policy or institutional improvement goals has led state legislators to seek legislation with "name recognition," to circumvent controversial issues, and to favor policies with immediate effects and clear benefits over those with longer term and more remote benefits. At the same time, state policy makers are making policy on many more important education issues than in the past, forcing them to pay less attention to each aspect of policy. With increased complexity comes specialization in the legislative process. Specialization creates more arenas in which politicians can claim credit, but specialization contributes to the fragmentation of the system.[25]

Waves of Education Reform

State education policy has been shaped by four waves of education reform: the accountability movement of the 1970s, the excellence and restructuring movements of the 1980s, the standards-based or systemic reform movement of the 1990s, and the school finance equity movement of the 1970s and 1990s.

Increased involvement of states in education policy dates to the 1970s when state financial support of education increased and policy makers began to question how, and how well, these funds were being used. This interest, coupled with concerns about students' inability to read and compute, led many states to implement minimum competency testing (MCT) programs to measure and report student performance. The idea behind MCTs was that requiring certification of competencies at critical grades would prevent schools from passing incompetent students through the grades simply on the basis of social promotion. These tests focused almost exclusively, however, on the minimum abilities necessary to functioning in society.[26] This emphasis on basic skills, coupled with federal funding of compensatory education programs through the Elementary and Secondary Education Act of 1965, increased the performance of minority students and, to a lesser extent, students from educationally disadvantaged families.[27] At the same time, however, student achievement on higher order reading skills and in areas of problem-solving and application of mathematics showed signs of decline.[28] These data, evidence of score declines on the Scholastic Aptitude Test (SAT), and the poor performance of American students on international assessments of mathematics and science led a major national commission to declare in 1983 that the "educational foundations of our society are presently being eroded by a rising tide of mediocrity," and that students were not receiving the type of education necessary to meet the demands of a technological society or to maintain the nation's competitive economic position internationally.[29]

This report, and nearly a dozen others that reached similar conclusions, generated an unexpected response from the press, the public, and President Ronald Reagan, who toured the country speaking about the need to reform the national education system. Governors, state boards of education, and state legislatures established nearly three hundred state-level study commissions, proposed countless education reform measures, and adopted many of the recommendations contained in the national reports. Forty-one states responded by raising course work standards for high school graduation, twenty-two states implemented or expanded their minimum competency testing programs, and many states began to test aspiring teachers.[30]

This set of state reform activities did little to change the content of instruction (especially its focus on basic skills), to directly involve teachers in the reform process, or to alter the reigning notions of teaching and learning.[31] In response to these deficiencies, another wave of reform rhetoric emerged, calling for a fundamental rethinking and restructuring of schooling, rather than a bolstering of the existing system. The key concepts of this reform movement were decentralization, professionalization, and "bottom-up" change, as reformers focused on the change process and on the active involvement of those closest to instruction. The school building became the basic unit of change, with an emphasis on producing changes in student outcomes.[32] Today, the dilemma we face is how to scale up from this small number of reforming schools so that all children have access to successful schools. Achieving this goal will require a major reorientation in content and pedagogy for students and teachers, as well as in the structure of schools. The fragmented, complex, multilayered nature of our educational policy system, however, makes success highly problematic.

The response to these challenges has been the development in the 1990s of "a coherent *systemic* strategy that can combine the energy and professional involvement of the . . . [school-based] reforms with a new and challenging state structure to generalize the reforms to all schools with the state.[33] The purpose of the *systemic* reform strategy, or standards-based reform as it is sometimes called, is to provide top-down [state-level] support of bottom-up [school-site based] reform." According to Marshall Smith and Jennifer O'Day, the strategy has three major prongs.[34] The first is a *unifying vision and goals* that provide a coherent direction/strategy for education reform throughout the system. States should establish student outcome goals that focus primarily on the core functions of the education system—teaching and learning—and they should encompass high standards. The vision and goals must promote equality as well as quality, and be applied to *all* students and schools.

The second prong is a *coherent system of state policy guidance* that promotes these ambitious student outcomes. This involves the coordination of key state policies affecting teaching and learning: curriculum and curriculum materials, preservice and inservice teacher training, and assessment. State-developed curriculum frameworks that set out the best thinking about what students should know and be able to do in core academic areas can provide the direction for locally developed curriculum and for state professional development and assessment policies. States must then assure that prospective and practicing teachers have the content knowledge and instructional skills required to teach the content of the frameworks through program certification and teacher licensure requirements. They must also offer programmatic and financial support of professional development opportunities that are aligned with the new curriculum content standards. An assessment system designed to measure student knowledge of the new content standards would provide information on student progress and stimulate and support good instruction in the schools.

The third prong is a *restructured governance system* that defines the responsibilities of the various levels of the system to facilitate classroom adoption of the new content and pedagogy. State government's role is to set system and student goals for the state, coordinate these long-term instructional goals across various state policies, and hold schools and school districts accountable for meeting these goals. Schools are then given the authority to develop the specific curricula, programs, and instructional approaches needed to achieve their goals. The main responsibility of school districts is to provide resources and support the efforts of schools to educate all of the district's children to meet state and district goals. In addition, states and school districts must ensure that all students within their boundaries are treated fairly, especially regarding the allocation of resources.

In tandem with these waves of education reform have been two waves of school finance reform. Wealth-based disparities in education spending evident in the 1960s led to a series of legal challenges to state education finance systems. (See Chapter 7.) This first wave of litigation, which continued into the 1970s and early 1980s, was characterized by *equity* cases that focused on the relationship between school district wealth and spending. The remedies were designed to equalize spending among school districts by providing additional state aid to low wealth communities. Seventeen state high court decisions were handed down in this period; seven overturned existing school finance plans, and ten upheld them.[35] Yet, this new judicial activism spurred states to restructure and expand their education funding systems. Twenty-eight states enacted school finance reform measures between 1971 and 1981,[36] state education revenues rose by one-third, and the state share of funding rose from 40 to 49 percent.[37]

States began to address a second kind of educational equity issue during the 1970s as well: meeting the needs of students with physical, mental, and environmental disadvantages. Led by the urban states of California, Massachusetts, and New York, by 1980 twenty-three states had enacted special funding programs to support services to educationally disadvantaged students; an equal number funded the instruction of limited English proficient students. All fifty states had enacted programs for students with disabilities that conformed to federal law, although they varied in how they were financed.[38]

School finance activity abated in the 1980s as state policy makers turned their attention to issues of excellence in education. The equity issue appeared to be dead until four new school finance decisions were issued in 1989 and 1990 in Kentucky, Texas, Montana, and New Jersey. These decisions led to a second wave of school finance cases that have focused on issues of *educational adequacy* as well as equity. School finance cases were filed in over half of the states between 1989 and 1994. Fourteen decisions have been rendered, nine of which declared their state's school funding systems unconstitutional.[39] Cases are pending in the other dozen or so states. Three issues appeared to have triggered this new round of litigation. First, in a few states—for example, in New Jersey—reform laws that were enacted after an earlier round of litigation failed to close spending gaps. Second, reformers were concerned that the excellence movement of the 1980s would leave educationally disadvantaged students further behind because their communities could not provide the level of education resources necessary to meet the new standards. Third, the adequacy theory reopened the legal door for states that had been unsuccessful in litigating an equity claim.

Major Issues in State Policy

Although the fifty states are socially, economically, and politically diverse, policy makers in every state must direct five major areas of education policy: curriculum and instruction, accountability, teachers, governance, and finance.

Curriculum and Instruction

States have used a variety of measures over the years to influence the content of the school curriculum, not the least of which was minimum competency testing. But until the 1990s, most state activity focused on instructional time and/or required courses or credits. All states mandate the minimum number of days students must attend school, and a majority of states (36) have set this minimum at 180 days. Another twelve states have mandated shorter school years, though all but one of these have at least a 175–day school year. Districts are free to extend their school year beyond this minimum, and a few states—California and Michigan, for example—offer financial incentives to school districts that lengthen their school year. Forty-four states also mandate the minimum length of the school day, with the length of the school day increasing as students get older. Again, districts may extend their school day beyond this minimum time, and many do.[40]

In 1983, the National Commission on Excellence in Education recommended that high school students take more courses in the "New Basics"—English, mathematics, science, social studies, and computer science. Specifically, the Commission recommended that high school graduates should complete four years of English, three years of mathematics, three years of science, three years of social studies, and one-half year of computer science. Two years of a foreign language were strongly recommended for college-bound students.[41] Forty-two of the forty-four states that mandate the number and type of courses students must complete for high school graduation raised their course work standards after the publication of the Commission's report. Yet, the course work requirements of most states still fall short of the National Commission's recommendations. While thirty-seven states require four or more years of English, only twenty-eight require three or more years of social studies, and few require three years of mathematics (10) or three years of science (4).[42]

States are beginning to explore the substitution of "outcome-based" high school graduation standards in place of "course-based" standards. Minnesota, for example, is developing a new outcome-based high school graduation rule that will shift the basis for matriculation from seat time to demonstrated achievement in two categories of learning outcomes: content knowledge in seven academic areas and more general learner expectations (for example, applying mathematical concepts to solve problems). While the state will require all students to pass competency tests in the seven content areas to receive a high school diploma, it has eliminated many of its other education mandates, including high school course work requirements.

Course work and instructional time requirements provide little substantive guidance in developing appropriate curricula. In an effort to provide students with a higher level of academic content and critical thinking skills, state and federal policy makers have turned increasingly to the establishment of challenging content and student performance standards and progressive state curriculum frameworks as the cornerstones of education reform. Federal education reform initiatives, such as the reauthorization of programs for disadvantaged students in the Improving America's Schools Act of 1994, the Clinton Administration's Goals 2000 program, and the National Science Foundation's Statewide and Urban Systemic Initiatives, require states to establish challenging learner outcomes in, at a minimum, mathematics, reading, writing, and science. States are then expected to align other policies, such as assessment and professional development, with these standards.

As states turn to a more results-oriented focus, they are looking to curriculum frameworks to serve as the intellectual core of state education policy. Nearly all states (45) report they are in the process of developing or revising curriculum frameworks that "outline the required knowledge, skills and processes to be taught to students."[43] States differ, however, in the focus, content, and prescriptiveness of their curriculum frameworks. Some states have adopted broad learner outcomes that emphasize general knowledge, skills, and attitudes students should acquire by the time they graduate from high school, rather than specifying content knowledge in the disciplines. For example, the first draft of Vermont's Common Core of Learning identified relatively abstract skill-based competencies under the rubric of communication, reasoning and problem-solving, citizenship, well-being, and global stewardship.[44] Minnesota's initial effort at revising the curriculum framework, the Model Learner Outcomes program, broadly set forth values, goals, and expected learning achievement in four subject areas. Pennsylvania's proposed learner goals and exit outcomes were also worded broadly; the former include items such as "adaptability to change." In contrast, curriculum frameworks such as those in California, Michigan, and Colorado contain more detailed, subject-matter-based content goals. Many states with broad learner outcomes have begun to develop subject-specific curriculum frameworks. In Vermont and Minnesota, for example, broad outcomes were deemed insufficient in providing an adequate foundation for an assessment system. In other states, the impetus to develop curriculum frameworks in mathematics and science came from the National Science Foundation's Statewide Systemic Initiative program.

The potential for curriculum frameworks to shape instruction is related to at least four factors. First, does the state mandate the use of these frameworks? Some states, such as Georgia, require districts to adopt state frameworks and to write local curriculum guides to implement these objectives. State curriculum resource guides aid local school districts with strategies to teach the state's objectives. Other states—New Jersey, for example—only require LEAs to incorporate state curriculum content standards; districts are given considerable leeway in the design of local curriculum. Curriculum guides in states such as Wisconsin are only advisory. While the new documents are comprehensive and have achieved national recognition, districts are under no obligation to adopt any or all of their content. Second, does the state have rewards or sanctions tied to local adoption of standards and/or frameworks? Are LEAs monitored on their implementation of these policies? Third, are the frameworks authoritative? Do they reflect a professional consensus on where teaching and learning should be going and/or the community's consensus about their content? Sometimes expert judgment and community values clash. In Pennsylvania, conservative religious groups viewed the state's proposed outcome-based education standards as interfering with and even challenging their own values. Similarly, Kansas' system of standards came under intense pressure from religious conservatives over the assessment of students' attitudes and beliefs, and Iowa halted its plans to move to outcome-based education to avoid a similar controversy. Fourth, are curriculum frameworks aligned with other state policies, such as textbook adoption and/or student assessment? South Carolina's attempts to generate higher order thinking and upgraded content are hampered by a basic skills assessment program that the legislature refuses to modify.

Accountability and Assessment

States have historically used systems of school accreditation as a means of monitoring and regulating education in their communities. Traditionally, accreditation has focused on compliance with input standards (for example, the proportion of certified staff and number of books in the library) and with process standards (for example, the method of handling student complaints). Districts were monitored periodically through a combination of district self-reports and site visits by state department of education personnel. In line with their increased attention to student standards and use of incentives and sanctions to improve school performance, states today are revising their accountability systems to focus more heavily on student performance and less on compliance monitoring, and more on the process of teaching and learning at the school level.

While over 80 percent of the states report they are developing, piloting, or implementing new approaches to accountability, there are few performance-based systems in operation.[45] Progress has been delayed in many states by issues of how to define and measure student performance and progress and by politics. A recent analysis of two states that have developed performance-based accountability systems—Kentucky and Mississippi—identified five challenges to their design and implementation. These are (1) making accountability systems understandable and defensible to policy makers, educators, parents, and students; (2) resolving issues of fairness when the composition of schools varies over time and across districts; (3) determining where to focus incentives for improvement—at the school or district level, and on low-achieving schools and districts or across a broader range of performance levels; (4) developing the state capacity in assessment and evaluation needed to implement and maintain these accountability systems; and (5) creating a stable political environment for standards-based reform.[46]

State assessments are at the center of most state education accountability systems. Thirty-nine states use state-developed, state-selected, or state-approved tests to assess student performance against state-established performance standards. But the states differ in the subject areas and grade levels assessed, number of students assessed (universe versus sample), type of test used (norm-referenced, criterion-referenced), test use (student diagnosis or placement, student promotion/high school graduation, school and district performance monitoring, program assessment), and test format (multiple choice, performance tasks, portfolios, writing samples). In twenty-three states, these tests have "high stakes" for students: students must meet state-established standards to graduate from high school (18 states) and/or to be promoted from one grade to the next (9 states).[47] State assessments have high stakes for school districts in Kentucky, New Jersey, and South Carolina as well, where low test scores are a major criterion in these states' decisions to intervene in and/or take over the administration of a school district.

As states shift to performance-based accountability programs, they are reevaluating the nature of tests and their effects on the system, particularly on classroom instruction. During the 1980s, state assessments were expanded to cover more grade levels and subject areas, but the primary focus remained on basic skills content. Research showed, however, that multiple choice, basic skills testing, and the high stakes use of assessment led to a narrowing of the curriculum and to drill-and-practice methods of instruction. Emphasis was placed on rote memorization of facts and not on problem-solving or application of facts to a real world context.[48] In addition, basic skills tests could not assess the more challenging curriculum advocated by national professional associations (for example, the National Council of Teachers of Mathematics) or by state policy makers.

Many states began modifying their testing programs in the late 1980s and early 1990s in response to these concerns. Vermont and Kentucky, for example, replaced their multiple choice testing programs with portfolio assessments where a student's work is presented in full detail, not just as test results. Other states, such as Colorado, suspended their state assessment programs until they could develop state content standards and new assessments aligned with these new standards. But the more common reaction was to move away from norm-referenced tests to criterion-referenced assessments and to add some form of nonmultiple-choice format to the test, such as writing samples, open-ended questions, and performance items. In 1992, twenty-eight states were implementing, and six more were in the process of designing or piloting, some form of alternative assessment.[49] These new assessments are designed to connect more directly to what students learn in the classroom and to encourage instruction that has students synthesize information and engage in problem-solving and other higher order thinking skills.

While many state and federal policy makers have embraced new assessment approaches, state testing policy faces three challenges. First, policy makers expect one assessment system to serve multiple purposes. These purposes include providing indicators of the performance of the education system, holding schools and educators accountable for their performance, certifying student performance as students move from grade to grade or out of the K-12 education system, motivating students to perform better and teachers to change their instructional content and strategies, and aiding in instructional decisions about individual students.[50] Yet, assessment experts question whether one test, no matter what the format, can address these multiple needs. For example, scores on assessments that are best suited for classroom instruction, such as portfolios, are difficult to aggregate on a district basis for accountability purposes. This first challenge leads to a second—developing alternative assessment formats that are reliable, valid, and generalizable. Studies of portfolio assessments in Vermont and Kentucky have raised a number of technical problems, including whether the scoring of portfolios is too subjective and inconsistent and whether changes in school scores from one year to the next are reliable enough for allocating monetary rewards or sanctioning school administrators.[51]

Third, while assessment reforms appear to have support from the education profession and many policy makers, the public position on the substance and use of alternative assessments is not as clear. A survey by the Public Agenda Foundation in 1994 found that only a bare majority of the public agrees with educators that multiple-choice exams should be replaced with essays.[52] In fact, the current education reform agenda generally is out of sync with the public's top concerns about safe and orderly schools and effective teaching of the basic skills. While the public supports setting higher academic standards for students, and having schools set clear guidelines on what students should learn, they are uncomfortable with many recent pedagogical reforms, such as using calculators to teach computation, teaching composition without teaching spelling and grammar, and grouping students of different abilities.[53] In California, for example, the education community failed to build broad public support for its reform efforts. As a result, political opposition led by the conservative right succeeded in killing that state's cutting-edge assessment program. California is now in the process of revising its assessment program to incorporate more traditional test items and is revisiting the content of its curricular frameworks.

Teacher Policy

State teacher policy encompasses three broad areas: the preparation and certification of teachers, professional development, and teacher pay.

Teacher Preparation and Certification.   States are responsible for assuring that individuals entering the teaching profession are qualified to teach the grades and subjects to which they are assigned. They use several policy instruments to meet this objective. First, all states require that teachers complete an approved teacher education program and/or a prescribed course of study. Program requirements differ by grade span and by subject area, but, like high school course work requirements, focus on the type rather than the content or quality of the courses taken. Forty states allow individuals with a college degree to seek certification through an alternative route.[54] In many states, this option is limited to critical shortage areas, such as mathematics and science. In others, such as New Jersey, the alternative route was developed to attract more qualified people into the teaching pool and is available for most certification areas. In that state, where nearly half of all newly hired teachers come through the alternative route, prospective teachers must pass a subject area test, receive mentoring from a school staff person, and complete a 200-hour professional development component.

Second, most states assess prospective teachers. In 1980, only a handful of states—primarily in the Southeast—required individuals to pass a test before becoming certified to teach. By 1990, thirty-nine states required aspiring teachers to pass a state-prescribed, standardized test before entering a teacher education program and/or before being certified to teach. Applicants are tested in basic skills (26 states), professional knowledge (27 states), and their teaching specialty (23 states).[55] In addition, seventeen states evaluate a beginning teacher's classroom performance before granting regular certification.[56] While the number of states assessing prospective teachers has stabilized in the last few years, the scope and substance of teacher assessments is changing. One major producer of teacher assessments, Educational Testing Service, is replacing its National Teacher Examination program with an assessment program that includes a computer-based assessment and instructional program in the basic skills and a mechanism for evaluating beginning teachers in the classroom.

Unlike high stakes tests in elementary and secondary education, teacher tests have little or no impact on teacher education curriculum. There appear to be two explanations for this. First, much of the tested material is basic skills, skills that individuals should have developed prior to entering college or a teacher preparation program. Second, the tests of pedagogy and subject matter are aligned with existing curriculum to meet state and federal legal requirements of content validity. Thus, teacher testing has followed, rather than led, teacher preparation curriculum. Institutions with high failure rates have adjusted their curriculum to increase the passing rates of their students, but this involves strengthening a traditional program rather than implementing an innovative program. Vermont is trying to address this problem by establishing a "results-oriented" process for the approval of teacher preparation programs that is based on student portfolios.

Third, states regulate the recertification of teachers. The last state (New Jersey) to grant a permanent license to first-year teachers ended this practice in 1991. Ten states, however, provide lifetime licenses to teachers who hold an advanced certificate. The remaining thirty-nine states require teachers to renew their certificates on a regular basis and, with one exception, base recertification on years of teaching experience and/or completion of additional formal education and/or in-service training. Most states' requirements do not specify that this additional training be in the individual's teaching area. The activities of the National Board for Professional Teaching Standards (NBPTS) may change the nature of teacher recertification in the future. Funded by foundations and the federal government, NBPTS is establishing demanding standards for what experienced teachers should know and be able to do and developing a national, voluntary assessment system to identify teachers who meet these standards. The National Board's certification system, which will eventually encompass more than two dozen different fields, is being phased in. Criteria for certification will include a minimum of three years of teaching experience and successful completion of state-of-the-art assessments in the individual's teaching area. It is not known what impact the NBPTS' standards and assessments will have on state teacher policy, though the National Board hopes that their work will drive reforms in both teacher preparation and teacher licensure practices at the state level.

Staff Development.   States generally play a limited role in teacher staff development. States may require districts to provide in-service opportunities and educators to develop plans for continued professional growth, and many states establish guidelines for or approve in-service activities used for recertification. But these guidelines do not specify content. Most districts must rely on local funds or federal categorical aid programs, such as Title I of the Elementary and Secondary Education Act and the Eisenhower Mathematics and Science Education Program, to support professional development activities. In 1990, only eight states reported funding district in-service programs or teacher professional development activities, although several states funded state academies or training programs.[57] And even those states that fund professional development provide too few dollars to support the kind of extended, long term staff development that the research shows to be most effective.[58] Part of the problem is that staff development has limited political support and is vulnerable at times of fiscal crisis. Minnesota, for example, required that school districts set aside a fixed percentage of their general state aid payments for staff development, but this funding mechanism became an issue in the legislature and school districts. The earmarking provision was eliminated in 1995, and professional development funds will now compete with other uses at the district level. Legislation that increased federal funding of professional development in 1994 is under attack by the current Congress.

Teacher Pay.   In the early 1980s, many states set out to raise teacher salaries to make teaching more competitive with other professions. By 1986, at least thirty states had set minimum teacher salaries.[59] In addition to upgrading salaries, state policy makers also experimented with a number of incentive systems to reward teachers for more, or better, performance. While a number of merit pay programs, career ladders, and similar initiatives have continued, the trend has been to transform these programs into less controversial school-based incentive programs. South Carolina and Kentucky, for example, provide financial rewards to schools that show gains in student performance on state tests. Schools in South Carolina receive a per pupil award for annual improvements in achievement test scores that exceed predicted gains, student attendance, and teacher attendance. In Kentucky, teachers receive cash awards if student performance in their schools exceeds state-determined improvement goals.

Governance

The systemic reform movement, with its focus on student outcomes, and a growing political call for the decentralization and deregulation of government have led states to reconsider many aspects of their education governance systems. State policy initiatives, which include the deregulation of state education policy, decentralization of control through site-based management (SBM), and the privatization of education through vouchers and contracting, are designed to give schools, their communities, and their clients greater control over education policy so they have the freedom and flexibility to improve student performance.

States began experimenting with the deregulation of state education policy in the mid-1980s as a way of promoting the school-based innovation and teacher professionalization called for in the wave of "bottom-up" reform. Initially, states permitted schools to seek waivers from regulation, but the early waiver programs were limited in their eligibility criteria and in the rules that could be exempted. Not surprisingly, they had limited impact on school practice.[60] Deregulation then evolved to charter schools and broad-scale deregulation of state regulations. In 1995, twelve states had charter school legislation and another twenty were considering it.[61] Charter schools operate under contract with sponsoring agencies (e.g., local school boards, universities, state boards of education) that specify the outcomes and how they will be measured and the nature and extent of the schools' freedom from state and district regulation. The degree of autonomy granted charter schools by state legislatures varies widely across the twelve states. For example, while Arizona and Minnesota grant superwaivers to charter schools, limiting state regulation to health, safety, and civil rights issues, charter schools in Colorado must specify what state and local rules they want waived. Most states, however, require charter schools to negotiate personnel, service, and budget decisions with their districts, and many limit the number of charters permitted.[62]

New accountability systems focused on student outcomes are also causing states to reexamine the substance and scope of their education regulations. Minnesota and Tennessee repealed large numbers of regulations to free schools to organize and manage instruction in ways they considered necessary to improve student performance. The Texas legislature allowed its state's education code to expire and then replaced it with legislation that scaled back the authority of the state education department and allowed districts to apply for "home rule" charters that would free them from most state mandates. In 1993, at least eight other states reported some form of formal review or advisory process to determine whether existing regulations should be modified to promote school and school district autonomy.[63] That number has grown since the 1994 elections placed more conservative governors and state school board members in office.

School restructuring or site-based management (SBM) is another approach to increasing school control over the content and delivery of education services. In its various forms, SBM provides greater school-site autonomy over some combination of budget, personnel, and program decisions. Most SBM plans also include a school-based governance structure that involves parents and teachers (and sometimes community members) in the decision-making process.[64] The first school-based governance initiatives were launched by innovative superintendents in a few large urban school systems, often with the support of their teacher unions. States then entered the arena, encouraging and/or mandating the adoption of school-based planning or SBM activities. Some states, such as Illinois, focused their restructuring initiatives on urban school districts. The Chicago Reform Act of 1988, for example, required that city to reallocate the resources of the system to the school level and created local school councils at each school with the responsibility to adopt a school improvement plan, devise a budget to implement that plan based on a lump sum allocation, and hire and fire the principal.[65] Others, such as Kentucky, required all schools to establish school site councils and assigned these bodies responsibility for curriculum, instructional materials, personnel, and other policies, many of which had previously been under the purview of the local school board.

The most radical forms of deregulation and decentralization place the control of education in the hands of a private contractor or in the hands of the parents. Over the years, school districts have privatized a number of education support activities, such as transportation and food service, but only recently have they decided to contract out the management of an entire school or schools. Like charter schools, private contractors are given leeway in how they manage schools or school districts in exchange for promises of raising student achievement.

Proposals to use parental choice as a way of improving the quality of public education date back more than two hundred years, when Adam Smith wrote in *The Wealth of Nations* that parents should pay part of the costs of schooling because if the state were to pay all the costs, the teacher "would soon learn to neglect his business."[66] Giving parents the power (and the dollars) to choose their schools shifts the production of educational services from the government to the marketplace. Proponents argue that the marketplace will provide educational programs that are more responsive to the needs and concerns of parents and their children and that the system will utilize resources more efficiently.

The most visible and controversial parental choice policy has been the tuition voucher program, but school choice plans come in many forms. Since 1985, when Minnesota passed a law permitting high school students to enroll in college courses for high school credit, more than half the states have passed school choice laws of one kind or another. Most provide for choice only within the public sector. These laws fall into six categories: (1) interdistrict transfer laws, which allow students to attend public schools in other school districts; (2) intradistrict transfer laws, which enable students to choose schools or programs within their district but outside their attendance zone; (3) postsecondary enrollment option laws; (4) state-supported residential and special high schools for academically talented students; (5) educational clinics and alternative programs for high school dropouts; and (6) tuition vouchers for use in private schools.[67]

Although many states have enacted choice statutes, most are limited in scope because of the political, fiscal, and legal constraints involved in the design of these programs. Choice programs seriously threaten the interests of school boards, administrators, and teacher unions and have the potential of draining scarce state aid funds from public schools. In interdistrict transfer laws, states must make basic fiscal decisions such as who will pay for the students' transportation and will state aid follow the student to his or her new district? In Massachusetts, for example, three school districts lost so much state aid as a result of student transfers that the legislature had to appropriate

Table 9-2 Educational Expenditures per Pupil and Revenues by Source and State, 1991–1992 (percent)

State	Source of Revenues		
	Federal	State	Local[a]
Alabama	11.4	58.8	29.8
Alaska	11.5	68.0	20.5
Arizona	8.8	42.4	48.8
Arkansas	10.8	59.9	29.3
California	7.5	65.9	26.6
Colorado	5.0	42.8	52.3
Connecticut	3.2	40.7	56.0
Delaware	7.6	65.9	26.5
District of Columbia	9.4	0	90.6
Florida	7.3	48.4	44.3
Georgia	7.7	47.7	44.6
Hawaii	7.5	90.3	2.2
Idaho	8.1	61.8	30.1
Illinois	6.8	28.9	64.2
Indiana	5.3	52.9	41.8
Iowa	5.3	47.3	47.4
Kansas	5.5	42.4	52.1
Kentucky	10.1	67.0	22.9
Louisiana	10.8	54.7	34.4
Maine	5.9	49.8	44.3
Maryland	5.1	38.2	56.7
Massachusetts	5.3	30.7	64.0
Michigan	6.2	26.6	67.2
Minnesota	4.5	51.6	44.0
Mississippi	17.0	53.5	29.5
Missouri	6.4	38.0	55.7
Montana	8.8	41.8	49.3
Nebraska	6.2	34.3	59.5
Nevada	4.2	38.7	57.1
New Hampshire	3.1	8.5	88.4
New Jersey	4.1	42.2	53.7
New Mexico	12.4	73.8	13.8
New York	5.6	40.3	54.1
North Carolina	7.2	64.6	28.2
North Dakota	11.1	44.8	44.1
Ohio	5.9	40.8	53.3
Oklahoma	4.6	62.2	33.2
Oregon	6.4	30.6	63.0
Pennsylvania	5.7	41.4	52.8
Rhode Island	6.0	38.5	55.5
South Carolina	9.0	48.3	42.6
South Dakota	11.1	27.0	62.0
Tennessee	10.5	42.2	47.3
Texas	6.6	43.4	50.0
Utah	6.9	57.2	35.8
Vermont	5.1	31.6	63.3
Virginia	5.8	31.1	63.1

Table 9-2   *(continued)*

| | Source of Revenues | | |
State	Federal	State	Local[a]
Washington	5.7	71.6	22.6
West Virginia	7.6	67.2	25.2
Wisconsin	4.4	39.4	56.2
Wyoming	5.3	52.5	42.2
U.S. Total	6.6	46.4	47.0

Source: Digest of Education Statistics, 1994 (Washington, D.C.: U.S. Department of Education, National Center for Education Statistics, October, 1994), Table 158.

[a] Local, intermediate, and private (e.g., revenue from gifts and tuition and fees from patrons).

emergency funds to blunt the financial impact of the choice law.[68] Finally, state constitutions and courts will determine whether school choice plans can extend to religiously supported schools and how these plans will interact with civil rights laws, such as court-ordered desegregation of schools.

School Finance

The state role in education finance dates to 1647 when the General Court of Massachusetts passed the Old Deluder Satan Act, requiring every town to set up a school or pay a sum of money to a larger town to provide educational services. The act required that these schools be supported by masters, parents, or the inhabitants in general.[69] Initially, local communities established one-room elementary schools, often fully supported by a small local tax. By the mid-nineteenth century, several states had created not only statewide systems of public education, but mechanisms for funding these schools. In New York State, for example, an 1849 statute provided for a state share of school funding of 52 percent. Yet, the fixed appropriation could not keep up with rising school costs, and local real property taxes had to bear an increasing share of the burden. State legislators 150 years ago thus faced the same vexing problems as legislators today: how to alleviate wealth-based disparities in education spending and taxation among school districts in their state.

School districts receive revenues from three sources: the federal government (6.6 percent), state government (46.4 percent), and local taxes (47.0 percent).[70] These national averages for the 1991–1992 school year mask major differences in sources of revenues across the states. As shown in Table 9-2, state support for elementary and secondary education ranges from a low of 8.5 percent in New Hampshire to 90.3 percent in Hawaii. Similarly, the local share of education funding varies from 88.4 percent to 2.2 percent in these two states, respectively. The level of local education revenues is driven by the interaction of the wealth and tax effort of a community. This close relationship between wealth and revenues makes it possible for a rich district to raise more revenue for education than a poor district, even though both are applying the same education tax rate. For example, a community with property wealth of $100,000 per student can raise only $1,000 per student in local tax revenues with a ten-mill tax rate, while a wealthier neighboring community with a tax base of $500,000 per student can raise five times as much, or $5,000 per student, with that same tax effort. Although most state aid systems are designed to compensate for these wealth-based disparities in education spending, state aid is generally insufficient to offset these differences in community wealth. The result of these school finance systems is that poor school districts cannot generate sufficient revenue for an adequate education program, or one that matches their more fortunate neighbors.

The school finance equity cases referenced earlier in this chapter (and discussed in Chapter 7) focused on whether school districts of different wealth and tax effort received similar levels of funding. In contrast, adequacy cases are concerned about whether that level of funding is sufficient to prepare all students for higher education, skilled employment, and other experiences of adult life.[71] While issues of educational adequacy are often raised in equity cases to illustrate the negative effects of inadequate funding on educational opportunities, educational adequacy claims relate the level of education resources provided to students to some measure of an adequate education, as defined by the state in its constitution, in a court's interpretation of that constitution, or in state statute. In the *Abbott v. Burke* decision, for example, the New Jersey Supreme Court defined the state's constitutional obligation as assuring that students in poor urban communities have the opportunity to compete in, and contribute to, the society entered by their relatively advantaged peers.[72] Courts in Kentucky, Alabama, and Massachusetts defined their states' obligation in terms of broad educational outcomes, such as "sufficient mathematical and scientific skills to function in [their state] and at national and international levels, . . . sufficient understanding of the arts to enable each student to appreciate his or her cultural heritage and the cultural heritage of others, . . . [and] sufficient support and guidance so that every student feels a sense of self-worth and ability to achieve."[73]

The continuing school finance litigation and the new focus on educational adequacy create a large number of education finance policy issues for states. First, states must address the continuing disparities in education spending that separate their poor and wealthy communities. They must decide how, and how much, to equalize these spending differences and how to raise the revenues to pay for greater equalization. In addition, states must find ways to fund programs for the growing number of students with special needs—those with disabilities, limited English proficiency, and economic and social needs. Second, states face growing opposition to the use of property taxes to fund education. Most taxpayers want the state to bear a larger portion of education funding, yet they are often unwilling to support higher state taxes. Michigan recently reduced its reliance on local property taxes to pay for schools, but raised the state sales tax by two cents to pay for the increased state share. In contrast, New Jersey cut its state sales and income taxes, forcing local communities to bear a larger share of education and municipal costs. Other states, such as Colorado and Oregon, have responded to taxpayer pressures by capping local property taxes, though without replacing this lost local revenue with increased state aid.

In addition to these traditional school finance issues, state policy makers face new challenges in responding to the new "adequacy" decisions by the courts.[74] The first issue is how to define and measure an adequate education. Should states use input standards, such as minimum class size, number of computers in a school, and/or minimum facilities standards, or should they determine what kinds of programs are necessary to help students achieve the outcome standards being established by state boards of education, legislatures, and courts? States have begun to define the parameters of an adequate education as they develop content and student performance standards in academic disciplines. What is unknown at this time, however, is the level and mix of educational services and resources required to enable all students to meet these new standards. Once a state determines the basis of an adequate education, it must determine the cost of this education for students with differing needs and design a state school finance system that supports an adequate education. To date, no state has revised its finance system along these lines. In New Jersey, the state supreme court addressed the issue by using the expenditure levels of wealthy (and usually high-performing) school districts as its measure of a constitutionally adequate education. In other states, such as Alabama, the court found that no district met the state's input-driven accreditation standards, thereby leaving states obligated to raise spending in all school districts.

Other finance issues are raised by nonfinance reform initiatives. As states encourage changes in education governance structures, such as site-based management, choice, and charter schools, they must consider how to allocate resources to school sites and parents, as well as, or instead of, school districts. Districts will have to develop school-based fiscal accounting systems that provide these sites with detailed information on revenues, budgets, and expenditures.[75] As states turn to outcome-based accountability systems, policy makers have become increasingly interested in the use of fiscal incentives to improve school performance. Incentive funding is still in the early stages of development, however, and little is known about how incentives work or how the allocation of incentive dollars will affect equalization policy. Policy makers must consider how they will measure the performance to be rewarded, how much state aid will be allocated through an incentive program, how an incentive program will be integrated with the general aid formula, and how incentive funds can be used by recipients.[76]

Conclusion

The state role in elementary and secondary education policy has expanded rapidly during the last thirty years. Today, states pay about half of the bill for education and increasingly drive decisions about how much is spent on education, what students and their teachers should know and be able to do, how this knowledge should be assessed, and how schools and school districts should be governed. With education representing one-third of states' expenditures, debate over how to allocate state education aid in ways that are equitable, politically feasible, and economically sound have come to dominate the state policy agenda. The growing state role in nonfiscal issues has also contributed to the development of a more complex and fragmented education policy-making structure. This fragmentation, policy makers' greater focus on elections, and policy overload and specialization reinforce the design of short-term solutions to long-term education problems.

State education policy through the latter 1990s will be shaped by a number of forces. These include the changing demographics of the student population, the changing structure of the nation's economy, and national education reform agendas. At a time when work force skills are growing increasingly complex and undergoing rapid change, the future workers of America are entering the educational system with greater economic and social disadvantages. Students in general are not learning the high level of skills needed for a post-industrial society, and students of color and/or of limited English proficiency are doing even more poorly. Reformers argue that dramatic improvements in student learning will require a more systemic approach to education policy. Most states have responded to this new wave of reform by developing more ambitious student outcomes and curricular frameworks, and many are revamping their basic skills assessment systems to align with these higher standards. States have been slower to redesign their teacher preparation and professional development policies and to significantly restructure their governance systems.

State policy makers still face a number of challenges, reflecting the continuing tensions between the reform values of equity, excellence, efficiency, and choice. As state courts increasingly link school finance reform to guarantees of an "adequate" education, policy makers must define and fund the mix of educational services and resources required to bring all students up to these new high outcome standards. As most students nationally perform well below these standards, the new finance reforms will require new funds or a redistribution of existing state aid. Both are politically unacceptable alternatives. The religious right is opposed to the substance of many of the reforms, and conservative interests, which gained control of many statehouses and state boards of education in 1994, argue that increased parental choice and a market-driven education system are more appropriate ways to improve the nation's schools. Their push to deregulate state education policy could facilitate the restructuring of education governance systems advocated by systemic reformers, or it could derail the reform movement. The fate of standards-based education reform lies largely in the hands of those who initiated the movement in their 1989 education summit—the nation's governors.

Notes

1. This chapter addresses only elementary and secondary education policy. It does not include a discussion of public higher education, which is also a responsibility of state government.
2. Henry J. Raimondo, *Economics of State and Local Government* (New York: Praeger, 1992).
3. Frederick M. Wirt, Douglas Mitchell, and Catherine Marshall, as cited in Frederick M. Wirt and Michael W. Kirst, *Schools in Conflict* (Berkeley, Calif.: McCutchan Publishing Company, 1989), 260; and James W. Guthrie, "United States School Finance Policy 1955–1980," in *School Finance Policies and Practices: The 1980's: A Decade of Conflict*, ed. James W. Guthrie (Cambridge, Mass.: Ballinger, 1980), 3–46.
4. *Digest of Education Statistics, 1994* (Washington, D.C.: U.S. Department of Education, National Center for Education Statistics, October 1994), Table 21.
5. Harold L. Hodgkinson, *A Demographic Look at Tomorrow* (Washington, D.C.: Institute for Educational Leadership, 1992).
6. *Digest of Education Statistics, 1994.*
7. 1976 data are drawn from the U.S. Department of Education, Office of Civil Rights 1976 Elementary and Secondary School Civil Rights Survey. 1992 data are reported in *Digest of Education Statistics, 1994*, Table 45.
8. Hodgkinson, *A Demographic Look at Tomorrow.*
9. Gary Orfield, *School Segregation in the 1980s* (Chicago: University of Chicago National School Desegregation Project, 1987).
10. *School-Aged Children: Poverty and Diversity Challenge Schools Nationwide* (Washington, D.C.: U.S. General Accounting Office, 1994).
11. Ibid.
12. James Gordon Ward, "The Power of Demographic Change: Impact of Population Trends on Schools," in *Who Pays for Student Diversity? Population Changes and Educational Policy*, ed. James Gordon Ward and Patricia Anthony (Newbury Park, Calif.: Corwin Press, 1992), 1–20.
13. Gary Natriello, Edward L. McDill, and Aaron M. Pallas, *Schooling Disadvantaged Children: Racing Against Catastrophe* (New York: Teachers College Press, 1990); Henry Levin, *Educational Reform for Disadvantaged Students: An Emerging Crisis* (West Haven, Conn.: National Education Association Professional Library, 1986).
14. Hodgkinson, *A Demographic Look at Tomorrow.*
15. Council for Economic Development, *Investing in Our Children: Business and the Public Schools* (New York: Council for Economic Development, 1985).
16. Ina V. S. Mullis et al., *NAEP 1992 Trends in Academic Progress* (Washington, D.C.: U.S. Department of Education, National Center for Education Statistics, National Assessment of Education Progress, 1994).
17. Michael Timpane, "Business Has Rediscovered the Public Schools," *Phi Delta Kappan* 65 (February 1984): 390.
18. Allan Odden, "Including School Finance in Systemic Reform Strategies: A Commentary," *CPRE Finance Briefs* (New Brunswick, N.J.: Rutgers University, Consortium for Policy Research in Education, May 1994).
19. Steven D. Gold, *The Outlook for School Revenue in the Next Five Years* (New Brunswick, N.J.: Rutgers University, Consortium for Policy Research in Education, 1995).

20. U.S. General Accounting Office, *Education Finance: Extent of Federal Funding in State Education Agencies* GAO/HEHS-95–3 (Washington, D.C.: U.S. General Accounting Office, 1994).
21. Wirt and Kirst, *Schools in Conflict.*
22. Susan H. Fuhrman, "State Politics and Education Reform," in *The Politics of Reforming School Administration: The 1988 PEA Yearbook*, ed. Jane Hannaway and Robert Crowson (Philadelphia: Falmer Press, 1988), 61–75.
23. For example, Wendell Anderson of Minnesota, Rubin Askew of Florida, and William Milliken of Michigan. Susan H. Fuhrman and Richard F. Elmore, "Governors and Education Policy in the 1990s," in *The Governance of Curriculum*, ed. Richard F. Elmore and Susan H. Fuhrman (Alexandria, Va.: Association for Supervision and Curriculum Development, 1994), 56–74.
24. This education summit led to the adoption of six national education goals that addressed school readiness, high school completion, competency in nine academic areas, preparation for responsible citizenship and productive employment, and school safety. In 1994, Congress codified these six goals and added two more that are directed at teacher professional development and parental involvement in the schools. *The National Education Goals Report: Building a Nation of Learners, 1994* (Washington, D.C.: National Education Goals Panel, 1994).
25. Susan H. Fuhrman, "The Politics of Coherence," in *Designing Coherent Education Policy: Improving the System*, ed. Susan H. Fuhrman (San Francisco: Jossey-Bass, 1993), 1–34.
26. Walt Haney and George Madeus, "Making Sense of the Competency Testing Movement," *Harvard Educational Review* (November 1978): 462–484.
27. Marshall S. Smith and Jennifer O'Day, "Educational Equality: 1966 and Now," in *Spheres of Justice in Education: The 1990 American Education Finance Association Yearbook*, ed. Deborah A. Verstegen and James G. Ward (New York: Harper Business, 1991), 53–100.
28. National Assessment of Educational Progress, *Three National Assessments of Reading* (Denver: NAEP/Education Commission of the States, 1981); and National Assessment of Educational Progress, *Changes in Mathematical Achievement, 1973–1978* (Denver: NAEP/Education Commission of the States, 1979).
29. National Commission on Excellence in Education, *A Nation at Risk: The Imperative for Educational Reform* (Washington, D.C.: National Commission on Excellence in Education, 1983).
30. Margaret E. Goertz, *State Educational Standards: A 50–State Survey* (Princeton: Educational Testing Service, 1986).
31. David K. Cohen, "The Classroom of State and Federal Education Policy" (East Lansing, Mich.: School of Education, Michigan State University, 1990).
32. Carnegie Forum on Education and the Economy, *A Nation Prepared: Teachers for the Twenty-first Century* (New York: Carnegie Corporation, 1986); and Richard F. Elmore and Associates, *Restructuring Schools: The Generation of Education Reform* (San Francisco: Jossey-Bass, 1990).
33. Marshall S. Smith and Jennifer O'Day, "Systemic School Reform," in *The Politics of Curriculum and Testing*, ed. Susan H. Fuhrman and Betty Malen (London: Falmer Press, 1991), 233–267.
34. Ibid.
35. Deborah A. Verstegen, "The New Wave of School Finance Litigation," *Phi Delta Kappan* 76 (November 1994): 243–250.
36. Patricia R. Brown and Richard F. Elmore, "Analyzing the Impact of School Finance Reform," in *The Changing Politics of School Finance*, ed. Nelda H. Cambron-McCabe and Allan R. Odden (Cambridge, Mass.: Ballinger, 1982), 107–138.
37. Verstegen, "The New Wave of School Finance Litigation."

38. Harold R. Winslow and Sarah M. Peterson, "State Initiatives for Special Needs Students," in *New Dimensions of the Federal-State Partnership in Education*, ed. Joel D. Sherman, Mark A. Kutner, and K. J. Small (Washington, D.C.: Institute for Educational Leadership, 1982), 46–62.

39. Julie Underwood, "School Finance Adequacy as Vertical Equity," *University of Michigan Journal of Law Reform* 28 (Spring 1995): 493–519. The nine states that declared their school finance systems unconstitutional during this period were Alabama, Arizona, Kentucky, Massachusetts, Missouri, Montana, New Jersey, Tennessee, and Texas. The five that found their systems constitutional were Minnesota, North Dakota, Rhode Island, Virginia, and Wisconsin.

40. Richard J. Coley and Margaret E. Goertz, *Educational Standards in the 50 States: 1990* (Princeton: Educational Testing Service, 1990).

41. National Commission on Excellence in Education, *A Nation at Risk*.

42. Coley and Goertz, *Educational Standards in the 50 States*.

43. Ellen Pechman and Kate G. Laguarda, *Status of New State Curriculum Frameworks, Standards, Assessments, and Monitoring Systems* (Washington, D.C.: Policy Studies Associates, March 1993).

44. Diane Massell, "Achieving Consensus: Setting the Agenda for State Curriculum Reform," in *The Governance Curriculum*, ed. Susan H. Fuhrman and Richard Elmore (Alexandria, Va.: The Association of Supervision and Curriculum Development, 1994), 84–108.

45. Richard F. Elmore, Charles H. Abelmann, and Susan H. Fuhrman, "The New Accountability in State Education Policy: From Process to Performance," in *Holding Schools Accountable: Performance-Based Reform in Education*, ed. Helen Ladd (Washington, D.C.: Brookings Institution, 1996).

46. Ibid.

47. Council of Chief State School Officers & North Central Regional Education Laboratory, *Annual Survey of the Association of State Assessment Programs* (Oak Brook, Ill.: NCREL, 1993).

48. Diane Massell and Susan H. Fuhrman, *Ten Years of State Education Reform: 1983–1993: Overview with Four Case Studies* (New Brunswick, N.J.: Rutgers University, Consortium for Policy Research in Education, 1994).

49. Ellen M. Pechman. "Use of Standardized and Alternative Tests in the States" (Washington, D.C.: Policy Studies Associates, Inc., 1992).

50. Lorraine M. McDonnell, *Policymakers' View of Student Assessment* (Santa Monica, Calif.: RAND, 1994).

51. Daniel M. Koretz et al., *The Reliability of Scores from the 1992 Vermont Portfolio Assessment Program, Interim Report* (Santa Monica, Calif.: RAND, 1992); and Lonnie Harp, "Ky. Student Assessments Called 'Seriously Flawed,'" *Education Week*, July 12, 1995, 12.

52. Jean Johnson and John Immerwahr, *First Things First: What Americans Expect from the Public Schools* (New York: Public Agenda, 1994).

53. Ibid.

54. Emily Feistritzer, "National Overview of Alternative Teacher Certification," *Education and Urban Society* 26:1 (November 1993): 18–28.

55. Coley and Goertz, *Educational Standards in the 50 States*.

56. Rolf Blank and M. Dalkilic, *State Policies on Science and Mathematics Education, 1992* (Washington, D.C.: Council of Chief State School Officers, State Education Assessment Center, 1992).

57. Coley and Goertz, *Educational Standards in the 50 States*.

58. Judith Warren Little, "Teachers' Professional Development in a Climate of Educational Reform," *Educational Evaluation and Policy Analysis* 15 (Summer 1993):129–151; and Thomas C. Corcoran, *Transforming Professional Development for Teachers: A Guide for State Policymakers* (Washington, D.C.: National Governors Association, 1995).

59. Linda Darling-Hammond and Barnett Berry, *The Evolution of Teacher Policy* (Santa Monica, Calif.: RAND, 1988).
60. Susan H. Fuhrman and Richard F. Elmore, *Ruling Out Rules: The Evolution of Deregulation in State Education Policy* (New Brunswick, N.J.: Rutgers University, Consortium for Policy Research in Education, 1995).
61. Mark Walsh, "12 States Join Move to Pass Charter Laws," *Education Week*, May 10, 1995, 1.
62. Priscilla Wohlstetter, Richard Wenning, and Karri L. Briggs, "Charter Schools in the United States: The Question of Autonomy," *Education Policy* 9:4 (1995): 331–358.
63. Fuhrman and Elmore, *Ruling Out Rules*.
64. Allan R. Odden and Lawrence O. Picus, *School Finance: A Policy Perspective* (New York: McGraw-Hill, 1992).
65. G. Alfred Hess, Jr., *School Restructuring, Chicago Style* (Newbury Park, Calif.: Corwin Press, 1991).
66. Quoted in Henry M. Levin, "Educational Vouchers and Social Policy," in *School Finance Policies and Practices: The 1980s: A Decade of Conflict*, ed. James W. Guthrie, 238.
67. Richard Fossey, "School Choice Legislation: A Survey of the States," *CPRE Occasional Paper* (New Brunswick, N.J.: Rutgers University, Consortium for Policy Research in Education, May 1992).
68. Ibid.
69. Odden and Picus, *School Finance*.
70. *Digest of Education Statistics, 1994*, Table 158.
71. Martha I. Morgan, Adam S. Cohen, and Helen Hershkoff, "Establishing Education Program Inadequacy: The Alabama Example," *University of Michigan Journal of Law Reform* 28 (Spring 1995): 559–598.
72. *Abbott v. Burke*, 119 N.J. 287 (1990) at 363.
73. *Harper v. Hunt*, Opinion of the Justices, 624 So.2d 107 (Ala. 1993).
74. Margaret E. Goertz, "Program Equity and Adequacy: Issues from the Field," *Educational Policy* 8 (December 1994): 608–615. Also, see other articles in this special issue of this journal and the special issue of the *University of Michigan Journal of Law Reform* on educational adequacy (Spring 1995).
75. Odden, "Including School Finance in Systemic Reform Strategies."
76. Lawrence O. Picus, "Using Incentives to Promote School Improvement," in *Rethinking School Finance: An Agenda for the 1990s*, ed. Allan R. Odden (San Francisco: Jossey-Bass, 1992), 166–200; Charles T. Clotfelter and Helen F. Ladd, "Picking Winners: Recognition and Reward Programs for Public Schools," in *Holding Schools Accountable: Performance-Based Reform in Education*, ed. Ladd.

10

State Welfare Policy

Irene Lurie

Few public functions are as closely shared by local, state, and federal governments as the provision of financial assistance to needy individuals and families. From colonial times until the early twentieth century, local governments and private charities bore primary responsibility for poor relief. Between 1910 and 1930, most states introduced welfare programs for poor mothers and their children, although local governments continued to pay a large share of their cost. With passage of the Social Security Act of 1935, the federal government lifted some of this burden from state and local governments by creating social insurance programs for the elderly, widowed, and unemployed and by contributing to the cost of state welfare programs. Today, the most visible of these welfare programs, Aid to Families with Dependent Children (AFDC), is operated by the states with federal financing. In the words of the U.S. Supreme Court, "The AFDC program is based on a scheme of cooperative federalism."[1]

Although this cooperative arrangement is a pillar of American federalism, critics across the political spectrum have proposed shifts in the weight borne by the states and the federal government. Arguments for greater decentralization to the states typically come from Republicans, while proposals that the federal government assume full responsibility for guaranteeing poor families a minimum income—or at least require states to provide a minimum welfare benefit—are, with some exceptions, the domain of Democrats. We should not be surprised that the Republicans, after gaining control over both houses of Congress in 1995, enacted a law abolishing the AFDC program and giving states greater flexibility in welfare policy. Nor was it out of character that a Democratic president vetoed it.

The Personal Responsibility and Work Opportunity Act of 1995, vetoed by President Bill Clinton in January 1996 during the long budget stalemate with Congress, was not in the nation's tradition of incremental policy change. It would have drastically altered the nature of the welfare system by replacing the AFDC program with a block grant that would cap federal funding, impose a five-year limit on a family's eligibility for welfare, and eliminate safeguards that give needy families an entitlement to assistance. Reforms of this enormity reflect the dissatisfaction of numerous critics, including President Clinton, who campaigned on a promise to "end welfare as we know it," and governors, local officials, welfare administrators, scholars, and welfare recipients themselves. Why have virtually all parties become disaffected with welfare policy and why has welfare become one of the most contentious issues in American politics?

To answer these questions, we will first present some basic facts about the AFDC program and then look at the program's structure and the perverse incentives it creates for recipients and for states. We will then review the history of federal and state efforts to reform the AFDC program in ways calculated to mitigate some of these incentives and analyze the states' most recent reforms. Finally, we will examine some of the political dimensions of welfare policy and the radical reforms proposed by President Clinton and the 104th Congress.

AFDC in Perspective

Sixty years after passage of the Social Security Act, an array of federal, state, and local programs transfer income to families and individuals. The AFDC program is among the smaller of these programs in terms of expenditures and in the mid-range in terms of number of recipients. Social Security is by far the largest, paying in 1993 $302 billion in cash benefits to 42 million elderly, widowed, or disabled people. In that same year, Medicare financed $147 billion in health care for the elderly and disabled. Unemployment insurance, which, like Social Security, calculates benefits on the basis of previous earnings rather than current income, paid out $35 billion to 3.9 million unemployed workers. Among the income-conditioned programs that provide benefits on the basis of current income, the largest is Medicaid, which paid $126 billion in benefits to assist 33 million low-income individuals and families with their medical expenses. The Food Stamp program, which is federally financed but administered by the states, gave $22.8 billion in food vouchers to 27 million low-income households in 1993. The Supplemental Security Income (SSI) program paid $24.6 billion to 6.1 million elderly, blind, or disabled individuals. AFDC paid $22.3 billion to 5 million families containing 14 million adults and children. Finally, general assistance or home relief programs, which operate in most states without any federal funds or guidance, assisted approximately 1 million cases.[2]

In the minds of many Americans, welfare expenditures absorb a large share, more than a tenth, of the federal budget.[3] In fact, the level of expenditures for AFDC is modest compared to expenditures for other government programs. Federal expenditures for AFDC accounted for only 1 percent of the $1.5 trillion of federal outlays in 1993, a minuscule share compared with the big-ticket items: 21 percent for Social Security, 20 percent for defense, and 14 percent for debt interest.[4] Federal subsidies to middle- and upper-income people through tax breaks also dwarf expenditures for welfare, such as lost tax revenues in 1993 of $49 billion from the deduction of home mortgage interest, $58 billion from the exclusion from taxable income of employers' pension contributions and personal savings, and $47 billion from the exclusion of employer contributions for health insurance and medical care.[5] State expenditures for the AFDC program comprised an average of only 3.2 percent of total state expenditures in 1994, and only in California and Michigan were AFDC expenditures more than 5 percent of total state spending.[6] The bulk of state spending was for other functions: 31 percent for education, 19 percent for Medicaid, and 9 percent for transportation.[7] In the vast majority of states, local government finances none of the cost of the AFDC program.

Although the AFDC program is not the largest income transfer program in terms of either costs or recipients, AFDC caseloads have grown at a disturbing rate over the past three decades, raising a concern that this growth may be caused by, or may result in, a fraying of the social fabric of the nation. AFDC caseloads began to rise rapidly during the 1960s and have continued to rise with few interruptions, increasing from 787,000 families in 1960 to 2,208,000 families in 1970, 3,712,000 in 1980, and 4,981,000 in 1993.[8] Critics accuse AFDC recipients, generally never married or divorced mothers, of irresponsible behavior in having children, failing to marry or remain married, and shirking employment. They contend that the AFDC program itself encourages this behavior by offering financial incentives to have children and remain single while providing few incentives to work.[9]

Federal legislation enacted in 1988 made significant reforms in the AFDC program, changes that were described at the time as the most sweeping revision in the nation's welfare system over the previous fifty years.[10] Yet they failed to stem the rise in caseloads or quell the public's discontent. The nation's experience with the 1988 reforms made clear what had been increasingly apparent—that there are no sure-fire ways to reduce welfare dependency without risking hardship to poor children. The program's structure does not lend itself to easy reform, but the dynamics of welfare politics, with its present inviting opportunities to government leaders, nevertheless brought Congress to the point of risking this hardship.

Structure of the AFDC Program

Assistance programs for poor children were already established in most states when the Social Security Act was written in 1935, and the need for assistance was expected to diminish as the Social Security program matured to cover most widows and their children, initially the primary group of AFDC recipients. The Act's authors saw no compelling reason for the federal government to assume full responsibility for the AFDC program, although they recognized that the poor financial condition of state and local governments justified some federal funding.[11] Hence, the beginning of the cooperative relationship: the AFDC program remains a state responsibility that receives financial support from the federal government. With this federal funding came federal rules regarding the structure of state programs.

Under current law, the federal government finances a share of AFDC benefits through categorical grants-in-aid to the states. The federal government matches a percentage of the benefits paid by the states, ranging from 50 percent of benefits in richer states to a potential 83 percent in poorer states, with no limit on the total amount of the grants. In 1995, for example, the federal share was 50 percent for New York and 78.58 percent for Mississippi. Because the federal grants are open-ended, depending only on the matching rates and the levels of state spending, the federal budget treats them as the states' entitlement.

Until the late 1960s, the states had considerable discretion in setting both the financial and nonfinancial rules governing eligibility. Federal law does not specify that all needy families with children be given assistance but requires only that states give assistance to dependent children "as far as practicable under the conditions in such State."[12] Some states imposed nonfinancial eligibility conditions designed to deny assistance to certain groups, particularly children born out of wedlock and African-Americans.[13] For example, some states used a rule requiring that a home be "suitable" to deny assistance to unwed mothers, and they used the "man in the house rule" to deny assistance to households containing a man, regardless of whether he was the father of the children or the husband of the mother. But court decisions and federal legislative and regulatory actions during the 1960s and 1970s not only eliminated these nonfinancial eligibility conditions but established guarantees of equal protection and due process in the administration of public assistance.[14] In doing so, these reforms established the principle that individuals who meet the eligibility criteria for welfare programs are entitled to benefits. With more nationally uniform eligibility conditions came an erosion of state authority and greater centralization of welfare policy in the federal government.

Eligibility and Benefits

After decades of evolution in the scheme of cooperative federalism, both the federal government and the states retain control over important features of the AFDC program. Federal law and regulations set most of the nonfinancial conditions governing eligibility for AFDC benefits. To receive assistance, a child must be deprived of the support or care of a parent due to death, incapacity, continued absence from the home, or unemployment. Federal regulations define unemployment as working less than 100 hours per month. This criterion denies eligibility to the families of the "working poor"—those working full-time but who, because of low wage rates, large families, or both, are unable to earn enough income to raise them out of poverty. These nonfinancial eligibility conditions are reflected in the characteristics of the AFDC caseload. Of the 9.4 million children receiving AFDC in 1992, 53.1 percent were born out of wedlock, 30 percent had parents who were separated or divorced, 8.2 percent had an unemployed parent, 4.1 percent had an incapacitated parent, 1.6 percent had a deceased parent, and 2.9 percent were categorized as other or unknown.[15] Of the 4.4 million adults receiving AFDC, 88.6 percent were women.[16] Of all AFDC families, 38.9 percent were white, 37.2 percent were African-American, 17.8 percent were Hispanic, and the rest were of another or unknown race.[17]

The popular image of families trapped in long-term welfare dependency oversimplifies a rather complex pattern of welfare use over time. Welfare recipients are heterogeneous in the characteristics that enable them to leave welfare, such as education, previous work experience, disability, motivation, and the ability to connect with a husband or other breadwinner. David Ellwood and Mary Jo Bane found that most people coming onto welfare are only in the program for a short time, although the long-timers comprise a large share of recipients at any moment. While 49 percent of all people going on welfare stay on it less than two years, and only 14 percent stay on it ten years or more, 48 percent of people on welfare at any moment will be recipients for ten years or more. These findings have been influential in shaping welfare employment programs by suggesting that services to encourage employment, such as educational opportunities, training, and assistance in job search, should be targeted toward people who are most likely to become long-term recipients.[18]

Although the states have lost much of the authority to set nonfinancial eligibility conditions, the setting of financial eligibility conditions and levels of welfare benefits remains largely a state prerogative. Members of Congress have periodically attempted to impose a nationwide minimum under the states' AFDC benefits, and Congress has increased the federal matching share to induce states to raise benefit levels, but states continue to have virtually complete authority to set AFDC benefit levels. The U.S. Supreme Court has upheld this authority, rejecting demands that states set adequate standards of need or pay a family a benefit sufficient to meet these needs.[19] According to the U. S. Department of Health and Human Services (HHS), "The Social Security Act is silent with regard to a definition of standard of need. The determination of need is left entirely to the states."[20] States are required only to determine need and benefits on "an objective and equitable basis."[21] As a result of the states' authority in this area, the definition of need is an expression of the states' preferences that reflect a complex set of political and economic characteristics rooted in history and resistant to change.[22]

The states' control over financial eligibility conditions and benefit levels now constitutes their greatest power regarding the cash assistance component of AFDC. States establish two sets of values: the income limits governing eligibility for welfare and the maximum amount of benefits paid. A family is eligible for AFDC if its income is less than the monthly "need standard" set by the state. States may then pay the full difference between the need standard and the family's income or a portion of this difference. The majority of states do not pay the full difference but either impose a dollar limit on the amount of the benefit or pay a percentage of the difference between the need standard and income. Setting a high need standard and then limiting payments enables states to extend eligibility broadly while restricting the total cost of the program.

As shown in Table 10-1, need standards in 1994 varied considerably from one state to another, from $320 for a three-person family in Indiana to

$1,648 for a similar family in New Hampshire. But what is more striking is that only eleven states paid a family the full difference between the need standard and the family's income, so that the maximum amount that states actually paid varied even more widely than the need standard, from $120 in Mississippi to $680 in Connecticut and to still more in Alaska and Hawaii, where the cost of living is particularly high. The variation in benefit levels was considerably wider than the variation in the cost of living, so that families with equal real incomes were not treated equally across the nation. Table 10-1 also shows the states' AFDC caseloads and total AFDC payments in 1994.

Even the most generous states failed to provide AFDC payments that were sufficient to lift families with no income out of poverty. As Table 10-1 indicates, no state's maximum benefit for a family of three was as high as the poverty line for a family of that size, $11,816 annually or $985 per month in 1994. Nor do many AFDC families have other sources of income to raise their total cash income up to the poverty line. In 1992, for example, only 7 percent of families on AFDC reported any earnings and only 15 percent reported unearned income such as child support or Social Security.[23] Low AFDC benefits and the lack of other sources of cash income for families on welfare help explain why many families headed by women, 35.6 percent, remain poor.[24] Their poverty rate is lower if noncash types of income such as food stamps and housing are counted, but the vast majority of AFDC recipients are still poor.

Another important parameter of the program, one that federal law governs closely, is the way earnings are treated in calculating the amount of the welfare benefit. The treatment of earnings is significant because the rate at which benefits are reduced as earnings increase affects the financial incentive for recipients to work. Current law requires states to deduct certain amounts from monthly earnings in calculating a family's benefit: $90 for work expenses, up to $200 for the day care of each child and, to encourage work, $30 of earnings a month for twelve months and one-third of earnings in excess of $30 for four months. These rules mean that many families realize little net financial gain from working. But if more earnings were deducted in calculating benefits, the amount of benefits paid to working families would increase and more families would be eligible for assistance. The tradeoff between providing financial work incentives and limiting program costs is inescapable.

Perverse Incentives and Inequities

In the jargon of insurance and economics, AFDC creates problems of "moral hazard," meaning that an insured individual has some control over the factors that trigger insurance benefits. Although strictly speaking the program is not insurance, since eligibility does not depend on prior contributions, it nonetheless distorts incentives, producing several moral hazard problems. By scaling benefits to the level of income, it reduces the reward for earning income and seeking child support from an absent parent. By limiting eligibility to families who are deprived of a breadwinner, it may encourage parents to

Table 10-1 AFDC Benefit Levels, Caseloads, and Total Payments, 1994

State	Three-Person Family, January 1994 Monthly need standard	Monthly maximum benefit	Average Monthly Caseload, FY 1994 (thousands)	Total Assistance Payments, FY 1994[a] (millions)
Alabama	$673	$164	50	$91.9
Alaska	975	923	13	112.2
Arizona	964	347	72	265.8
Arkansas	705	204	26	57.3
California	715	607	909	6,088.3
Colorado	421	356	42	158.2
Connecticut	680	680	59	397.0
Delaware	338	338	11	39.6
District of Columbia	712	420	27	126.2
Florida	991	303	247	806.2
Georgia	424	280	141	427.9
Hawaii	1,140	712	20	163.0
Idaho	991	317	9	30.2
Illinois	890	367	240	913.5
Indiana	320	288	74	228.1
Iowa	849	426	40	169.2
Kansas	429	429	30	123.0
Kentucky	526	228	80	198.3
Louisiana	658	190	87	168.3
Maine	553	418	23	107.4
Maryland	507	366	80	313.7
Massachusetts	579	579	112	729.7
Michigan	551	459	224	1,132.1
Minnesota	532	532	63	379.4
Mississippi	368	120	57	81.7
Missouri	846	292	92	286.9
Montana	511	401	12	48.9
Nebraska	364	364	16	61.5
Nevada	699	348	14	48.0
New Hampshire	1,648	550	11	61.8
New Jersey	985	424	122	531.3
New Mexico	357	357	34	143.8
New York	577	577	455	2,913.0
North Carolina	544	272	131	352.5
North Dakota	409	409	6	25.5
Ohio	879	341	250	1,015.8
Oklahoma	471	324	47	165.1
Oregon	460	460	42	196.7
Pennsylvania	614	421	210	934.7
Rhode Island	554	554	23	136.0
South Carolina	440	200	52	115.0
South Dakota	491	417	7	24.5
Tennessee	426	185	111	215.0
Texas	574	184	284	544.3
Utah	552	414	18	77.2
Vermont	1,124	638	10	64.8
Virginia	393	354	75	253.0
Washington	1,158	546	103	609.8
West Virginia	497	249	41	125.8
Wisconsin	647	517	77	424.6
Wyoming	$674	$360	6	$21.4
U.S. median/total	$579[b]	$366[b]	5,046[c]	$22,797[c]

Sources: U.S. Department of Health and Human Services, *Overview of the AFDC Program, Fiscal Year 1994,* 6, 13, 20; Committee on Ways and Means, U.S. House of Representatives, *1994 Green Book: Overview of Entitlement Programs,* July 15, 1994.

[a] Excludes administrative costs of $3,235 million.

[b] Excludes Guam, Puerto Rico, and Virgin Islands.

[c] Includes Guam, Puerto Rico, and Virgin Islands.

divorce, separate, or never marry. By limiting eligibility to people with children and raising benefits when another child is born, it rewards childbearing.

The magnitude of the response to these incentives by recipients and potential recipients has been the subject of considerable research, much of it suggesting that families do not respond strongly to the program's perverse incentives. Studies that investigated the role of AFDC in the growth in the number of families headed by single women showed mixed results. Earlier studies demonstrated no consistent pattern of effects from AFDC. While later studies showed stronger effects, these were too small to explain all of the increase in female-headed families.[25] Other factors, such as the deterioration in the labor market for low-skilled young men, may also have played a role in the growth in the number of female-headed families on welfare. Once on welfare, women have fewer children than the general population, negating the notion that women have additional children to obtain larger welfare benefits.[26] Studies also failed to find a strong relationship between AFDC benefit levels and benefit reduction rates, on the one hand, and work effort, on the other. Although studies showed that the AFDC program reduced work effort, the magnitude of this effect was uncertain, potentially too small to account for much of the increase in the poverty rate of female-headed families. Thus, economist Robert Moffitt concluded that the problem of welfare dependency could not be ascribed to the work disincentives of the program.[27]

Another incentive for recipients and potential recipients stems from the variation in the need standards and benefit levels set by the states. The more generous a state's program, the greater the incentive for recipients to remain in the state despite a lack of earning opportunities and the greater the incentive for residents of lower-benefit states to migrate to a higher-benefit state. High-benefit states, in other words, become welfare magnets. Again, the magnitude of the response to this incentive is a subject of debate. Studies of the effects of interstate differentials in benefit levels in encouraging migration have been inconclusive, and although more recent studies have found welfare to have a greater effect on mobility and residential location than did the earlier studies, they suffer from methodological difficulties.[28]

Regardless of the strength of these effects, analysts argue that states keep their welfare benefits low at least in part to avoid becoming welfare magnets.[29] In making welfare a state rather than a federal function, the Social Security Act sets up a "race to the bottom" in which states compete by lowering benefits to keep out the poor and lowering taxes to attract business. The large differential between states in their levels of benefits also gives rise to the charge that the AFDC program creates interstate inequities among the poor population.

Unlike the moral hazard problems, problems created by interstate differences in benefits point to a ready solution: a national standard of benefits. In enumerating the appropriate roles of each level of government in a federal system, economists have long counted income distribution as a federal-level function. "The heart of fiscal federalism," argues economist Richard Musgrave, lies in the proposition that the distribution and stabilization functions "require primary responsibility at the central level."[30] Alternatives to the AFDC program proposed in the 1960s and 1970s included a nationwide minimum benefit financed by the federal government. The major reform to be enacted in that era, the SSI program, provides such a minimum benefit. But the SSI program, which supports elderly or disabled people who are not expected to work, has few potential impacts on low-wage labor markets. A nationwide minimum benefit for AFDC, in contrast, could put upward pressure on the wages of low-paid workers and reduce the ability of low-wage states to lure businesses from higher-wage states.

General Assistance

For low-income people who fall through the safety net of the federally supported cash assistance programs, state and local governments, on their own initiative and without any federal funding, operate general assistance or home relief programs. People eligible for general assistance include two-parent families with a low-wage earner, childless couples, and individuals who are poor but neither elderly nor disabled. Because the federal government plays no role in these programs, their administration and structure vary considerably among states and, in some cases, within states. In 1992, general assistance programs operated in 42 states. In only 22 of these were uniform statewide regulations in effect. No statewide program operated in the other 20, although some or all of these states' local governments operated a program. Eligibility for general assistance was extended to all needy people in 11 of the states, while the other 31 states restricted benefits to certain categories of people.[31]

The federal government and the states clearly show greater concern for poor families with children than for equally poor non-aged, able-bodied, and childless adults. Not only are these latter individuals frequently ineligible for assistance, but when they do qualify, their benefits are less generous than those to AFDC families, and they face more stringent requirements vis-à-vis work in exchange for a welfare grant. In recent years, several relatively high-income industrial states, including Michigan, Ohio, and Pennsylvania, have eliminated their general assistance programs, leaving former recipients to subsist on food stamps or to apply for federally supported disability programs.

Welfare Reform

The search for solutions to these perverse incentives and inequities has generated a stream of reforms in the AFDC program. Since the 1960s, when AFDC caseloads began their upward spiral, the federal government has required states to make significant changes in their program. With regularity— in 1967, 1971, 1975, 1981, and 1988—federal legislation or regulation has sought to mitigate one after another of its perverse features. In response to federal mandates, states have reformed the structure of welfare benefits, the design of employment and training services, and the administration of their cash and services programs, yet they have failed to realize desired goals.

Advocates for welfare reform apply a variety of criteria for judging policies. Most agree that reducing families' need for welfare and governments' welfare costs are overarching long-term goals and that the welfare system should encourage work and family cohesion. Yet they disagree on the means toward these ends, the time frame for achieving them, and the importance of protecting children from destitution. People sympathetic to the plight of the poor believe reforms should aim primarily on increasing the earning capacity of disadvantaged people, expanding employment opportunities, financing necessary child care costs, and raising the incomes of families so they are no longer in poverty. In the hope of long-term savings, they are willing for government to incur higher short-term costs, since the cost of expenditures on education, training, and child care often exceed the welfare benefits to mothers who simply stay home with their children. People who are less sympathetic or patient see welfare as stifling work effort and breeding welfare dependency. They argue for reforms that enforce work immediately, even if it does not result in higher incomes, and for reforms that discourage out-of-wedlock births, even if children are left without public support. Conservative critic Charles Murray, for example, attributes the rise in out-of-wedlock childbearing to the availability of welfare and is willing to pull the social safety net out from under poor children.[32]

Values and ideology clearly influence the general public's criteria for judging the welfare system, while the more practical consideration of attracting voters may enter the calculations of politicians. Public opinion polls consistently show that welfare has less popular support than any other social program. Lawrence Bobo and Ryan Smith argue that "the term 'welfare' has become a red flag, apparently signaling waste, fraud, and abuse to many Americans."[33] People do not oppose helping the poor—their responses to polls about their willingness to assist the poor are quite positive—but their responses change when questions use the "W" word. In addition, there is evidence that the public tends to believe that most of the poor are African-Americans and that some of the negative connotations about "welfare" stem from individuals' feelings about African-Americans and racial discrimination.[34]

The stream of reforms over the past three decades generally sought to increase the earning capacity and work effort of recipients while maintaining the safety net, albeit one that sagged as inflation eroded the value of benefits. They were orderly and systematic reforms, in the sense that federal law or regulations required or enabled all states to make the same changes in their programs. Beginning with the Bush administration, however, states began to take the initiative by requesting waivers from federal laws and regulations to implement their own version of welfare reform. This phase of reform has been chaotic, with states moving in different directions in attempts to resolve some of the problematic incentives in the AFDC program.

Orderly Reform to Encourage and Require Work: Early Programs

The first federal legislation that required states to provide welfare recipients with employment and training was the Work Incentive (WIN) program enacted in 1967. WIN authorized states to offer a range of activities, including basic education, institutional and on-the-job training, unpaid work experience, public jobs, and job placement services. WIN funds also financed child care for program participants. Complementing the WIN program, the 1967 legislation created a financial incentive for recipients to work. Instead of reducing a recipient's benefits by one dollar for each dollar of earnings, leaving the recipient with the same total income regardless of her work effort, the law required states to disregard a portion of the recipient's monthly earnings—$30 plus one-third of earnings above $30—so that the work effort would be rewarded by an increase in total income. Legislation in 1971 added the requirement that all recipients, except those specifically excluded by law, register for the WIN program when they applied for welfare and accept a job if one was available. For the first time, recipients of AFDC could be required to work and, if they refused, could be sanctioned by a reduction in their welfare benefit.

Despite WIN services, the financial work incentive, and the work requirement, welfare caseloads continued to rise. Critics of all political persuasions found fault with both the federal laws and regulations governing the WIN program and their implementation by the states. They argued that federal funding was sufficient to finance services for only a small fraction of the people required to register for the program, so that for many recipients the program was only a paper process of registering for services that were unavailable. State welfare agencies and employment security agencies, which were jointly responsible for operating the program, were poorly coordinated and inefficient in moving individuals through the steps of the program. Welfare caseworkers lacked the motivation to urge recipients to participate in the program and to sanction them if they refused. Critics argued that labor markets for low-skilled workers were slack, available jobs paid low wages, and child care was unavailable or costly.[35] Despite several changes in the federal laws and regulations, this litany of criticism continued throughout the 1970s.

Along with these criticisms of WIN was a growing perception that the AFDC program was inherently flawed in denying eligibility to two-parent families and thereby encouraging out-of-wedlock births and marital instability. Presidents Richard Nixon and Jimmy Carter each proposed liberal welfare reforms that would have extended eligibility to all low-income families with children, including intact families with a working parent, and would have provided a minimum nationwide benefit. These changes were expected to encourage family formation and stability and to discourage interstate migration. But they would also have increased caseloads and costs, extended AFDC's financial work disincentive to two-parent families, and put upward pressure on wage levels, particularly in low-wage, low-benefit states. Members of Congress, particularly southern senators, prevented enactment of these reforms.

After a decade of fruitless debate about these liberalizing reforms, Ronald Reagan's 1980 election led to a turnabout in the direction of presidential proposals and the rapid enactment of legislation. Reagan's first budget reduced the financial reward for working by permitting states to disregard a portion of recipients' earnings for only a limited time period. Reagan's legislation also gave states new options for their welfare employment programs. States could operate a "workfare" program, in which a recipient works without wages in a public or nonprofit agency in exchange for the welfare grant. States could also require both AFDC applicants and recipients to search for a job, and they could pay a recipient's benefit to an employer to subsidize his or her wages.

The years following this legislation saw much initiative and innovation on the part of the states. The new federal options gave them an opportunity to reexamine their WIN program and to create a program that met each state's own vision of welfare reform. The optional nature of these initiatives also gave states a sense of ownership of these programs, facilitating the changes needed to implement them.[36] Many states altered and expanded their welfare employment programs in significant ways. New names helped to highlight the reforms and put each state's individual stamp on their program. GAIN (Greater Avenues for Independence) in California, MOST (Michigan Opportunity and Skills Training) in Michigan, REACH (Realizing Economic Achievement) in New Jersey, and PEACH (Positive Employment and Community Help) in Georgia are just a few examples. Evaluations by independent research organizations found these programs were feasible to operate and yielded benefits that, while typically small, were generally positive.[37]

The Reagan years were also notable for a shift in attitude away from those of the late 1960s and early 1970s, when legal challenges to the states gave welfare recipients the constitutional rights of due process and equal protection and turned AFDC into an entitlement program. The rise in labor force participation among married women with children, the rapid growth in the number of families headed by single mothers, and the continued rise in the number of welfare dependents led many political leaders, policy analysts, and scholars to argue that government should place greater demands on single parents. Government has an obligation to give financial assistance to poor parents, they argued, but parents have an obligation to help themselves become economically self-sufficient.[38] The idea that welfare involves a set of *mutual* obligations gained popularity in statehouses and Congress. Supported by the National Governors' Association and its chair, Gov. Bill Clinton, Congress sought to put this idea into place with the Family Support Act of 1988.

Orderly Reform to Encourage and Require Work: The JOBS Program

The Family Support Act was hailed as landmark legislation that represented a new consensus on the nature of the social contract between government and welfare recipients. As Sen. Daniel Patrick Moynihan, a chief architect of the legislation, described the contract: "Congress laid down a set of mutual obligations. Society owed single mothers support while they acquired the means of self-sufficiency; mothers owed society the effort to become self-sufficient."[39] To enable parents to become self-sufficient, the Act eliminated the much-maligned WIN program and created the Job Opportunities and Basic Skills Training Program (JOBS).

The JOBS program is like the WIN program in many respects, but it is stronger in that it provides more federal funding for services and child care, requires states to offer a greater variety of services, and sets clear goals that states must meet to receive their full share of federal matching funds. States can provide a wide range of services under the JOBS umbrella, including virtually any type of education, training, or employment activity available to the general public and several work programs designed around the welfare grant. The Act emphasizes education by requiring states to offer any educational activity below the postsecondary level that is appropriate to a participant's employment goal. The Act also strengthens the financial incentive for recipients to take a job by continuing to finance their child care and Medicaid coverage for a year after they earn enough to become ineligible for welfare.

A ten-state study of the implementation of the JOBS program found that it fostered the development and expansion of education, training, and employment services for welfare recipients while allowing states the flexibility and discretion to design programs that are responsive to their social, political, and economic environments.[40] By laying out clear goals regarding recipients' participation in the program, the federal legislation encouraged states to expand existing programs or develop new ones that would serve more recipients for more hours per week. The emphasis on education led most states to increase efforts to offer AFDC recipients the opportunity to pursue education, although some states chose to move many recipients directly into the labor force or a work activity. Overall, the study concluded that the federal legislation for the JOBS program is generally well-designed and that providers of JOBS services are willing to supply services if they are paid in exchange.

Although expenditures for the JOBS program and its attendant child care substantially exceed those for the WIN program, inadequate funding was a significant factor in slowing the pace of JOBS implementation. Available federal matching funds for JOBS services in 1993 were $1 billion, but states spent enough of their own funds, $477 million, to draw down only $736 million. Only about one-third of the states drew down all of their potential match, and total spending was only $1,213 million. Federal matching for child care is open-ended at the same rate as AFDC benefits, between 50 and 83 percent, and total federal and state spending was $1,003 million, almost as much as spending for JOBS services. Lack of services, child care funds, and staff in the welfare agencies left many states unable to demand that recipients participate in the JOBS program and accept available employment. States learned that imposing an obligation on recipients requires that they first assume the costly obligation of financing needed services.

Chaotic Reform in the 1990s

As states were implementing the JOBS program, a few governors, most notably John Engler in Michigan and Tommy Thompson in Wisconsin, began to make a national name for themselves with a campaign to cut welfare dependency. Both governors proposed that the JOBS program be supplemented with additional approaches to reducing welfare caseloads and costs. These approaches called for changing the rules determining AFDC eligibility and benefits to increase the incentive for recipients to work and prepare for work and to place pressure on them to change their behavior in ways that would reduce the cost of welfare. Perhaps most importantly, states were seeking to restructure their programs not only to increase the incentive to work but to make work a necessity.

To implement these changes, states needed waivers from the federal law governing the structure of the program. Section 1115 of the Social Security Act, an amendment enacted in 1962, permits the federal government to grant waivers from certain sections of the Act to states wishing to operate demonstration or experimental projects. Initially, because states requested waivers for their intended purpose of conducting research on alternative welfare policies, use of the waiver process generated little controversy. But waivers began to serve another purpose in 1992, when President George Bush encouraged the states to request them by promising to streamline the process for approving waiver applications and to approve a wide range of projects. Under the guise of research, the demonstrations gave states the opportunity to pursue their own version of welfare reform. Many governors, both Republicans and Democrats, responded to the challenge.

Some of the waivers ease current restrictions on eligibility and benefits, while others tighten restrictions. To ease restrictions that may discourage recipients from working, states have increased the amount of earnings disregarded in calculating the AFDC benefit and have permitted unemployed parents to work more than 100 hours per month before declaring them ineligible for assistance. To encourage continued employment by people who have earned their way off of welfare, states have extended the number of months of subsidized child care and Medicaid that a family can receive after leaving welfare from the standard limit of twelve months. Many states have increased the dollar limit on the value of a welfare family's automobile to facilitate employment requiring transportation. To give mothers and fathers more equal access to education and training, states have made noncustodial fathers eligible for JOBS services. Some states have increased the amount of assets an eligible family may hold to encourage recipients to save for their education and training. They have "cashed-out" food stamps by giving money instead of stamps, so that recipients have a greater choice in how they spend. To give welfare agencies flexibility in assisting families in crisis—for example, a breadwinner risking job loss as a result of a car breakdown—waivers permit "welfare diversion": a one-time payment to welfare applicants that addresses their immediate problem—in this example, lack of funds for car repairs—so they do not need to become welfare recipients.

Many of these waivers restrict eligibility and benefits as a means by which to alter recipients' behavior. States with a "family cap" do not give a mother an increased benefit when she has another child. States with "learn-fare" decrease benefits when children or teen parents fail to attend school or increase benefits by giving bonuses for good attendance. Some states also fingerprint recipients to prevent welfare fraud or require recipients to perform unpaid community service as a condition of eligibility. Immunizations against childhood diseases are a condition of eligibility in several states. States have also exercised the option in existing law to require mothers under age eighteen to live with their parents. Although thwarted by the courts, some high-benefit states have also attempted to discourage in-migration by implementing a "welcome stranger" policy that gives recent immigrants into the state the amount of welfare paid by their previous state of residence. Finally, and most controversial, are the waivers that permit states to impose a time limit on a family's eligibility for AFDC benefits.

Why Waivers Now?

Welfare waivers quickly became fashionable, attracting even states where welfare reform was usually a low priority. By 1995, HHS had approved the applications of more than thirty states. The timing of these waiver applications is curious because Clinton had campaigned on a promise to "end welfare as we know it"—welfare reform was already back on the federal agenda. States could have been expected to wait for Congress to act before making reforms of their own; instead, they took the initiative. What were their motivations in requesting these waivers and why did the federal government approve them?

Certainly some governors had given careful thought to welfare reform and believed they could create an alternative that was superior to the current system. Other factors may also have led to a desire for reform, such as a recognition that the JOBS program was neither cheap nor rapid in its payoff, a continuing rise in welfare caseloads, and an increase in the incidence of teenage out-of-wedlock childbearing. But, to a greater degree, the waiver movement was an appeal to voters. Once started, this show of toughness generated a bandwagon effect among governors, legislators, and welfare officials who wanted to avoid being seen as easy on welfare.

The politics of welfare reform is well illustrated by the ten-state study of the implementation of the JOBS program cited earlier. The study found that governors implemented JOBS in 1989 and 1990 without fanfare. Further, governors made little effort to convince the general public that the program significantly expands opportunities for recipients or calls for the mutual obligation of government and welfare recipients to make efforts to reduce welfare dependency. In the majority of states, this low profile was possible because recent reforms in their welfare employment programs in response to the options

created in the early 1980s enabled them to meet the immediate new requirements for JOBS without major restructuring. In those states that had not
taken significant action, welfare was typically viewed as a no-win issue for politicians, one that did not warrant a high-profile public stance.

State leaders were more aggressive in pursuing the waivers than in implementing the JOBS program. Without giving the JOBS program sufficient
time to demonstrate the magnitude of its effect in reducing welfare expenditures, governors and state legislatures introduced measures to limit eligibility
and benefits directly and to condition benefits on certain behavior. Impatience
with solutions such as the JOBS program, which will yield benefits over the
long term, might explain the states' actions, as might rising caseloads and
costs. But other features of the political landscape also contributed to the constant call for welfare reform and the continual churning of welfare policies.

As demonstrated during the years since Reagan's first budget, governors,
legislators, and welfare commissioners prefer to take the initiative in seeking
welfare reform rather than to respond to mandates imposed by the federal
government. During the 1980s, many state leaders were enthusiastic in designing their own welfare employment programs and claiming ownership of
their creations. But when federal legislation in 1988 forced states to implement the JOBS program, which consisted of services that many states were already providing, state officials saw it as another federal mandate requiring
program changes and additional expenditures. Some state leaders, rather than
devoting political capital to increasing expenditures for the JOBS program,
chose to restrict welfare eligibility and benefits as a way of generating political
capital. One state welfare commissioner explained that officials stand to benefit from this tough approach because "the public blames the welfare system
for problems in their own life." At low cost to the majority of voters, a hard-
line stance on welfare policy offers state leaders an easy opportunity for political gain.

Two close observers of the waiver process reached a similar conclusion.
Michael Wiseman argued that "waiver-based demonstrations make governors
look good. Waivers are so politically popular that some of the innovations proposed in waiver applications do not require waivers at all."[41] Mark Greenberg
agreed: "A state that can only point to its accomplishments in implementing
the Family Support Act tends to be quite vulnerable to the charge that it is not
'doing' welfare reform. In contrast, a state that has done little to implement the
Family Support Act can jump to the forefront of welfare reform simply by
filing a controversial waiver application."[42]

The motivation at the federal level was much the same, leading both the
Bush and Clinton administrations to approve waivers even though the reforms
articulated no consistent theme or vision. President Bush, in his State of the
Union address at the start of his 1992 campaign, demonstrated his toughness
on welfare by announcing his administration's willingness to approve state
waiver requests that met only two conditions, cost neutrality to the federal
government and an acceptable research component to evaluate the waiver. The

Clinton administration, committed as it was to ending the status quo on welfare, was compelled to follow this precedent.

Welfare reform, which appeals to the majority and imposes costs on the minority, has obvious political value. In his 1992 address, President Bush denied such a motivation: "Our intention is not scapegoating or finger-pointing."[43] But House Speaker Newt Gingrich later responded to Democratic attacks on his welfare proposal by saying,

> The people on the other side who are attacking our effort to reform welfare should be made to bear the burden of the system they would keep. Every night on television, everywhere in America, people see on their local news the deaths, the drug addiction, the rapes, the child abuse, the spouse abuse, the despair. This is a failed system. It's a failed system for the very poor who are trapped in it.[44]

Such rhetoric plainly makes welfare reform a scapegoat for other problems in our society.

Ending Welfare as We Know It

As governor of Arkansas, Bill Clinton took an active interest in welfare reform at both the state and federal levels. He introduced into Arkansas many of the options enacted during the early Reagan years and led the National Governors' Association in its advocacy for legislation that finally became the Family Support Act of 1988. He then brought welfare into his presidential campaign, promising to "end welfare as we know it" by imposing on it "a two-year limit." Once elected, his administration proposed legislation that would give young AFDC mothers up to two years to prepare themselves for work, after which they would be expected to find a regular job or, if jobs were unavailable, to take subsidized private sector jobs, jobs in nonprofit organizations, or government jobs. Although his administration's proposal will be remembered for its two-year time limit, the bill's fine print actually created safeguards to protect families from destitution at the end of that limit.

In the 1994 elections, with the Clinton bill and competing alternatives under consideration by Congress, welfare reform proved to be an attractive campaign issue. After gaining control of Congress, one of the first bills passed by the new Republican House sought to reform welfare dramatically, upping the ante on the administration's proposal. The House bill not only contained time limits but denied any assistance to certain individuals. For example, states would be unable to give assistance to a child born out of wedlock to a girl under age eighteen or to one born to a woman already receiving welfare. Neither would they be able to give assistance to the family of an individual who, after attaining age eighteen, had received aid for sixty months, consecutive or otherwise. The House bill also took the revolutionary step of creating a block grant to replace the AFDC program and the JOBS program. Under the rules of the block grant, individuals' entitlement to assistance would be eliminated.

States would have no duty to assist individuals who meet the eligibility rules: families could be put on waiting lists or turned away. The bill sought a tough, brute force way of modifying the behavior of both the states and recipients so they would increase work and decrease out-of-wedlock childbearing.

Because the Senate favored fewer restrictions, the bill finally enacted by Congress was a compromise giving states the options to deny assistance to a child born out of wedlock to a girl under age eighteen and to one born to a woman already receiving welfare, rather than mandating denial, and requiring states to set aside funds for child care. Yet the compromise followed the broad design of the House bill, creating a block grant and time-limiting welfare eligibility so that states and recipients would have to bear the burden of increased welfare costs and long-term poverty. President Clinton then vetoed the Republican measure, citing shortcomings in its provisions supporting work and financing child care.

At the start of 1996, it was unclear whether Clinton and the 104th Congress would compromise or leave welfare reform as an issue for debate in the 1996 elections. If postponed until the elections, voters would have the opportunity to rethink two basic premises concerning responsibility that underlie the current welfare system. One is the premise that AFDC benefits are an entitlement for eligible individuals, implying that parents are not fully responsible for their own financial well-being or that of their children. This raises the question of whether or not welfare recipients should bear more of this responsibility so that welfare programs entail not just an obligation of government but the mutual obligation of both government and the poor. The second premise is that welfare for families with children is a scheme of cooperative federalism, a joint responsibility of the federal government and the states in which both governments have zones of authority over the program. The question here is should the nation reverse this historical relationship and give greater authority to the states?

Entitlement or Personal Responsibility

"Entitlement" was not in the welfare lexicon until the 1960s, when legal scholars argued that welfare should be considered an entitlement rather than a gratuity. In *Goldberg v. Kelly*, Supreme Court Justice William J. Brennan drew upon this legal scholarship to express the view that "such [welfare] benefits are a matter of statutory entitlement for persons qualified to receive them."[45] When the 1974 Congressional Budget and Impoundment Control Act established special procedures to deal with entitlement programs, the use of the term became more widespread. Entitlement programs now refer to "legislation that requires the payment of benefits to any person or unit of government that meets the eligibility requirements established by such law." In the case of AFDC, the payment obligation is at the state level, but statutes require the federal government to pay a share of the states' costs.[46] Today, there is widespread agreement that the entitlement to welfare is a statutory right rather than a constitutional right.[47] As such, federal law could presumably curtail it.

During the 1980s, support grew for limiting the entitlement for AFDC by conditioning eligibility on the assumption of obligations. Advocates for this view argued that government has an obligation to assist the needy but in turn recipients have an obligation to try to help themselves. Recipients must work or prepare for work and must cooperate with government in obtaining child support from absent parents to receive their full welfare benefit. The Family Support Act responded to these sentiments, not only by creating the JOBS program but by strengthening the system for child support enforcement. Recent waivers are evidence that states have now extended this view of personal responsibility to childbearing, education, immunizations, and other behavior.

If it were not for the children receiving AFDC benefits, narrowing entitlements might be an easy political task. Several states do not provide general assistance to childless, able-bodied adults, and some others have recently eliminated their general assistance programs. But cutting children off welfare, leaving them destitute, is difficult to imagine in a country as rich as the United States. If the federal government reduces its role in the scheme of cooperative federalism, the states and localities will be under pressure to fill in the gaps. The constitution of New York State, for example, requires the state to assist the needy, so that people cut off AFDC would continue to be eligible for assistance. Recognizing that the congressional bill could leave county and city governments with the responsibility of absorbing some of the cuts resulting from the block grants, the National Association of Counties adopted guidelines on welfare reform: "Our overriding concern is the *protection of children*. NACo therefore supports maintaining the federal entitlement for these programs."[48] The U.S. Conference of Mayors urged the president: "Don't sign *any* legislation that hurts our children, our elderly, our families."[49]

Changing the Scheme of Cooperative Federalism

The balance between federal control and state autonomy has always been delicate in welfare policy, shifting subtly in response to a host of political and fiscal forces. States have been unwilling to relinquish the power to set the income levels determining eligibility or the amount of welfare benefits, although they have been willing to accept federal funding and the mandates regarding eligibility conditions and work programs that accompany this support. But the tide toward centralization began to turn with the election of Ronald Reagan and his proposal to give the states full responsibility for the AFDC program in exchange for federal assumption of responsibility for Medicaid. Although this "swap" was defeated, the idea of devolving responsibility to the states did not die. The legislation passed by the 104th Congress would turn both AFDC and Medicaid into block grants with strings attached, giving the states primary responsibility for both programs.

Scholars have argued both for and against a strong state role in setting welfare policy. On the one hand, state power to tax, spend, and redistribute income creates diversity among the states and a greater range of choice for people and firms deciding where to locate. This line of reasoning implies that states should help set welfare policy. On the other hand, the federal government is able to redistribute income without provoking a race to the bottom in which states compete with each other to lower taxes, lower welfare benefits, and discourage the poor from residing within their boundaries. A 1990 study examined these effects and concluded that a national minimum welfare standard is desirable.[50] Accordingly, block grants to the states would be a step backward.

Implications for the States

For both Clinton and the congressional Republicans, the ultimate goal of "ending welfare as we know it" is to reduce welfare caseloads and costs. But as the Clinton administration learned in developing its welfare proposal, reducing welfare caseloads and costs in the long run requires higher expenditures in the short run.[51] Subsidized child care, which the administration proposed for participants in education, training, and work programs and for people who have found employment, represents a particularly large share of the cost. When elected officials have a short time horizon, the delay in the return to programs designed to increase earning capacity becomes another item for the list of difficulties inherent in welfare reform.

It is not clear how turning welfare over to the states with block grants would cut through these difficulties. One argument for decentralization is that the states are closer to recipients and can better ascertain their needs and serve them. But the operation of welfare-to-work programs and other social services is by necessity decentralized, and although states differ in the degree of discretion given to local welfare offices, states and localities already exercise a high degree of discretion in responding to individual circumstances. If states were set free to design their own programs, they would remain constrained by the perverse incentives inherent in the AFDC program.

This reality is not lost on the governors, but they, too, are under pressure to be tough on welfare, particularly Republican governors. Torn between two forces—the welfare reform bandwagon on the one hand and their states' best interests on the other—the governors have not presented a united front. As one of Moynihan's aides explained, "The governors are in a daze, not sure whether to follow Thompson and Engler or to heed the advice of every expert on the subject as well as their own welfare directors: putting recipients to work is expensive, and they will need adequate federal funding to pull it off."[52]

Governors realize that block grants would be risky for the states. The welfare reforms implemented under the waivers are being evaluated, but it is too early to tell how successful they will be in increasing recipients' earnings and achieving other behavioral changes. In the absence of clear guidance from research, governors and state legislatures would make decisions based on ideology and hope. If healthy economies reduce welfare caseloads and maintain state revenues, they will have leeway to experiment with untested approaches.

If they are less fortunate and face rising caseloads and declining revenues, they may begin to agree with Musgrave that welfare is properly the function of the federal government.

Notes

Author's Note: The author thanks David R. Connelly for his assistance in preparing this chapter.

1. *King. v. Smith*, 392 U.S. 309 (1968) at 316.
2. Data for all programs except AFDC are from the *1994 Annual Statistical Supplement to the Social Security Bulletin* (Washington, D.C.: Government Printing Office, August 1994). AFDC data are from the House Committee on Ways and Means, *1994 Green Book, Overview of Entitlement Programs* (Washington, D.C.: Government Printing Office, July 15, 1994), 392.
3. In a May 1994 survey by Yankelovich Partners for *Time*/CNN, 44 percent of people polled said that more than 10 percent of the total federal budget is spent on the AFDC program. Quoted in the Roper Center for Public Opinion Research, *The Public Perspective* 6 (February/March 1995): 38.
4. *Budget of the United States Government, Historical Tables, Fiscal Year 1994* (Washington, D.C.: Government Printing Office, 1993), 41.
5. *Budget of the United States Government, Analytical Perspectives, Fiscal Year 1995* (Washington, D.C.: Government Printing Office, 1994), 54–55.
6. National Association of State Budget Officers, *1994 State Expenditure Report* (Washington, D.C.: National Association of State Budget Officers, April 1995), 87.
7. Ibid., 18.
8. *1994 Annual Statistical Supplement to the Social Security Bulletin*, 343; and *1994 Green Book*, 392.
9. Lawrence M. Mead, *Beyond Entitlement* (New York: Free Press, 1986); and Charles Murray, *Losing Ground* (New York: Basic Books, 1984).
10. Julie Rovner, "Congress Approves Overhaul of Welfare System," *Congressional Quarterly Weekly Report*, October 8, 1988, 2825–31.
11. Paul E. Peterson and Mark C. Rom, *Welfare Magnets* (Washington, D.C.: Brookings Institution, 1990).
12. 42 USC 601.
13. See Winifred Bell, *Aid to Dependent Children* (New York: Columbia University Press, 1965).
14. Michael R. Sosin, "Legal Rights and Welfare Change, 1960–1980," in *Fighting Poverty: What Works and What Doesn't*, ed. Sheldon H. Danziger and Daniel H. Weinberg (Cambridge, Mass.: Harvard University Press, 1986).
15. U.S. Department of Health and Human Services, *Characteristics and Financial Circumstances of AFDC Recipients, FY 1992* (Washington, D.C.: Government Printing Office, 1994), 34.
16. Ibid., 42 and 46.
17. Ibid., 28.
18. Mary Jo Bane and David T. Ellwood, *Welfare Realities* (Cambridge, Mass.: Harvard University Press, 1994), chap. 2.
19. *Rosado v. Wyman*, 397 U.S. 397 (1970); *Jefferson v. Hackney*, 406 U.S. 535 (1972).
20. U.S. Department of Health and Human Services (HHS), *Characteristics of State Plans for Aid to Families with Dependent Children, 1990–91 Edition* (Washington, D.C.: Government Printing Office), 10.
21. 45 C.F.R. 233.20.
22. For factors influencing welfare policies see Peterson and Rom, *Welfare Magnets*, 52–58.

23. HHS, *Characteristics and Financial Circumstances of AFDC Recipients*, 60 and 64.
24. Council of Economic Advisers, *1995 Economic Report of the President* (Washington, D.C.: Government Printing Office, 1995).
25. Robert Moffitt, "Incentive Effects of the U.S. Welfare System: A Review," *Journal of Economic Literature* 30 (March 1992): 27–31.
26. Mark R. Rank, "Fertility Among Women on Welfare: Incidence and Determinants," *American Sociological Review* 54 (April 1989): 296–304.
27. Moffitt, "Incentive Effects," 13–18.
28. Ibid., 34–36.
29. Peterson and Rom, *Welfare Magnets*.
30. Richard A. Musgrave, *The Theory of Public Finance* (New York: McGraw-Hill, 1959), 181–182.
31. Marion Nichols, Jon Dunlap, and Scott Barkan, *National General Assistance Survey, 1992* (Washington, D.C. and Denver, Colo.: Center on Budget and Policy Priorities and National Conference of State Legislatures, December 1992).
32. Murray, *Losing Ground*.
33. Lawrence Bobo and Ryan Smith, "Antipoverty Policy, Affirmative Action, and Racial Attitudes," in *Confronting Poverty: Prescriptions for Change*, ed. Sheldon Danziger, Gary Sandefur, and Daniel Weinberg (Cambridge, Mass.: Harvard University Press, 1994), 372.
34. Ibid., 391.
35. Margaret Malone, *Work and Welfare*, U.S. Senate, 99th Cong., 2d sess., August 1986.
36. Judith Gueron and Edward Pauly, *From Welfare to Work* (New York: Russell Sage Foundation, 1991).
37. Ibid.; Moffitt, "Incentive Effects."
38. Mead, *Beyond Entitlement*; National Governors' Association, *Making America Work: Productive People, Productive Policies* (Washington, D.C.: National Governors' Association, 1987); and Michael Novak et al., *The New Consensus on Family and Welfare* (Washington, D.C.: American Enterprise Institute for Public Policy Research, 1987).
39. Daniel Patrick Moynihan, "The Children of the State," *Washington Post*, November 25, 1990, C1.
40. Jan L. Hagen and Irene Lurie, *Implementing JOBS: Progress and Promise* (Albany, N.Y.: Rockefeller Institute of Government, 1994).
41. Mark Greenberg and Michael L. Wiseman, "Fixing Welfare Waiver Policy," *Public Welfare* 53 (Winter 1995): 13.
42. Ibid., 15.
43. *Weekly Compilation of Presidential Documents* (Washington, D.C.: Government Printing Office, February 3, 1992), 176.
44. Jennifer Dixon, "GOP's Welfare Reform Nears Passage," *Daily Gazette* (Schenectady, N.Y.), March 24, 1995, A5.
45. *Goldberg v. Kelly*, 397 U.S. 254 (1970) at 262.
46. Kent Weaver, "Controlling Entitlements," in *The New Direction in American Politics*, ed. John E. Chubb and Paul E. Peterson (Washington, D.C.: Brookings Institution, 1985), 308.
47. Ibid.; R. Shep Melnick, *Between the Lines: Interpreting Welfare Rights* (Washington, D.C.: Brookings Institution, 1994), 37; and Aaron Wildavsky, *The New Politics of the Budgetary Process* (Glenview, Ill.: Scott, Foresman, 1988), 266.
48. Letter from Randy Franke, president of the National Association of Counties, to Robert Packwood, Chairman of the U.S. Senate Finance Committee, April 25, 1995.
49. *New York Times*, December 11, 1995, A13.
50. Peterson and Rom, *Welfare Magnets*, 4.
51. U.S. Department of Health and Human Services, "Work and Responsibility Act of 1994, Detailed Summary" and "Work and Responsibility Act of 1994, Costs," unpublished.
52. Paul Offner, *Washington Post*, March 26, 1995, C5.

11

Power to the States

Carl E. Van Horn

Thirty years ago, in *Storm over the States*, Terry Sanford, former governor of North Carolina and later a U.S. senator, described profound changes that swept state governments in the 1960s as they adjusted to federal statutes and Supreme Court rulings that forced them to modernize.[1] Today, the state government scene seems more like a tornado of political, administrative, and policy change. The whirling activism of state governments in the 1980s was followed by a crash of the American economy in the early 1990s and diminished federal government involvement in domestic policy innovation.

The economic recovery that followed has not renewed federal government aid to the states. Instead, a Republican-controlled Congress has taken bold steps to curb government spending and put states at the cutting edge of radical social policy reform. It is, arguably, the most significant domestic policy development in at least thirty years. States will be struggling to absorb this rapid pace of change in the foreseeable future—change that is likely to further batter the foundation of state political institutions and threaten not only incumbent office-holders but also the representative functions of governors and state legislatures.

Political Reform

For many years, state government leaders were in the driver's seat of political activism. The origins of this enlarged state role in domestic politics and policy were changes in representation, governmental organization, and professionalization spawned in the late 1960s. The states' activism was tested when federal officials began cutting aid to states and local governments in the late 1970s. Interest groups shifted their focus from Washington, D.C., to the state capitals, repeating a phenomenon that has occurred before in American history.

Rewriting state constitutions, restructuring political institutions, and assembling professional expertise enabled state governments to design and implement far-reaching public policies.[2] Furthermore, the policy-making circles—in legislatures, courts, bureaucracies, and governors' mansions—were no longer exclusively filled with the upper-middle class white males that dominated government for most of American political history.

Landmark reapportionment decisions and changes in social attitudes transformed state governments from unrepresentative, homogeneous institutions to more representative bodies.[3] The U.S. Supreme Court in *Baker v. Carr* and *Reynolds v. Sims* removed barriers to direct representation of voters and re-apportioned legislatures according to the principle of "one person, one vote." The Voting Rights Act of 1965 eliminated obstacles to full political participation by African-Americans. Black registration in the deep South grew by more than 1 million between 1964 and 1972, an increase from 29 percent to 57 percent of eligible voters.[4]

State legislatures and administrative agencies today have greater numbers of women and minorities than twenty years ago but still far fewer than men or Caucasians. Women holding legislative office, for example, increased from 4 percent in 1969 to 20.6 percent in 1995.[5] In Arizona, Colorado, Nevada, Vermont, and Washington, women hold 30 percent or more of the seats in the legislature. Women's participation in state government positions also has risen at the appointive policy-making levels. Women have been less successful in obtaining statewide elected office. In 1996, only one woman was serving as a governor—Christine Todd Whitman of New Jersey.[6]

Minority participation in elected and appointed policy-making positions in state government also has grown, but very slowly. Even so, blacks, who account for 12 percent of the U.S. population, held no governorships and just 5 percent of the state legislative positions in 1992. In 1970, none of the governors was black and less than 2 percent of legislators were black.[7] Hispanics increased their share of elected positions in several states where they make up a significant part of the population—Arizona, California, Colorado, and New Mexico. Florida and New Mexico have elected governors of Hispanic origin.

Representatives of these newly empowered groups demanded greater government intervention to ameliorate social and economic problems in their communities. Elected officials' policy priorities reflect their life experiences and professional training. More teachers and working women in elected and appointed positions encouraged greater attention to family leave programs, child care, and women's and children's health care.[8]

Business, labor, local governments, school boards, and other traditionally powerful groups still wield the most influence in state politics, but environmentalists, consumer advocates, and senior citizens have become more effective. Citizen participation in state policy making has exploded since the early 1970s. State agencies now routinely allow citizens to voice concerns through public boards and commissions, ombudsmen, public advocates, and public hearings. Newly active groups raise money and contribute to candidates, advertise in the mass media, and exert considerable influence over governors and legislatures.[9]

The initiative process has been employed with increasing frequency by political leaders, interest groups, and citizens groups. Ballot initiatives doubled between 1976 and 1990. Sometimes the initiative is used as a method of circumventing the legislative process. In other cases, the mere threat of mounting such a campaign is used to spur the legislature to act.

In 1990, 236 ballot questions appeared in forty-three states—the largest number since 1914. Sixty-seven proposals were launched by citizens groups.

In recent years, voters weighed important and controversial proposals, including the regulation of pornography, acid rain, abortions, drug use, and the length of time legislators may remain in office.[10] Some state officials have concluded that joining initiative battles is better than fighting them.

Political institutions also have expanded their staffs to achieve their policy agendas and to compete with rival institutions in the struggle for power. Governors expanded staffs overseeing the bureaucracy, monitoring developments in Washington, D.C., and shepherding the flock of legislative proposals in the statehouse. Legislatures bolstered staffs to keep a watchful eye on the executive branch and to provide more effective service to constituents.

The cumulative impact of state governments acquiring more expertise and the renewed focus on state government has been dramatic. State officials now are able to fulfill their ambition and to meet the expectations of others in carrying out their responsibilities in the federal system. States now plan and execute complex policy initiatives: water supply and quality improvement programs, pollution prevention programs, education reform, science and technology development, and energy conservation initiatives.[11]

To some extent, the concern of some federal lawmakers that states are not up to the task of carrying out large-scale governmental reforms is unwarranted. The capacity to make complex choices and to implement difficult programs exists already in many states. States have been managing such large federal programs as welfare and Medicaid for decades. Steve Gold, director of the Center for the Study of the States, offers a balanced observation about the states: "They have more ability to make the important decisions, but that doesn't mean they're magicians."[12]

What is more controversial, and a source of concern to some and celebration for others, is the matter of what state governments will do with programs that used to be ruled by the federal government establishment. Proponents of greater state control, such as Illinois' Republican governor Jim Edgar, assert that the states "can run the programs at less cost than it costs us now."[13] Opponents of broad decentralization, such as Democratic senator John Breaux of Louisiana disagree: "We might as well just throw the money up in the air and hope it falls down and does good."[14]

State courts matched the activism of legislators and governors. The courts hired more judges, law clerks, and administrative officers to meet the rising demands for court review of policy and administrative cases. They took aggressive action on several public policy fronts, including expanding the rights of women, minorities, and criminal defendants. In doing so, state judges often relied upon state constitutions to establish rights that the U.S. Supreme Court has not found in the U.S. Constitution. State courts also expanded the rights of individuals to recover for personal injuries and imposed strict liability rules for faulty products. However, the conservative backlash now resident in many state legislatures has also found its way into the courtrooms around the country.

From Entrepreneurship to Crisis

During the 1980s, state governments brimmed with an entrepreneurial spirit. No longer passive partners in the federal system, states eagerly became a driving force in American politics. They levied and spent vast sums of money, hired hundreds of thousands of new employees, managed tough public problems, sought out new policy frontiers to conquer. The states aggressively set policy agendas for the nation and fashioned innovative solutions for some of the most important policy problems.

State governments were imperialistic in the 1980s. Governors and legislators clamored for new ideas and expanded government spending and regulation. State officials displayed no sustained interest in controlling government's spiraling costs. State leaders were more concerned with improving public education, protecting the environment, and rebuilding roads, bridges, and sewers.

The rosy fiscal picture became clouded when the U.S. economy lapsed into a long and deep recession in the early 1990s. Because the federal government was unable to prime the state government pump with new dollars, the burden of the recession fell squarely on the states. Following the path taken in the 1982 recession, states responded to the 1991 recession by raising $16 billion in additional taxes and by cutting $10 billion in state programs. States scaled back their plans for greater government intervention. Unlike the federal government, which can defy fiscal gravity by borrowing money, state budgets are tethered to the reality of declining revenues. States cannot spend what they do not collect.

With the new ideological winds sweeping the nation, governmental activism at the state level is no longer in vogue. State government spending continues to grow for such basic services as education, prisons, health care, and transportation. But large-scale innovations that come with big price-tags have been shelved—at least for now. The election of 1994 brought in the largest number of Republican legislators and governors since 1968. Republicans are more likely than Democrats to stake their political futures on government downsizing or at least holding the line against rapid expansion. In 1995, for the first time in a decade, state tax cuts exceeded state tax increases: twenty-five states cut taxes by $2.1 billion and fourteen states increased taxes by $910 million.[15]

The changes adopted by the Republican-controlled Congress in 1994 are likely to help deepen the ideological divisions between Republicans and Democrats running state governments. Issues such as policies about welfare programs and environmental regulation are likely to join tax policy as matters that deeply divide representatives of the two parties. This is a change worth noting. In the 1980s, state government leaders were characterized more by pragmatism than partisanship. For example, Democratic and Republican governors and legislators developed similar strategies for reforming welfare programs for the poor.[16] Today, however, partisan disagreements about the purpose of government action are rising.

Consider the reactions of two Florida legislators—one Republican and one Democrat—to proposed revisions in the Medicaid program. Republican Senate President James Scott said: "We'll now have the challenge and opportunity to be creative, to do more with less, without all these Federal restrictions." His Democratic counterpart in the Florida House, Speaker Peter Rudy Wallace, disagreed: "Certainly in Medicaid there is the prospect that reductions are going to mean very, very difficult decisions between funding for Medicaid nursing home beds and funding for health services for children and younger people in this state."[17]

Fiscal Policy Squeeze

State officials operate in a volatile environment with a public concerned about both taxes and spending. Unfortunately, the public remains ambivalent about fiscal policy. Most voters want lower taxes, but they also support higher spending for most programs. State officials are constantly buffeted by the need to reconcile competing priorities. When revenues declined, as in the 1990s, the pressures on state officials grew more intense.

In the early 1980s, tax-limitation initiatives, most notably California's Proposition 13, were adopted by several states. The reigning government buzzwords were zero-based budgeting, executive reorganization, and cutback management. But the "limited government" movement, the love affair with curbing government growth, did not last through the decade. State government spending soared at rates higher than inflation through the 1980s. Ironically, this spurt of government growth was rooted in the economic crisis of 1982. Faced with the prospects of greater social welfare spending and reduced tax collections, twenty-eight states increased their income taxes, and thirty increased sales taxes.[18] Even without additional tax increases, these actions eventually would have yielded a fiscal bonanza. But nineteen states raised either their income or sales taxes again in 1984 and 1985. In addition, the 1986 federal tax reform law brought millions of additional dollars rolling into state treasuries.

The 1980s-style budgets could not be balanced with the revenues collected during the depressed economy of the 1990s. Facing a rising tide of red ink, more than thirty-five states turned to tax increases and program cuts to bring their budgets into balance. Despite these drastic measures, states had difficulty achieving equilibrium. Within six months of enacting the largest tax increases in decades, more than half the states were still facing budget deficits in their current year budgets.[19]

The sustained economic recovery of the mid-1980s contributed to reduced spending on some government services, such as unemployment insurance and welfare, and increased revenue collections. When the state treasuries bulged, most states spent the windfall instead of giving it back to the taxpayers. Several states established so-called rainy-day funds to cushion the shock of another recession, but typically the increased state revenues were quickly committed to new or expanded programs.[20]

The economic troubles of the 1990s reversed the trends of the 1980s and resulted in fewer revenues but increased demands for government spending. As the recession deepened, states spent more to meet the swelling demand for social services. Revenues dropped sharply as unemployment rose and as the corporate bottom line changed from profit to loss. The economic recovery that begin in mid-1992 and continued through 1995 created a fiscal windfall. But a 1980s-style spending binge did not occur this time. Why? Because state policy makers are now more conservative in their outlook about the role of government. In addition, policy makers are mindful of the past and wary of repeating the mistakes of the 1980s when rapid expansion brought a heavy price when recession gripped the economy.

Power Struggles

Reforms fashioned in the 1960s and 1970s to strengthen the competence of state government simultaneously encouraged governors, legislators, judges, and bureaucrats to boldly assert power. As power fragmented, state politics became more conflict-ridden. Policy makers who wanted to tackle tough problems struggled to find consensus for specific actions. Distrust deepened as governors, judges, legislators, and administrators jealously guarded their prerogatives.

Unfortunately, the positive developments that made state governments more democratic and responsive also caused some troubling problems. Personal conflicts often escalated into battles for institutional control and the agenda of government. Fragmented policy making sometimes blurs clear lines of responsibility and thus decreases institutional accountability.

The reforms that fostered modern political institutions carved up power into bits and pieces and undermined the ability of any one institution or political leader to dominate state politics. Individualism was encouraged at the expense of institutional responsibility. With more at stake in the governance of states, everyone has a greater incentive to seek power and control.

Prevailing attitudes about the responsibilities of legislators also changed during the 1980s and 1990s. Modern legislators are much more likely to pursue their own agendas instead of those dictated by party leaders. Legislators feel they must aggressively champion their districts' interests even if they come in conflict with county party organizations, governors, and legislative leaders.[21] With their antennae tuned to the voters back home and campaign contributors, legislators often feel free to ignore appeals for party discipline.

The dispersion of power within political institutions has resulted in fierce battles for the control of policy agendas and outcomes. More intense competition is apparent in all phases of state political life from elections to state budget decisions. More legislators, judges, bureaucrats, and interest groups have sufficient clout to engage in the struggle, but few have enough power to rule.

The desire to hold on to power strongly shapes the political process within institutions, especially in legislatures where electoral considerations are paramount. The quest for power is hardly a new phenomenon, but career-oriented politicians are more intent on winning because they are more intent on remaining in office for a long time. "Permanent" legislators must constantly deliver benefits, claim credit for accomplishments, and attack opponents in the executive branch or elsewhere.[22] They undertake new legislative initiatives, examine administrative rules and regulations, scrutinize the state budget, and investigate government agencies. Clearly, these strategies serve their intended purpose; incumbents rarely lose.[23]

Incumbents and challengers also have stepped up the intensity of campaigns. Costs are rising because people are willing and able to spend huge sums of money to gain elective office. The staples of modern campaigns—media consultants, pollsters, and television advertising—are expensive. Statewide candidates must collect substantial sums of money or have a large personal fortune. Even legislative candidates now are required to assemble substantial resources, except in the smaller states.

A candidate who cannot afford to participate in high-cost elections is less likely to be heard. Those who form political action committees and contribute money or political support or both get special attention from the candidate and from officeholders who want to keep their jobs. Educators, dentists, senior citizens, labor leaders, builders, and others are effective advocates for their interests because they supply the campaign funds and the reliable voters that keep incumbent politicians around to serve them another day.

State politics is locked in a spiraling institutional "arms race." Governors, legislators, bureaucrats, judges, and interest groups are employing new techniques and strategies to achieve their goals. Governors assert greater control over the bureaucracy. Legislatures step up efforts to oversee executive government agencies. Interest groups bypass representative institutions and pursue goals through the initiative process. State courts adjudicate disputes between legislators and governors and make policy independently.

Nothing is inherently wrong with conflict. Representative government and deliberation are well served by sharp clashes of strongly held views. Few observers of American politics are nostalgic for a return to an era when a handful of party bosses and top ranking elected officials called the shots. But, unfortunately, many political conflicts result from ambiguous authority and personal political ambition instead of from disputes over competing policy visions. Institutional conflicts have sidetracked the policy process into a round robin policy game as the court, legislature, and governor fight with one another for leadership.

The more strident politics of the 1990s has soured many incumbent officeholders and led to a rash of early retirements. Consider the remarks of Democratic governor Bruce Sundlun of Rhode Island:

> It's not fun to be governor. You can't have fun shutting the state down, abolishing positions, laying off personnel, and balancing the budget by cutting expenditures. Nobody likes any of these those things.[24]

Divided party control of the legislature and governorship exacerbates institutional conflict. Voters in most states do not seem to be bothered, however. A remarkable increase in split-ticket voting has taken place in the last thirty years. Split control of state legislatures has increased from four states in 1982 to twelve states in 1994. In thirteen states in 1996 where one party dominated the entire legislature, the governor was from the other party.

As battles for power intensify, others are drawn into the fray. When legislators and governors cannot reach clear decisions, they often delegate hard choices to the bureaucracy or create new administrative entities. This policy-making-by-other means has caused a proliferation of commissions and "independent" authorities created through legislative and gubernatorial appointments. State courts, as a result, frequently are forced to mediate between the other branches of government. For example, courts have ruled recently on the authority of governors to exercise their line-item veto and extent of gubernatorial appointment and removal powers.

By entering into disputes between representative institutions, the courts allocate political power, shed the role of referee, and become policy makers.[25] For example, the state courts have handed down dozens of liberal decisions in civil rights cases and other fields. But this activism has come with a price. Many legislators, governors, and voters perceive that courts have thwarted majority preferences. And they have sought to reverse the courts by amending the constitution, passing new laws, or removing judges from office.

State courts have become a battleground for competing ideologies and policy agendas. Interest groups, legislators, and governors have tried to overturn court decisions. The courts successfully have fended off challenges to their authority in the interpretation of constitutional law. But their power to interpret common law has not been so well defended. For example, state legislatures have narrowed the rights of injured parties, but they have been less successful in curbing the state courts' support for the rights of women in sex discrimination cases.

Recently, liberal judges have been challenged in judicial confirmation elections as a way of reining in the courts. Decisions on hot-button issues, such as the death penalty, frequently are central issues in campaigns to oust judges. Spending on judicial elections and the number of direct challenges have risen substantially. Ballot initiatives have overturned liberal court decisions affecting criminal defendant rights. While the defeat of incumbent judges and anti-court initiatives still are rare, the fear of defeat may curb the courts' liberal leanings. In California, the defeat of three Supreme Court justices resulted in new appointees who affirmed more death penalty sentences—the outcome sought by voters in statewide referendums.

Bureaucracies also are embroiled in disputes over their activities, purposes, and performance. Legislatures have sharpened their oversight of agency decisions through sunset laws and reviews of administrative rules and regulations. Governors have exerted greater control through executive reorganizations, a reduction in the number of boards and commissions, centralization of budgeting techniques, and executive orders mandating direct accountability to the governor.

Governing During a Revolution

State governments are facing unprecedented challenges in the 1990s. The "Devolution Revolution" will make effective governing extremely difficult. Republicans in Congress are cutting federal aid to the states, consolidating programs and turning control over to governors and legislators. Republican governors and legislatures appear to be unwilling to raise taxes to fill the void. Interest groups—from environmentalists to advocates for the poor—are girding for new battles in the state capitals. State government officials are going to have to do more with less and to make dozens of new choices that previously were settled elsewhere. According to political scientist Don Kettl, states are being asked to "do things that no American government has ever done before.... The governors and legislatures will not only have to figure out how to manage these programs. They will have to learn to dance the intricate minuet of connecting them."[26]

The rise of governmental, institutional, and individual entrepreneurship makes meeting these new challenges more difficult. Institutional accountability has been overshadowed by individual accountability. When incumbent governors and legislators deny responsibility for the actions of their own governments or institutions, they are trying to avoid responsibility. When no one is willing to accept responsibility, people are less willing to act responsibly.

Legislators have tried to insulate themselves from executive domination, party leaders, and legislative leaders. Governors increasingly portray themselves as the clarion of the people, not the head of state government. They play to the press and go over the heads of party and legislative leaders. Political parties have been shoved aside by candidate-centered politics, where the incumbent, not the party, is judged. Partisanship is on the rise, but responsible party governance is on the decline. Even judges now are more wary of voter reactions to their judicial decisions.

When political officials act like independent agents in the political system, leadership becomes difficult. Legislative leaders serve at the pleasure of the partisans who selected them, so they wield influence by distributing campaign funds rather than through persuasion. Legislators and governors used to be primarily concerned with governing. Now, they are more likely to be preoccupied with power. And they are dismantling local party organizations and taking over electoral functions through leadership caucuses and political action committees.

The high price tag of elections means that elected officials are more accountable to those with money and less accountable to the public at large. The deep public resentment of special interest politics helps explain why proposals to limit the terms of officeholders have caught fire in more than twenty states.

Political fund raising diverts time from governing responsibilities and compromises elected officials. Legislators and governors commonly hold large fund-raising events while important policy issues are under consideration. Elected officials regularly solicit and receive campaign contributions from companies that either have contracts with the state or want to do business in the future. Partisan staff in the executive and legislative branches are routinely deployed to work on election activities.

Warfare between legislatures and governors enhances the power of bureaucracy and courts and thus reduces accountability to the public. More decisions are delegated from democratic institutions to administrative agencies. While these agencies are somewhat more responsive to the public than before, they are less responsive than governors or legislatures. And bureaucracies often obscure clear lines of responsibility and make establishing who is in charge difficult. Ultimately these conflicts may generate more contradictions, delay, rigidity, and uncertainty. As more decisions are thrown into the courts, the "judicialization of state administration" may result.

The new state politics also puts its stamp on public policy. As the power of narrow special interests rises, policies serving the public interest suffer. Policy makers concerned with their political survival are likely to choose the safest course and are less likely to confront difficult choices.

When governors and legislators are driven by short-run political needs, they may ignore the long-term needs of their state. Electoral expediency crowds out other important values. State officials may ensure their reelection but undermine their state's future and further cripple democratic institutions.

If more fiscal restraint had been exercised in the 1980s when the economy was booming, the 1990s recession would not have wreaked so much havoc on state budgets. Unlike the federal government, the states cannot borrow their way out. So when they raised taxes and cut programs, voters were angry. Incumbent officeholders paid the political price for the loose-money politics of the 1980s; many are declining to run for reelection.

The reliance on statewide initiatives to resolve public policy disputes represents a troubling development. In some of the nation's more populous states, such as California and Florida, state elected officials are passing the responsibility for tough decisions to initiative campaigns. These "issue elections" seldom are grass-roots citizens movements. Instead, they are dominated by interest groups that spend lavishly on television advertising, direct mail, and tracking polls. For example, the insurance industry and its opponents spent $80 million on campaigns for and against a proposal to cut insurance premiums in California.

The erosion of accountability raises serious implications for the ability of political institutions to effectively handle public policy problems. Expansion and innovation are popular, but power struggles reduce the possibilities for reaching consensus on matters involving difficult trade-offs. The fragmentation of power and the reluctance to assume responsibility produce policy gridlock and delegation of the hard choices to administrative agencies.

How will state leaders manage the difficult realities of the late 1990s? Opponents of enhancing power to the state paint a grim picture. They claim that the safety net for poor people will be shredded and that incompetence and corruption will run rampant.[27] Advocates of greater state control naturally envision a different future. They see innovative and efficient programs operated by officials who have greater understanding of the needs of intended beneficiaries. They say it is high time for states to take over responsibility for problems that the federal government has been unable to solve.

Both proponents and opponents of devolution are exaggerating their positions to score political points with voters and interest groups. Giving greater responsibility to state governments while cutting federal aid will not usher in the dark ages. Nor will it be a panacea. It is difficult to predict what will happen because the scope of reform is unprecedented and because states are so diverse. It is safe to say, however, that the late 1990s will be chaotic for state governments as they adjust to expansions in responsibilities, reductions in federal resources, and higher expectations from various constituencies. As we near the end of this century, basic assumptions about the size and standard operating procedures of state governments are ripe for challenge and change. State governments are going to endure the tornado of policy reform, but not without sustaining serious damage to the reputations of state government officials and institutions.

Notes

1. Terry Sanford, *Storm over the States* (New York: McGraw-Hill, 1967).
2. Ibid.; Larry J. Sabato, *Goodbye to Good-time Charlie: The American Governorship Transformed* (Washington, D.C.: CQ Press, 1983).
3. Timothy G. O'Rourke, *The Impact of Reapportionment* (New Brunswick, N.J.: Transaction Books, 1980).
4. Charles S. Bullock and Charles M. Lamb, eds., *Implementation of Civil Rights Policy* (Monterey, Calif.: Brooks/Cole, 1984), 20–54.
5. Center for the American Woman and Politics, National Information Bank on Women in Public Office, Eagleton Institute of Politics, Rutgers University, November 1995.
6. Ibid.
7. Personal communication from the Joint Center for Political Studies, Washington, D.C., December 5, 1992.
8. See, for example, Alan Ehrenhalt, "In Alabama Politics, The Teachers Are Sitting at the Head of the Class," *Governing* (December 1988): 22–27.
9. William T. Gormley, Jr., "The Representation Revolution: Reforming State Regulation through Representation," *Administration and Society* 18:2 (August 1986): 179–196.
10. Patrick B. McGuigan, *The Politics of Direct Democracy in the 1980s* (Washington, D.C.: Free Congress Research and Education Foundation, 1985); Patrick B. McGuigan, ed., *Initiative and Referendum Report* (Washington, D.C.: Free Congress Research and Education Foundation, December 1986/January 1987); Carol Matlack, "Where the Big Winner Was the Status Quo," *National Journal*, November 10, 1990, 2748–49.
11. See, for example, Advisory Commission on Intergovernmental Relations, *The Question of State Government Capability* (Washington, D.C.: Advisory Commission on Intergovernmental Relations, 1985).

12. Same Howe Verhovek, "State Lawmakers Prepare to Wield Vast New Powers," *New York Times*, September 24, 1995, 24.

13. David Rosenbaum, "Governors' Frustration Fuels Effort on Welfare Financing," *New York Times*, March 21, 1995, B7.

14. E. J. Dionne, Jr., "50 Ways to Waste Money," *Star-Ledger*, October 10, 1995, 15.

15. Robert Pear, "Federal Impasse Saddles States with Uncertainty," *New York Times*, January 2, 1996, A1.

16. Julie Rovner, "Welfare Reform: The Issue That Bubbled Up from the States to Capitol Hill," *Governing* (December 1988): 17–21.

17. Verhovek, "State Lawmakers Prepare to Wield Vast New Powers."

18. David S. Broder, "States Make Hard Decisions as Reagan Fantasies Wane," (Raleigh) *News and Observer*, August 5, 1987, A17.

19. National Association of State Budget Officers, *Looking for Light at the End of the Tunnel: States Struggle with Another Difficult Budget Year* (Washington, D.C.: National Association of State Budget Officers, January 1992), 2.

20. Steven D. Gold, ed., *Reforming State Tax Systems* (Denver, Colo.: National Conference of State Legislatures, 1986).

21. See, for example, Malcolm Jewell, *Representation in State Legislatures* (Lexington: University of Kentucky Press, 1982).

22. See, for example, Joel A. Thompson, "Bringing Home the Bacon: The Politics of Pork Barrel in the North Carolina Legislature," *Legislative Studies Quarterly* (February 1986): 91–108.

23. Richard Niemi and L. R. Winsky, "Membership Turnover in State Legislatures: Trends and Effects of Redistricting," *Legislative Studies Quarterly* 12 (1987): 115–124.

24. David Sherman, "Governors of Fiscally Strapped States, Seeing No Sign of Relief, Yearn for the Good Old Days," *Wall Street Journal*, August 19, 1991, 12.

25. Dave Frohnmayer, "The Courts as Referee" (Paper delivered at the State of the States Symposium, Eagleton Institute of Politics, Rutgers University, December 15–16, 1988).

26. Robert Pear, "Shifting Where the Buck Stops," *New York Times*, October 29, 1995, 4–3.

27. See, for example, Richard Cohen, "States Aren't Saints, Either," *Washington Post Weekly Edition*, April 3–9, 1995, 28.

Index